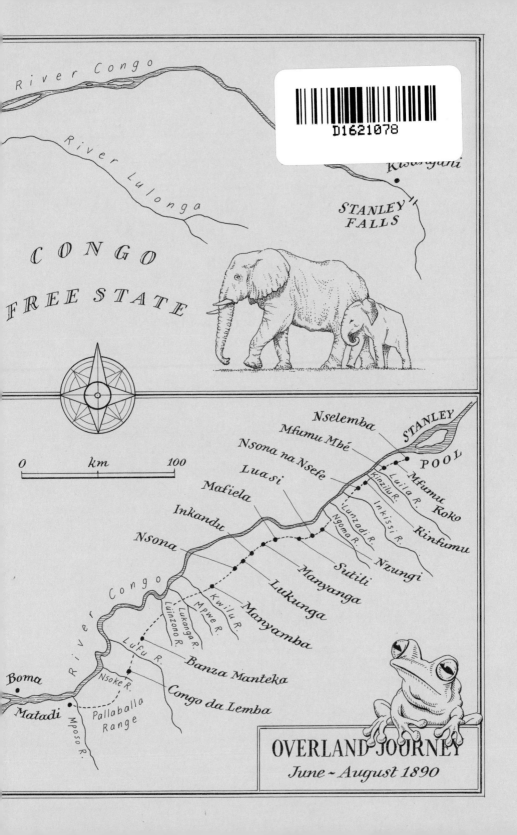

CONRAD'S CONGO

CONRAD'S CONGO

JOSEPH CONRAD'S EXPEDITION TO
THE CONGO FREE STATE, 1890

Edited and introduced by
J. H. Stape

Preface by
Adam Hochschild

London
THE FOLIO SOCIETY
2013

This edition published by The Folio Society Ltd
44 Eagle Street, London WC1R 4FS
www.foliosociety.com

This selection © The Folio Society Ltd 2013

Introduction and editorial matter © J. H. Stape 2013
Preface © Adam Hochschild 2013

Frontispiece: Józef Teodor Konrad Korzeniowski (Joseph Conrad) in 1882

Endpaper map by Neil Gower

Typeset at The Folio Society in Minion.
Printed on Abbey Wove paper at TJ International,
Cornwall, and bound by them in cloth blocked
with a design by Neil Gower

Contents

Illustrations

Facsimiles of Conrad's hand-drawn maps in 'The Congo Diary' and the 'Up-river Book' are reproduced from his original 1890 manuscripts.
(*Houghton MS Eng 46 (1) and (2) Houghton Library, Harvard University*)

Joseph Conrad. Photograph by C. Potier, 1882.
(*Beinecke Rare Book and Manuscript Library, Yale University*)   *frontis*

Steamer workshops, Bolobo. Photograph by Rev. George Grenfell, *c*.1882–9. (© *Royal Geographical Society (with IBG)*)

The riverbank near Irebu. Photograph by R. Dubreucq, *c*.1900. (*A.P.0.0.1089, Collection RMCA Tervuren*)

Assembly of people in the forest, on the route of the *Roi des Belges*, on the Sankuru river. Photograph by M. F. Demeuse, *c*.1888. (*Arnaud Delas/adoc-photos*)

Forest area on the bank of the River Congo. Photograph by M. F. Demeuse, *c*.1890. (*Arnaud Delas/adoc-photos*)

BETWEEN PAGES 118 AND 119

Bangala tribesmen. Photograph by M. F. Demeuse, *c*.1890. (*Arnaud Delas/adoc-photos*)

Portrait of two mutilated children, victims of atrocities committed under Leopold II's terror regime in Equateur, *c*.1905. (*Images of Empire/Universal Images Group via Getty Images*)

Portrait of two manacled men, members of a chain gang enslaved under Leopold II's terror regime, *c*.1904. (*Images of Empire/Universal Images Group via Getty Images*)

Portrait of Joseph Conrad. Pencil drawing by Sir William Rothenstein, 1916. (© *estate of Sir William Rothenstein/National Portrait Gallery, London*)

JOSEPH CONRAD was born Józef Teodor Konrad Korzeniowski in 1857 in Berdyczów, in Russian-occupied Ukraine, to Polish parents. Following his parents' deaths after the family returned from exile in northern Russia he began a career as a sailor in the 1870s by joining the French merchant marine and, eventually, the British merchant navy. After twenty years at sea, including his influential time in the Belgian Congo, Conrad became a British subject and settled in England to devote himself to writing fiction in English, his third language. His works include *Almayer's Folly, An Outcast of the Islands, The Nigger of the 'Narcissus', Heart of Darkness, Lord Jim, Typhoon, Nostromo, The Secret Agent, Under Western Eyes, Chance* and *The Rover*.

J. H. STAPE is a Conrad scholar of international standing and a Research Fellow at St Mary's University College, Twickenham, London. He is the author of *The Several Lives of Joseph Conrad* (2007) and is co-General Editor of *The Cambridge Edition of the Works of Joseph Conrad*, for which he co-edited *Notes on Life and Letters* (2004), *A Personal Record* (2008), *Last Essays* (2010), *Lord Jim* (2011) and *Tales of Unrest* (2012). He also co-edited volumes 7 and 9 (2007 and 2009) of the Cambridge *Collected Letters of Joseph Conrad* and is a contributing editor of *The Conradian: The Journal of the Joseph Conrad Society* (UK).

ADAM HOCHSCHILD is a journalist, author and teacher of writing at the Graduate School of Journalism at the University of California at Berkeley. His books have been translated into twelve languages and include *King Leopold's Ghost: A Story of Greed, Terror and Heroism in Colonial Africa* (1998), from which his preface is, in part, adapted, and which won the Duff Cooper Prize in Britain, the Lionel Gelber Prize in Canada and was a finalist for the 1998 National Book Critics Circle Award in the United States; *Bury the Chains: The British Struggle to Abolish Slavery* (2005); and *To End All Wars: A Story of Protest and Patriotism in the First World War* (2011).

Preface

At the beginning of August 1890, the steamboat *Roi des Belges* –
'King of the Belgians' – a boxy, wood-burning stern-wheeler with a
funnel and pilot-house on its upper deck, began a four-week journey
up the Congo River. At the captain's side was a thirty-two-year-old,
black-bearded ship's officer, whose eyes, in some photographs, look
as if they were perpetually narrowed against the tropical sun. Józef
Konrad Korzeniowski had arrived in the Congo some weeks earlier,
his previous nautical experience limited mainly to the sea, on vessels
very different from the steamer that, he wrote, 'resembled an enormous sardine box with a flat-roofed shed erected on it'. This was his
first trip on the river, and his logbook is filled with businesslike notes
about such matters as shoals, sandbars and refuelling points not
included on the primitive navigational chart available.

It would be some years before he got onto paper other features of
the Congo not shown on the map, and by that time, of course, the
world would know him as Joseph Conrad. The outstanding result
of his river journey would be *Heart of Darkness,* probably the most
widely read short novel in English. The documentary record of
Conrad's life-changing months in the Congo is frustratingly scanty,
but the volume in your hands collects what there is of it, plus much
else as well: his first working of these travels into fiction, in 'An Outpost of Progress', recollections by others and excerpts from the
enormously influential report on the colony's atrocities by Conrad's
one-time Congo housemate, Roger Casement.

What, exactly, was it that Conrad saw in Africa, which made his
nightmare voyage such a turning point in his life? What is often
called the 'Scramble for Africa' was the greatest land grab in history,
and one of the swiftest. In 1870, some eighty per cent of Africa
south of the Sahara desert was still under the control of indigenous
kings, chiefs or other rulers. Thirty-five years later, virtually all of
it, only a few territories excepted, would be European colonies or
protectorates. Britain, France, Germany, Portugal, Spain and Italy

all seized pieces of what King Leopold II of Belgium – who took an enormous slice for himself – called 'this magnificent African cake'. The Scramble for Africa redrew the map, enriched Europe and left tens of millions of Africans dead. But it is glaringly absent from the work of first-rank European novelists of the day. It would be as if no major nineteenth-century American writer dealt with slavery, or no major German one later wrote about the Holocaust. Joseph Conrad was a rare and brave exception.

It is often said that there were two great totalitarian systems of the twentieth century: Fascism and Communism. But we too often ignore a third: European colonialism, especially in Africa, where it could be just as brutal and deadly as the other two systems. Hitler's top deputy Hermann Göring, sentenced to death at Nuremberg for his role in the murder of Europe's Jews, was the son of the colonial governor of German Southwest Africa (today's Namibia), where the authorities carried out a deliberate genocide against the Herero people who had rebelled against German rule. And as late as the 1950s the British imprisoned tens of thousands of Kenyans in harsh concentration camps, executing some and castrating others in the course of ruthlessly suppressing an anti-colonial revolt. The list is far longer, and at the top of any tally of atrocities is what Conrad saw in the Congo.

Orchestrating this particularly bloody chapter of the Scramble for Africa was the man whose formal title was the name of Conrad's steamboat: Leopold II, King of the Belgians. Brilliant and charming, ruthless and avaricious, a public relations genius who cloaked his greed in the rhetoric of Christian philanthropy and anti-slavery crusading, Leopold was openly frustrated with being king of such a small country. '*Petit pays, petit gens*', he once said of Belgium, meaning, 'Small country, small-minded people.' He wanted a colony, a big one, where he could rule supreme, without interference from politicians or voters. The king began by hiring the famous explorer Henry Morton Stanley to explore the Congo River and its tributaries for him. Next he successfully lobbied first the American government and then all the major nations of Europe into recognising the Congo – a vast territory more than seventy times the size of

Belgium – as belonging to him *personally*. It was the world's only privately owned colony, and in 1885 he proclaimed himself its 'King-Sovereign'.

In the early years of the Congo Free State, as Leopold inaccurately christened his new domain, the major commodity he coveted was ivory. Elephant tusks were highly prized because they could be easily carved into piano keys, statuettes, jewellery, false teeth and much more. The king ordered a network of ivory-gathering stations, like the one in 'An Outpost of Progress', set up along the colony's river banks, and white men who wanted to make their fortunes flocked to the Congo. These adventurers were often eager not just for riches but for combat. Much of the ivory they seized at gunpoint and, as Congolese resisted the king's private army that was taking over their land, there were countless rebellions to put down. For a young European or American, going to the Congo promised the thrills of joining both a gold rush and the French Foreign Legion.

Like much of the European colonisation of Africa, the entire ivory-gathering system was based on compulsion. It was forced labourers who carried the white men's supplies into the interior on their backs and Congolese conscripts who were dragooned into the ranks of the king's army. In the years after Conrad's visit, the toll of this forced-labour system would swell to unimaginable proportions. Although ivory remained valuable, by the late 1890s wild rubber would supplant it as the colony's most lucrative treasure. The army went into village after village, holding the women hostage in order to force the men to go into the rainforest, for days and eventually weeks at a time, to gather a monthly quota of rubber. Many male rubber gatherers were worked to death; many women hostages starved. Tens, possibly hundreds of thousands of Congolese died in doomed uprisings against Leopold's well-armed military. Hundreds of thousands more fled the forced-labour system by going deep into the rainforest, where there was little food and no shelter, and they died. And, with so many Congolese turned into forced labourers, hostages or refugees, there were few able-bodied adults left to hunt, fish, or plant and harvest food crops. In the resulting famine, disease took a horrendous toll among people who otherwise would have survived. The birth rate plummeted. From all these causes, the best estimates today are that the territory's population was slashed from somewhere around twenty million in 1880 to approximately half of that in 1920. Conrad was an eyewitness to the beginnings of one of the great human catastrophes of modern Africa.

Paradoxically, the most richly revealing document to survive from Conrad's odyssey, the 'Congo Diary', is not from the river trip immortalised in *Heart of Darkness*, but from the weeks before he was able to board the *Roi des Belges*. For several centuries, European explorers and fortune-seekers had been frustrated that just upstream from where the Congo River pours into the Atlantic its enormous torrent of water – in volume second only to the Amazon – is a long, impassable succession of thundering rapids that the river tumbles down on the last part of its journey from the central African plateau. Soon after disembarking at the end of the voyage from Europe, Conrad set off, accompanied by one other white man and a caravan of thirty-one forced-labour porters, on the arduous 230-mile trek around these rapids. (Only eight years later would Belgian robber baron Albert Thys, who had interviewed Conrad in Brussels, succeed, at a cost of thousands of lives, in building a railway around the rapids. The ship Conrad took to Africa carried the first batch of rails and sleepers for this line.) It was on this caravan route that Conrad first recorded signs of the immense violence that underlay the colony's operations. In his diary on 4 July 1890, for example, he noted, 'Saw another dead body lying by the path.' And on 29 July: 'On the road to day passed a skeleton tied-up to a post.'

After more than a month of walking, in shaky health, he arrived at the small trading post of Kinshasa; from here, just above the rapids, it was clear steaming for a thousand miles upstream. On that trip up the river, the *Roi des Belges* passed only half a dozen other steamers. Typically these riverboats would travel by daylight and then tie up onshore for the night, either at one of the militarised ivory-gathering posts where firewood for the boilers could be loaded, or on the river bank where a crew of forced labourers, usually towed on a barge behind the steamer, could chop trees during the night for a day or two's supply of fuel.

Finally the steamer reached Stanley Falls, today Kisangani, a settlement of ivory warehouses, army barracks and the headquarters for officers who controlled the eastern part of the colony. A week later, Conrad and the *Roi des Belges* headed back downstream – with the current, the voyage would only take some two weeks. Back in Kinshasa, some bitter disappointments punctured Conrad's Congo dreams. He hit it off badly with a key official, Camille Delcommune, and found that he was not slated to take part, as he had been hoping, in an exploring expedition up one of the Congo's major tributaries, the Kasai River. The venality and greed of the ivory hunters dismayed him. And his malaria and dysentery, which he had already been fighting for some weeks, grew worse, landing him in a primitive hospital at a Baptist mission station where he may have had to endure some proselytising. 'He is a gentlemanly fellow,' wrote an American missionary in his diary. 'An English [New] Testament on his table furnishes a handle I hope to use on him.' Europeans still had few medicines for most tropical diseases, and roughly a third of the white men who came to the Congo in this era died there – a statistic that King Leopold II did his best to keep secret. Finally, at the end of October 1890, Conrad decided to abandon his Africa venture and head home. On the long trip around the rapids his illness was at its worst, and he had to be carried by porters. He arrived back in Europe early the next year, his health permanently weakened and his view of humanity for ever darkened.

Conrad struggled for many years to make sense of his Congo experience, and in some ways he never completely did. On the one hand, the clear-eyed observer who produced *Heart of Darkness* saw the colonial Scramble for Africa for what it was, and got all of its cruelty and lust for riches onto paper. On the other, he himself invested (and lost) money in another greedy scramble of the era, the South African gold rush, and all his life believed that the colonialism of his adopted country, Britain, was constructive and benign. But great artists abound in great contradictions – think of Tolstoy's extolling the virtues of marriage in his novels at the same time as he was the father of some dozen illegitimate children – and the raw materials in this volume may help us better understand the mixture of temptations, illusions, hopes and experiences that were the building blocks of Conrad's genius.

ADAM HOCHSCHILD

Introduction

In late January 1891, Captain Józef Korzeniowski – not yet reborn as the writer Joseph Conrad – returned to a cold and grey Brussels from an eight-month stint in the Congo Free State where he had been working as a riverboat pilot for the Société Anonyme Belge pour le Commerce du Haut-Congo (the Belgian Limited Company for Trade on the Upper Congo). The firm's trading interests, linked to far-distant Europe by waterway, depended upon a series of trading stations thinly scattered along the Congo River. That Conrad's experience proved an unhappy one for both him and his employers is an understatement. The fragmentary remains of the company's documents dismiss their erstwhile employee in the pithy phrase: *ne convient pas pour nous* (does not suit us). Conrad's bitterness towards, and his dislike and scorn of, the company are registered in 'An Outpost of Progress' and *Heart of Darkness*, masterly works that together comprise a major and moving statement about the late nineteenth century's 'Scramble for Africa'.

The blandly named Société Anonyme Belge was involved in several highly profitable (and conscienceless) ventures that were making Leopold II, King of the Belgians, and his cronies who managed it, enormously wealthy. Under terms agreed upon at the Berlin Conference of 1884–5, the territory was his personal property. (It passed to the Belgian state only in 1908, when it became a colony under the name the Belgian Congo.) Engaged for three years to captain a steamer along the river, Conrad found himself mainly occupied in menial tasks in the uncongenial company of freewheeling adventurers and dried-out company hacks. While in the Congo he witnessed, and quickly became disgusted with, the brutality that was commonplace in a part of the world then known as the 'White Man's Graveyard'. Roger Casement, whom he met in Matadi, would expose Belgian atrocities just over a decade later in a report commissioned by Parliament (extracted in the present collection). This would help to bring an era of egregious misrule that had variously posed as civilising mission and as the development of trade, not only to European but also to wider international attention.

Having come down with dysentery and malaria, the latter disease not at the time fully understood, Conrad managed to obtain a medical certificate that allowed him to wriggle out of his three-year contract. He returned to Europe physically and psychologically exhausted, in ill health and sick at heart. Shortly after arriving in England in early 1891, he entered the German Hospital in London's Dalston district to convalesce and, not long after, went to Geneva for a water cure to treat 'neurasthenia' (the day's word for clinical depression). In some sense, as he told Lady Ottoline Morrell, he never really 'recovered' from Africa, and bouts of illness and depression plagued him until his premature death, aged sixty-six, in 1924.

As the slightly loopy phrenologist in his *Heart of Darkness* quips to Captain Charlie Marlow who is about to set out for Africa: 'The changes take place inside, you know.' And, as Conrad recognised, they had. He famously – even somewhat shockingly – observed to his friend Edward Garnett, 'Before the Congo I was a mere animal.' His first-hand involvement in empire-building red in tooth and claw momentously altered his perspective on himself, his values and his life experience. Even more, it nourished a view of all human endeavour, which, as he later said, could be summed up on a cigarette-paper: 'They were born, they suffered, they died.'

An ironic realist, Conrad in his 1924 essay 'Geography and Some Explorers' characterised Europe's 'conquest' of Africa as 'the vilest scramble for loot that ever disfigured the history of human conscience'. The 'loot' he himself brought out – he tellingly described it as such – consisted of two fictions: the short story 'An Outpost of Progress', written during his honeymoon in Brittany in the summer of 1896, and the novella *Heart of Darkness* (1899). The terse but compelling 'Congo Diary' and the severely observant 'Up-river Book' also survive from his time in Africa. Hardly indicative of a nascent writer's descriptive powers – 'saw at a camping place the dead body of a Backongo – Shot? Horrid smell', 'Mosquitos', 'Night clear and starry' – the former document is none the less of signal interest both in itself and as a source-book for anyone reading *Heart of Darkness* (a work so dense, so intricate, that it demands to stand on its own and is thus not included in the present selection of documents).

The actual journey to Africa took slightly more than a month, with Conrad travelling from Brussels to Bordeaux by train to catch a steamer that had already left Antwerp and that had, at Brest, boarded French troops bound for Senegal and Dahomey (now Benin), the latter colony then engaged in a rebellion. Conrad's trip down Africa's Atlantic coastline in the company of soldiers sent to enforce France's colonial presence invests the image in *Heart of Darkness* of a French naval man-of-war firing into the continent with added, autobiographical potency.

By any measure, Conrad's trip to the Congo had been an extra-ordinarily circuitous one. Born in the Ukraine not far from Kiev in 1857, the son of Polish gentry whose short lives had been devoted to patriotic endeavour, an orphan privately educated, he had played the life of a young *boulevardier* in Marseilles before going out to the French Antilles, his first experience at sea. He drifted into the British Merchant Service, then heavily dependent upon foreign labour, and travelled to the entrepôts of the Far East – Singapore, Bombay, Calcutta, Bangkok – to Australia and Mauritius, collecting along the way the experience that led, in 1886, to a Master's certificate that mainly proved an over-qualification, steam by then replacing sail. Conrad was armed with this achievement when he sought out employment in Belgium; but, in the event, the post of captain of a river steamer was his only briefly and temporarily aboard the *Roi des Belges* (King of the Belgians), a tinpot little boat that plied the stations of the Société Anonyme Belge on the Congo River.

Along the way, he also 'collected' English. His third language, after Polish and French, it was the one he chose to write in, declaring in *A Personal Record* (1912), his most sustained autobiographical piece, that he had been 'adopted' by English, in much the same way that the Red Ensign, the flag of the British Merchant Marine, had provided him a 'home' during his years as a professional seaman. Languages do not 'adopt' people; but the word, if fanciful, is also deeply poignant, simultaneously recollecting his orphanhood and expressing an ardent desire for belonging.

And then there was that other transformation, the one that counts most: his desire to write. People write for many reasons – for money, fame, because they have something to say. The reasons are often elusive, sometimes imperfectly understood even by the writer. Conrad's depiction of his own great moment deliberately eschews high drama and opts, instead, for fiction: one morning in London, after breakfast, the remains of his repast cleared away, he sat down . . . and began to write, communing, as he puts it, with the 'shades' of the past – 'Malays, Arabs, and half-castes' – that had appealed to him for expression. They were patient. His first novel, *Almayer's Folly* (1895), took some five years to write. And he nearly lost the manuscript – the unique copy – twice: there was misadventure in a Berlin railway station, and it narrowly escaped the waters of the Congo River precisely at a point where a young officer had earlier drowned, giving his name to the spot.

There must have been earlier writing. A novel influenced by Flaubert's *Madame Bovary* and winning so much praise from the London press that it launched a career does not emerge full-blown and without some tentative forays into fiction. But of those earlier writings – in Polish? in French? – we know nothing at all. A solid education in the Classics, reading in Shakespeare, Cervantes and Dickens, a thorough mastery of the French language and wide reading in contemporary French literature and Polish Romantic poetry are good equipment but in themselves no guarantee that one could call upon them to earn one's bread in late nineteenth-century England, let alone win lasting fame.

A mid-Victorian by birth with a foot solidly in the early twentieth century, Conrad will always remain something of a mystery. The most assiduous scholarly research – a worldwide critical industry is devoted to him – has pinned down only fragments of him. Like Dickens's Mr Gradgrind, we know lots of facts; but Conrad always recedes from view, and tends to do so the closer we approach him. The one-time 'animal' turned writer gives away little, even when writing so directly from and about his own experience. *A Personal Record*, a short extract of which is reprinted here, is an impressionistic account, with the rare date and the occasional worked-up fiction, of what appear to be at times randomly selected moments of a life. As has long been recognised, *Heart of Darkness*, that other piece of 'loot' that Conrad dragged out of Africa, is 'highly autobiographical', set firmly in experienced and observed realities in the Congo Free State (never, in fact, mentioned by name either in that novella or in 'An Outpost of Progress').

The documents brought together in this volume variously and richly illuminate aspects of Conrad's encounter with Leopold II's Congo. The letters that pre-date his journey offer sparse yet privileged glimpses into a man notoriously private and reserved, and establish a sense of the importance of his family relationships that were maintained by rare correspondence and the still more infrequent visit. That Conrad was orphaned at eleven and had virtually no contact as an adult with his familial and cultural past gives, perhaps, a greater intensity to these letters, some written aboard the ship that took him southwards, to the mouth of the Congo. Travelling down the African coast, he ponders the welfare and doings of his relatives in Austrian Poland and the Russian Ukraine, themselves subject peoples living in colonial conditions and under foreign domination.

Vividly glimpsed here as well are colonialism's long tentacles, the hard necessity of having to earn one's daily bread out of others' sufferings and the mordant irony of a small, unimportant and upstart European nation arrogantly appropriating a large swathe of land and its inhabitants, whose culture stretched back to time immemorial. Conrad's retrospective appreciation of his time in Africa and his use of his experience for fiction is finely demonstrated in 'An Outpost of Progress', which is here at last reprinted without a division into two that its author had found disfiguring and disruptive, but to which he bowed because of editorial pressure.

'The Congo Diary' and 'Up-river Book' meticulously document the bare facts observed at first hand; but they also urge one to look beyond them, to contextualise both one man's complex personal experience and that of a whole generation of Europeans leaving their countries to make money and to fulfil ambitions, strange dreamers in a strange land with death or psychological disintegration frequently the price of their gamble. One sees in these two records as well, even if at some slight distance, the missionaries fired by a potent vision of a world transformed (and smoothed out), with Christianity seeking to extinguish age-old native cultural beliefs and practices. Of no less importance to the reader's understanding of the historical and cultural circumstances in which Conrad's own brief encounter with Africa occurred are the supplementary documents made available here in the testimonies of his friends and colleagues, wherein his Congo experience is variously recollected and refracted, and, with much more directness and immediacy, in Roger Casement's influential Congo Report of 1903.

To peruse these documents is necessarily to engage in an adventure of one's own: one is rapidly immersed in facets of a complex, now distant past – a moment of African and European history – and one is forced to contemplate, too, the ways in which hard facts can be imaginatively reworked as fiction. As to the facts themselves, there are a number of new ones offered in this volume. Several of the individuals mentioned in Conrad's correspondence are provided with dates here for the first time as well as with contextualising information not available in the standard edition of his letters (*The Collected Letters*, published by Cambridge University Press, 1983–2007). For the first time as well, it is revealed that Conrad's outward voyage to the Congo was in a vessel that had been co-opted to become, in effect, a troop-ship.

Captain Józef Korzeniowski made a journey up the Congo River, but it was 'Joseph Conrad' who came back from it. The raw facts, the carefully honed observational skills, the rich – sometimes clotted and tangled – style, the intense allusiveness add up to much, much more than the sum of their parts in 'loot' from that place, from which, as Pliny observed, something new is always coming. 'Come and find out,' whispers the land to Captain Marlow. 'Come and find out' all right, about that darkest of places, intractable to mapping, ever-shifting and inveterately elusive. A century after the challenge was issued, though to a time and place now long gone, that invitation to explore still stands.

J. H. STAPE

Editorial Note

The central texts of this selection are Joseph Conrad's 'Congo Diary' and 'Up-river Book', written during his eight-month journey in the Congo Free State in 1890. The 'Diary' extends from his arrival in Matadi to the end of his overland trek to Nselemba, whereas the 'Up-river Book' concerns Conrad's journey on the *Roi des Belges*. The principal source for both texts is *Last Essays*, edited by Harold Ray Stevens and J. H. Stape (Cambridge University Press, 2010). Conrad's spellings and punctuation have been retained, with minor editorial emendations.

Interspersed with these texts are Conrad's letters to family, friends and colleagues which illuminate his journey. These date from before he commenced his post with the Société Anonyme Belge pour le Haut-Congo and continue for many years after he returns from Africa. The source for these is *The Collected Letters of Joseph Conrad*, edited by Frederick R. Karl, Laurence Davies, et al (Cambridge University Press, 1983–2008).

Also included in this selection of documents is Conrad's short story 'An Outpost of Progress', which was strongly influenced by his time in the Congo and is the only work of fiction, except the novella *Heart of Darkness* (1899), which directly draws upon his experiences there.

Chronology

1857

3 December   Józef Teodor Konrad Korzeniowski born in Berdyczów, Russian-occupied Ukraine, son of the poet, playwright and translator Apollo Korzeniowski and of Ewa (née Bobrowska).

1861

21 October   Apollo Korzeniowski arrested and imprisoned in Warsaw by Russian police for involvement with the nationalist conspiracy movement.

1862

9 May   The Korzeniowskis are exiled to Vologda, Siberia.

1865

18 April   Ewa Korzeniowska dies of tuberculosis.
17 December   King Leopold II accedes to the throne of Belgium.

1868

January   Apollo Korzeniowski, seriously ill, is reprieved and leaves Russia with his son.

1869

23 May   Apollo Korzeniowski dies in Cracow; Tadeusz Bobrowski becomes Konrad Korzeniowski's guardian.

1874

26 September   Konrad leaves Austrian Poland for Marseilles.
15 December   Joins, as a passenger, the barque *Mont Blanc* sailing from Marseilles to Martinique.

1875

25 June   Joins the *Mont Blanc* as a trainee seaman on journey to Haiti.

1876

8 July   Works as steward aboard the *Saint Antoine* from Marseilles to Martinique, Haiti, and in the Caribbean.

1877

July–   Claims to have been involved in Carlist plot, smuggling
December arms to Spanish rebels.

1878

February   Unsuccessfully attempts suicide by shooting himself in the chest.
11 July   Joins his first British ship, the *Skimmer of the Sea*.
12 October Joins the *Duke of Sutherland* en route to Australia.

1884

28 April   Joins the *Narcissus* as second mate in Bombay.
3 December Qualifies as first mate.

1885

5 February Following the Berlin Conference, the Congo Free State is established under the personal rule of Leopold II.

1886

19 August   Becomes a British subject.
10 November Passes his examination for Ordinary Master of the British merchant marine.

1888

24 January Conrad receives command as master of the *Otago*.

1889

26 March   Resigns command of the *Otago*.
2 July   Released from Russian citizenship.
Autumn   Begins work on *Almayer's Folly*.

1890

10 May   Leaves Bordeaux to take a position on the *Roi des Belges*

for the Société Anonyme Belge pour le Commerce du Haut-Congo.

12 June	Conrad reaches Boma.
13 June	Alights ship at Matadi.
28 June	Begins inland trek to Kinshasa.
2 August	Reaches Kinshasa.
3 August	Takes substitute command of the *Roi des Belges*.
1 September	Reaches Stanley Falls.
16 November	Returns to Matadi and obtains a release from his contract on medical grounds.
4 December	Departs for Europe.

1891

February–March	In a London hospital suffering from fever and rheumatism.
19 November	Becomes first mate of the *Torrens*.

1894

17 January	Leaves his position on the *Adowa*, his final post as a seaman.
8 October	Meets Edward Garnett.

1895

29 April	*Almayer's Folly: A Story of an Eastern River* published in London. Korzeniowski adopts 'Joseph Conrad' as his pen name.

1896

4 March	*An Outcast of the Islands* published.
24 March	Conrad marries Miss Jessie George, born 22 February 1873.

1897

2 December	*The Nigger of the 'Narcissus'* published.

1898

15 January	Conrad's first son, Borys Alfred, is born.
26 March	*Tales of Unrest* ('Karain', 'The Idiots', 'An Outpost of Progress', 'The Return', 'The Lagoon') published.

1899

February,   *Heart of Darkness* published as a three-part serial
March, April   in *Blackwood's Magazine*.

1900

15 October   *Lord Jim* published.

1901

26 June   *The Inheritors*, written in collaboration with Ford
          Madox Ford, published.

1902

13 November   *Youth and Two Other Stories* published.

1903

22 April   *Typhoon and Other Stories* published.
16 October   *Romance*, written in collaboration with Ford Madox
             Ford, published.

1904

15 February   The Casement Report published by the Foreign Office.
14 October   *Nostromo* published.

1906

2 August   Conrad's second son, John Alexander, is born.
4 October   *The Mirror of the Sea* published.

1907

12 September   *The Secret Agent* published.

1908

6 August   *A Set of Six* published.
15 November   Leopold II forced to cede his personal control over the
              Congo Free State to Belgium, thus creating a Belgian
              colony under parliamentary control known as the
              Belgian Congo.

1909

May — Conrad and Ford Madox Ford quarrel and end all collaborative projects.

17 December — Leopold II dies at Laeken, Belgium.

1910

January–April — Conrad undergoes a severe nervous breakdown owing to poor health and financial problems.

1911

5 October — *Under Western Eyes* published.

1912

19 January — *Some Reminiscences* (later renamed *A Personal Record*) published.

14 October — *'Twixt Land and Sea* published.

1913

September — Introduced to Bertrand Russell by their mutual friend Lady Ottoline Morrell.

18 September — *Chance* published.

1914

25 July–2 November — Conrad travels to Poland with his family.

28 July — Outbreak of the First World War.

1915

24 February — *Within the Tides* published.

26 March — *Victory* published.

20 September — Conrad's son, Borys, joins the British Army.

1917

19 March — *The Shadow-Line* published.

1919

6 August — *The Arrow of Gold* published.

1920

21 May   *The Rescue*, a novel begun by Conrad in 1896, published.

1921

25 February   *Notes on Life and Letters* published.

1923

1 May–2 June   Conrad travels to the United States, staying in New York and Boston.

1 December   *The Rover* published.

1924

26 May   Conrad is offered a knighthood, which he declines.

3 August   Conrad dies of heart attack at his home near Canterbury.

CONRAD'S CONGO

CONRAD'S CORRESPONDENCE about his forthcoming trip to the Congo and his experience there offers glimpses of his preparations for and stay in Africa. This correspondence is incomplete, letters having gone astray at the time, whilst others are also known to have been lost. All those he sent to his maternal uncle Tadeusz Bobrowski (see letter of 27 December 1889) were destroyed during the Second World War. Conrad was typically reserved in expressing his feelings, and his letters are largely concerned with comings and goings, with plans and immediate events. The anxiety and excitement he must have felt goes unrecorded, and is to be sensed between the lines.

Conrad's expedition to the Congo began circuitously. The Great Dock Strike that by the end of August 1889 had paralysed the Port of London motivated him to consider looking abroad for a berth, and he apparently even toyed with the idea of joining Belgian ships in the Caribbean trade. Having returned to England in June after resigning his captaincy in the Australian ship *Otago*, he found himself in a transitional period; he was at work on his first novel – *Almayer's Folly* (1895) – but unsettled as regards short- and long-term professional prospects and his future. Fluent in French and with his experience – if, in fact, it had occurred – in Antwerp's *John P. Best* in his favour, he obtained an interview in Brussels with Albert Thys (1849–1915), managing director of the newly founded Société Anonyme Belge pour le Commerce du Haut-Congo (the Belgian Limited Company for Trade on the Upper Congo). One of several interlinked firms in the Congo Free State, the company, located at 9, rue Brederode (immediately behind the Royal Palace), operated a fleet of steamers to supply its stations along the river and ship goods between Léopoldville (now Kinshasa) and Belgium. Conrad's interview with Thys is immortalised in *Heart of Darkness*: Marlow – partly Conrad's surrogate – meets with 'an impression of pale plumpness in a frock-coat. The great man himself. He was five feet six, I should judge, and had his grip on the handle-end of ever so many millions.'

TO ALBERT THYS

4 November 1889
London

M. Deputy Director
Belgian Company of the Upper Congo

Sir,

I have the honour to inform you that I have withdrawn from the voyage to Mexico and the West Indies in the service of the house of Walford & Co. – naturally with the permission of these gentlemen.

I think that, considering my prolonged stay in the torrid zone (from which I have just returned) and my probable departure for Africa within a few months, it would be wise to profit from the European climate for as long as possible.

I hasten to apprise you of this change in my plans, for I consider that at present it is my duty to keep you informed of my movements.

Letters to the address below will reach me without delay.

I have the honour of being, Monsieur l'Administrateur, with the greatest respect, your very obedient servant

Conrad Korzeniowski

c/o Messrs. Barr, Moering and Co.,
36, Camomile Street, London E.C.

Conrad was temporarily employed by Barr, Moering & Company, a Stuttgart-based warehousing firm and shipping agent in the City of London, in which he had a small interest and a connection through his first 'English' friend, Adolph Krieger, a partner in the firm. Although holding a Master's certificate from the Marine Department of the Board of Trade, Conrad had only once – and quite recently – held a captaincy, his career characterised by berths below his rating and thus also at a pay lower than he should have received. G.-C. (Guillaume-César) de Baerdemaecker d. 1903), a Ghent shipping figure, had written to Thys on 24 September recommending Conrad on the basis of a good word from friends in London, asserting that Conrad was an educated gentleman who had good references. Conrad's French (idiomatic though not error-free) cannot account for a confusion about his being employed by G. P. (George Paget) Walford (1843–1936), who had extensive business connections in Antwerp and Ghent.

TO ALBERT THYS

28 November 1889
London

Sir,

I have just learned from a letter of M. de Baerdemaecker to Messrs. Barr, Moering & Co. that you thought I had served M. Walford as captain of one of his ships.

I hasten to apologize to you for having expressed myself so badly during the interview which you were kind enough to grant me in Brussels. My intention was to inform you that I was employed by M. Walford for the time being: I was not even aware he was a ship-owner. I dare to hope you will grant me your indulgence for this misunderstanding, caused simply by the unfamiliarity of expressing myself in French.

As doubtless there would be the question of qualifications for the post you have been so kind as to promise me, I take the liberty of informing you that I possess a commission from the Board of Trade, qualifying me absolutely to command sailing ships and steamers of the British merchant service (obtained by examination in London, 1885).

I am ready to produce copies of the certificates signed by the captains and shipowners who have employed me during my fifteen years of sea service, witnessing my competence in matters of seamanship and my good conduct in general.

I have also been – for the last four years – a member of the Society of Captains (Shipmasters' Association, London, 60 Fenchurch Street) where my standing is of course known.

G. F. W. Hope, Esq., Director of the South African Mercantile Co., member of the London Chamber of Commerce, 39 Coleman Street, will give you all the information about this matter you may judge it necessary to request.

I have the honour to be, Monsieur l'Administrateur, with the highest respect,

C. Korzeniowski

Having been invited by his maternal uncle and former guardian Tadeusz (Wilhelm Jerzy) Bobrowski (1829–94), a landowner and gentleman farmer, to visit him at his estate, Kazimierówka, in the western Ukraine, Conrad, in early February 1890, travelled to Russia via Brussels, Warsaw and Lublin. He recalls parts of his journey and two-month visit in *A Personal Record* (serialised in 1908 and published in book form in 1912).

TO ALBERT THYS

27 December 1889
London

M. Deputy Director
Belgian Company of the Upper Congo

Sir,

I have just received an invitation from one of my relatives to spend some time on his estate in Southern Russia.

It would please me very much to accept it, but before deciding I would like to know precisely how much time I have at my disposal.

Communications within that country are rather difficult in winter, and even the telegraph often does not function properly. On the other hand, a short visit would not be worth the trouble and expense of travelling.

Under these circumstances I venture to address you in the hope that you will please do me the favour of informing me (approximately) of the date when you will need my services. I could then take measures to return to London punctually, where I would hold myself at your disposal.

Please, sir, accept in advance my thanks for your answer, as well as my very sincere apologies for thus taking up your time.

I have the honour of being, Monsieur l'Administrateur, with the highest respect, your very obedient servant

J. C. Korzeniowski

Conrad's plan to visit his uncle Tadeusz Bobrowski gave him the opportunity to call on his distant cousin Aleksander Poradowski (1835–90) – his maternal grandmother's first cousin, not, in fact, his 'uncle', as he addresses him. A former cavalry officer, Poradowski left Poland in the wake of the 1863 Insurrection and lived in exile, first in Germany and then in France. He returned to his homeland to live in Lemberg (today Lviv, in Ukraine); but his Belgian-born wife of French descent, the novelist and bluestocking Marguerite(-Blanche-Marie) Poradowska (née Gachet de la Fournière, 1848–1937), found the climate too rigorous, and they left Galicia to settle in Belgium in 1884.

TO ALEKSANDER PORADOWSKI

16th January, 1890
[letterhead: The British and
Foreign Transit Agency. Barr,
Moering & Co., Shipping and
Custom House Agents, 36,
Camomile Street, London, E. C.]

My Dear Uncle.

I have just had a letter from Kazimierówka, in which, in reply to my inquiry, Uncle Tadeusz tells me that you are living in Brussels and gives me your address. I am terribly sorry that I did not know this earlier, as I was in Brussels in October last year. It is possible, however, that before long I shall have to visit Brussels again. The object of this scrawl to you is to remember myself to the relation whose great kindness to me in Cracow I have certainly not forgotten. I do not ask whether you will permit me to visit you – for I permit myself not to doubt it; but I would very much like to be certain that you are in Brussels and that I shall be able to find you there in the course of the next month.

I returned to London six months ago after a three years' absence. Of these three years I spent one among the islands of the Malay Archipelago, after which I spent two years as master of an Australian vessel in the Pacific and Indian Oceans. I am now more or less under contract to the 'Société Belge pour le Commerce du Haut

Congo' to be master of one of its river steamers. I have not signed any agreement, but Mr A. Thys, the director of that Company, has promised me the post. Whether he will keep his promise and when he will send me to Africa, I do not yet know; it will probably be in May.

I intend to visit Uncle Tadeusz soon; that is to say I want to, and he also wants me to; but he says that it is difficult during the winter. I am expecting a letter from him in a few days' time, which will decide the matter. If I do go home it will be via Hamburg – returning via Brussels. If, however, my visit is postponed I shall nevertheless be going to Brussels in March in connection with the post in the Congo. Therefore in any case I shall have the pleasure of seeing you, my dear Uncle, and of making myself known to Aunt Poradowska whom I only know from that portrait of her which you had with you in Cracow.

In the meantime, my dear Uncle, a most cordial embrace from your affectionate relation and servant,

Konrad Korzeniowski

A letter care of Messrs. Barr Moering will always find me.

Perhaps worried by his cousin's deteriorating health, Conrad quickly altered his travel plans to include a brief stopover in Brussels on his way to the Ukraine rather than upon his return trip to London. A British subject from August 1886 and, by petition, formally released from any connection with Russia in July 1889, he none the less required travel permits that, as a former Russian subject, were proving – at least in the short term – difficult to obtain.

TO ALEKSANDER PORADOWSKI

20 January, 1890.
[letterhead: Barr, Moering]

Dear Uncle,

My most affectionate thanks to you and to Aunt for the kind expressions contained in your letter. The sight of your handwriting gave me inexpressible pleasure, but, alas, my joy was short-lived! The news of your poor state of health has grieved me greatly. Please, do not trouble to answer this letter. I hasten to inform you that in view of the state of your health, I have decided to come home via Brussels. I realize that after the operation you will need not visits but a complete rest. This morning I received, simultaneously with your letter, one from Uncle Tadeusz that says 'come'. However, those villains in the Russian Consulate do not want to grant me a visa – which means further delay, inconvenience, and visits to the Embassy, perhaps to no avail.

I shall let you know how I am getting on as soon as I settle matters with these pirates. And so, au revoir to you, my dearest Uncle. I kiss the hands of dear Aunt.

Your loving and devoted nephew and servant.
Konrad

My apologies for the scrawl, but I have barely time to catch the post.

TO ALEKSANDER PORADOWSKI

31 January, 1890.
[letterhead: Barr, Moering]

My Dearest Uncle,

I am already in possession of all the necessary documents and intend to leave London next Tuesday or, at the latest, Wednesday, but not later, via Brussels of course. I shall, therefore, arrive at your place on Wednesday or Thursday and if you allow me I shall stay there 24 hours. I would not like to cause any embarrassment to dear Aunt – especially as you are not well. I could spend the night at an hotel and the day with you both 's'il n'y a pas d'empêchement'. When I leave you we shall say to each other 'see you soon', for I shall come back again shortly, via Brussels of course. A thousand embraces.

I shall come to you directly from the station.

Your loving,
K. N. Korzeniowski

Having travelled by boat train to the Belgian capital, Conrad called on the Poradowskis at their home at no. 48, rue Veydt, in Ixelles, a residential quarter of Brussels favoured by artists, intellectuals and the professional classes. The meeting proved a signal personal event in that Conrad quickly became friendly with Marguerite Poradowska. They began a correspondence that stretched over a decade, only part of which survives. Despite a lack of documentary evidence, some commentators have speculated that the relationship strayed into romance.

TO MARGUERITE PORADOWSKA

Tuesday, 4 February 1890
[London]

My dear Aunt,

Many thanks for your card. I am leaving London tomorrow, Friday, at 9 a.m. and should arrive in Brussels at 5.30 p.m. I shall therefore be with you at about six. Believe me, with the liveliest gratitude, your very affectionate nephew and very devoted servant

Conrad Korzeniowski

Aleksander Poradowski died at his home in the early morning of 7 February. News of this had reached Karol Antoni Tadeusz Zagórski (*c.*1850 – 98), the late Poradowski's nephew and a distant cousin of Conrad, and Conrad's visit to his relatives in Lublin was overshadowed by Poradowski's death. Having just been in Brussels, he was able to provide an up-to-date account to Gabriela Zagórska (*c.*1830 – ?), one of Poradowski's five sisters. The news, however, was not immediately shared with another of his sisters, 'Aunt Jeanette' (Joanna Konstancja Poradowska, *c.*1829 – 91). Nor was it imparted to Karol Zagórski's father – 'Uncle Jean' (Jan Antoni Nepomucen Zagórski, *c.*1825 – 91), apparently also in fragile health. His widowed 'aunt' – as he called her in letters – was much in his mind, as Conrad was also reading Poradowska's novel *Yaga* (1887), about life in the Ukraine (then called Ruthenia).

TO MARGUERITE PORADOWSKA

11 February 1890
Warsaw

My dear and good Aunt,

I am writing you this line to tell you that Charles Zagórski has left Warsaw for Lublin, so that I have not yet seen anyone in the family.

I was with you in thought and spirit yesterday, sharing, though far from you, your sorrow, as indeed I have not stopped doing since I left you. I am leaving tomorrow evening, and I shall have to find Charles before paying my respects to the Zagórskis. He hasn't left his address in Warsaw – at least with anyone I know.

I called at the offices of *Słowo* without finding the editor. I left the announcement and my card there. I shall call again tomorrow.

Au revoir, my dear aunt. If I do not know how to express all that I feel, you will believe me none the less your affectionate nephew and very devoted friend and servant

C. Korzeniowski

I shall write from Lublin or Kazimierówka as soon as I arrive.

TO MARGUERITE PORADOWSKA

Saturday, 14 February 1890 [15 – 16? February 1890]
at Lipowiec. En route to
Kazimierówka.

My dear Aunt Marguerite,

I left Lublin yesterday without being able to find a free moment to write to you as I promised. Excuse this twenty-four-hour delay in narrating my sad mission.

All those good souls, tried so much by sorrow, never cease thinking of you. Some hours before my arrival they learned the news from the obituary in the newspaper, but they hid it from Aunt Jeanette and poor Uncle Jean, who is, alas, very ill. And all those unhappy people crushed by the blow striking them, living in almost daily expectation of another death in the family, pressed around me asking, 'And Marguerite?' 'Poor Marguerite'. Aunt Gabrielle wanted to know everything, and with a grief-stricken heart I had to give her the account of your sorrowful ordeal. I described you as I have known you, kind, loving, devoted and spirited. But they know you so well! Appreciate you so much! All of them, Gabrielle and Angèle and Charles, possess hearts of gold. The announcement of your visit to Poland was like a lightening in the blackness of our meeting. Aunt Gabrielle expects you. I have told them all that I know of your plans. They will write to you. They await you with open arms.

That is all, dear Aunt. I leave here in ten minutes. My uncle expects me. His servant – who is accompanying me – says that the dear old man has hardly slept since receiving my telegram last Tuesday. I shall write to you soon.

Sincerely and affectionately yours
Conrad Korzeniowski

Excuse this letter, my dear little Aunt. I write to you in French because I think of you in French; and these sentiments, so badly expressed, come from the heart, which knows neither the grammar nor the spelling of a studied sympathy. That is my excuse. I have finished *Yaga* – twice. I shall write nothing to you about it while I am still under its charm. Presently, dispassionately; but soon,

Yours
J.C.K.

Conrad's friendly relations with Marguerite Poradowska continued in earnest, with letters exchanged during his stay with his uncle. (Apart from three letters, her side of their correspondence does not survive.) Her husband's death still fresh, she shared with Conrad an account of an obituary oration delivered by the vice president of the Polish Relief Society of Brussels at her home on the morning of her husband's funeral, and recalled as well the sympathies of the Princess de Ligne (née Hedwige Julie Wanda, Princess Lubomirska (1815–95)). The oration briefly sketched Poradowski's military career, his painful exile after the failed 1863 Insurrection, his involvement in Polish circles in Brussels and his 'austere' patriotism.

TO MARGUERITE PORADOWSKA

10 March 1890
Kazimierówka

My dear Aunt,

Only yesterday I received your letter of 15 February, through the agency of our good Aunt Gabrielle. The delay is explained by our absence from Kazimierówka, to which we returned yesterday after an excursion in the immediate area that lasted ten days.

Many thanks for the kind memory you carry of me. My admiration and friendship for you are increased by a feeling of deep gratitude for the goodness you show me. The thought of seeing you again in Brussels will console me when the time to part from my uncle arrives. I leave him on 15 April, and I will have the happiness of seeing you on the 23rd of the same month, if all goes well.

I am very happy to know that the Princess has been altogether so kind and friendly to you, but I venture to hope you will not make any hasty decision. Besides, you will not have to decide until near the end of April. By that time I should be with you and in a position to give you news of the Polish visit in person.

I have read M. Merzbach's speech with melancholy pleasure. He has not made any fine phrases, but he has recounted that simple and noble life in words brief but springing from the heart; and he has recognized (I do not say appreciated) – he has recognized the part you played in that life. I ask your pardon for such a short letter. The post leaves today and I have received a pile of letters which must be answered promptly. I believe that my recommendation to the Company of the Congo was not strong enough and that the matter will not succeed at all. That vexes me a little.

To our next meeting, dear Aunt – soon, for time goes quickly. I kiss your hands, and I embrace you warmly. Your affectionate nephew

C. Korzeniowski

My address: Mr T. Bobrowski, Lipowiec post office, Kazimie-rówka, Gov't of Kiev, South Russia. – (for Conrad)

Do not write unless you feel so inclined, for we shall be able to chat a little within a few days.

Marguerite Poradowska's proposed journey to Russian Poland to visit her late husband's relatives would involve her arranging appropriate travel documents, passports not being common prior to the First World War. Belgian by birth, she was by marriage a subject of the Austro-Hungarian Empire, Aleksander Poradowski having been born in Galicia, which since the late eighteenth-century partitions of Poland had become part of that sprawling and ethnically diverse empire.

TO MARGUERITE PORADOWSKA

23 March 1890
Kazimierówka

My dear Aunt,

I have just received your letter, which I read with much sorrow. Life rolls on in bitter waves, like the gloomy and brutal ocean under a sky covered with mournful clouds, and there are some days when to the poor souls embarked on the desperate voyage it seems that not a ray of sun has ever been able to penetrate that sad veil; that never again will it shine, that it never even existed! We must forgive those eyes which the harsh wind of misfortune has so filled with tears that they refuse to see the blue; we must forgive those lips which have so tasted life's bitterness that they refuse to express words of hope. Above all, we must forgive the unhappy souls who have elected to make the pilgrimage on foot, who skirt the shore and look uncomprehendingly upon the horror of the struggle, the joy of victory, the profound hopelessness of the vanquished; or those souls who receive the castaway with a smile of pity and a word of wisdom or reproach on their lips. We must especially forgive the latter, 'for they know not what they do!' This is my thought about him, about you, about those who surround you; but I beg you to consider, I beg you to understand that a soul living in a body tormented by suffering and worn out by illness is permitted to have such aberrant moments. Under the pressure of physical suffering, the intellect sees wrongly, the heart deceives itself, the unguided soul strays into an abyss. You must grant it, entirely, unreservedly, with complete disregard of your personal suffering; not as a sacrifice, but as a duty. So granted, your pardon will move a little nearer the human ideal of Divine Justice, nearer the Justice which is the only hope, the only refuge of souls who have fought, suffered, and succumbed in the struggle with life.

And since this letter is on the theme of forgiveness, I ask it also for myself. If this letter occasions disappointment or pain, do not pass sentence on me. Wait! Later you will perhaps see that I have tried to tell you only what I believed to be true; and if I annoy you now, you will pardon me then. Au revoir, my dear and good Aunt. I am eternally your very sincere and very devoted servant and friend

J. C. Korzeniowski

I asked my uncle to give his opinion about your visit to Russia. There won't be any difficulty. You can return, as an Austrian or a French subject, without the least fear.

I hesitate to send you this but 'fiat justicia ruat coelum'. You will understand me! Yours.

25 March.

A contact initiated by Gustaw Adam Sobotkiewicz (1824–94), a long-time friend of Conrad's uncle, Tadeusz Bobrowski, stirred memories of Conrad's Cracow days and of a youthful, now distant past. Conrad had made an excursion with Sobotkiewicz into the Carpathian Mountains also in the company of the tutor whom Bobrowski had arranged for his orphaned nephew – Adam Marek Pulman (1846–91), then a student in the Faculty of Medicine at Cracow's Jagiellonian University and later a physician. Conrad went on his first trip abroad with Pulman – to Switzerland and Italy – in May 1873.

TO GUSTAW SOBOTKIEWICZ

17/29 March, 1890
Kazimierówka

Dear and Honourable Sir,

I thank you heartily a thousand times for the kind and friendly words addressed to me in your letter to my Uncle. That I have not forgotten those who in their kindness remembered me may be witnessed by my letters to Uncle, in which I frequently asked after you and your daughter – not out of good manners – a quality which my way of life has not done much to develop – but out of a yearning from my heart which has not forgotten the good old times. And were they really so long ago? My later life has been so different, so unlike the life that I began, that those earlier impressions, feelings and memories have in no way been erased. And now, reading your letter, they are revived more clearly than ever.

I am extremely sorry that circumstances do not permit me to return through Cracow. I came here through Warsaw in order to reach my Uncle as soon as possible, and now I must go back the same way, so as to see the family in Radom, and to get back to London in time.

Although I am sorry to hear you speak of your journey to the last port of call in this life – a port from which there is no return, I have seen so many people living long years on the edge of eternity; indeed I myself have so often seen, as I thought, its portals, that I well know how illusory those presentiments are.

Your health will surely mend, and you will stay fit! Please allow me – as I set out on a long journey, with your blessing – to go away in the hope that in the near future – a year or two – I shall have the joy of seeing you and of thanking you personally for your kindness – which is so dear to me.

I thank Mrs Dębowska – whom I remember so well as Miss Marya sitting in a highlander's carriage together with you, somewhere on the Hungarian frontier – with all my heart for remembering me so kindly. Of our comrade on that excursion – Pulman – who so determinedly ran from mountain hut to mountain hut asking the way – I have news only from my Uncle, who refuses to accept the tragic story of his death in the flames of the burning Vienna theatre as not being in accordance with the documents in the archives of Kazimierówka. Probably he is living in Sambir, but I do not know how he is getting on.

Hoping that both you, honoured Sir, and your daughter will continue to remember me, I am,

Your grateful and humble servant,
K. N. Korzeniowski

If *Heart of Darkness* can be trusted, Conrad's interview with Thys was formal and almost comically perfunctory, his more extensive conversation about employment with the Société Anonyme Belge pour le Commerce du Haut-Congo being with its secretary general, A.-J. (Alphonse-Jules-Marie) Wauters (1845–1916), an acquaintance of Marguerite Poradowska (see letter of 10 June 1890 below). In addition to his post under Thys, Wauters, a geographer and cartographer, was editor-in-chief of *Le Mouvement géographique* from 1884 and the founding editor of *Le Congo illustré* (1892–5), the latter, in effect, a company magazine.

TO ALBERT THYS

11 April 1890
district of Kazimierówka

M. Albert Thys,
Brussels
M. l'Administrateur,

I have just been advised by my agents that your letter sent to my address in London has been forwarded to me in Russia – according to my instructions. I thought I had taken all possible precautions with my correspondence; unfortunately it seems that this letter has been mislaid, or perhaps it is entirely lost. I have inquired at the Provincial Post Office, but up to now unsuccessfully.

I am unaware, therefore, of the contents of the communication with which you have honoured me, but I dare hope that – if it contained a decision favourable to my candidacy – the regrettable accident of its loss will not carry any prejudice.

As I informed the Secretary of the Company during the interview that he so kindly granted me on 5 February of this year, I shall return towards the end of April.

I shall therefore be in Brussels on the 30th of this month at the latest, and shall present myself without loss of time at the offices of the Company of the Upper Congo, in order to learn your decision concerning my affairs.

I have the honour of being, Monsieur l'Administrateur, with the highest respect, your very obedient servant

J. C. Korzeniowski

Conrad seemingly drew upon Poradowska's efforts to help him, with Marlow confessing in *Heart of Darkness*: 'I, Charlie Marlow, set the women to work – to get a job! . . . I had an aunt, a dear enthusiastic soul . . . determined to make no end of fuss to get me appointed skipper of a river steamboat.' Well connected in intellectual circles in Brussels, Poradowska lived in the same street as Camille Janssen, governor-general of the Congo Free State. Whether or not she knew him or his family is, however, unknown; and what effect her efforts had is similarly a matter of conjecture. In any event, the Société Anonyme Belge was in need of a captain for its ship the *Florida* to replace a Dane – Johannes Freiesleben (born *c*.1861) – who had been killed by natives at Chumbiri in the Upper Congo region in late January. News of confirmation of a post came rapidly after this letter was posted, and Conrad also left Kazimierówka shortly after to return to London and begin his preparations to leave for Africa.

TO MARGUERITE PORADOWSKA

14 April 1890
Kazimierówka

My dear Aunt,

I have received your kind and charming letter, and this proof of friendship you give me in concerning yourself with my African plans touches me more than I can express. Many thanks for your kind attention. With impatience I await the moment when I shall be able to kiss your hands while thanking you in person.

I am leaving my uncle's in four days. I have some visits to make on the way (among others, one of forty-eight hours to Lublin) so that I shall not be in Brussels until the 29th of this month. – Then we shall talk of your plans to visit Poland and your future projects, which interest me a good deal – as you can well believe.

Have you received my last letter? I wonder. I have some doubts now. Did I understand you correctly? Has my reply offended you? In reading it, please think of the deep attachment I feel for you and also for the memory of my poor dear Uncle Alexander. So be indulgent, my dear and kind aunt.

Au revoir, then, for the time being. We have visitors and I have just escaped for a moment to write these few words. They are calling for me!

> I kiss your hands. Your very devoted friend and nephew
> J. C. Korzeniowski

Still immersed in the family relationships he had renewed during his visit to the Ukraine, Conrad updated his first cousin, Maria – the daughter of his late mother's brother Kazimierz (1837–86) – about his plans to leave for Africa. His use of the diminutive ('Maryleczka') may suggest a bond. She was also about to make a change in her life: then engaged, she married Teodor Tyszka (here 'Mr Tyszka') in July. The state of his aunt's health – her widowed mother, Zuzanna (née Hajęcka) – could not have been a matter for serious concern, as she was still living in 1894. Mention of Maria Bobrowska's brothers and sisters – Zuzanna ('Zunia', 1866–1942), Marta ('Marcia', 1869–1944), Stanisław (1865–1939) and Tadeusz ('Tadzio') – suggests the lively social life in which Conrad had recently been involved with his younger relatives.

TO MARIA BOBROWSKA

London, 2nd May, 1890.

My dear Maryleczka.

I could not write any sooner. I have been extremely busy and in fact still am so. In four days' time I am sailing to the Congo, and I have to prepare myself for a three years' stay in Central Africa. You can, therefore, imagine how precious each minute is to me. I hope that your Mother is better now and that you, my dear, will soon be writing to me. Probably your letter will be too late to find me in Europe, but it is certain to be forwarded to me. Do not be surprised by the delay in getting a reply; no one can tell where your letter will eventually catch up with me.

Please explain to Zunia and Marcia my reasons for not writing to them. I am sorry indeed! My photographs will not be ready till after my departure. I am leaving addressed envelopes ready for posting them. That is why you will find the photographs unsigned and no letter enclosed. So you see, my dear Maryleczka, how sad the situation is. I doubt even if I shall have time to write a few words to Stanis. and Tadzio. Please act as my intermediary with the family. Embrace them all on my behalf and ask for kind remembrances of the wanderer.

My best regards for Mr and Mrs Meresch, Mr and Mrs Dąbrowski, and Mr Tyszka. I kiss my Aunt's hands and embrace you a thousandfold, commending myself to your heart.

Your loving,
K. N. Korzeniowski

This brief note enclosing promised photographs is, in effect, a farewell to the past, with affectionate regards to his cousins and aunt. Conrad's journey to Africa began with a brief stopover in Brussels, where he again saw Poradowska and finalised arrangements for his employment – according to company documents, his formal engagement commenced on 7 May 1890. Taking his leave of her and the Belgian capital, he travelled to Bordeaux, where he and Prosper Harou (see introductory note to the 'Congo Diary') shipped for Boma, the Congo Free State's administrative capital, and Matadi in the Compagnie des Chargeurs Réunis (United Shipping Company) *Ville de Maceio*. (The French 1,771-ton steamer had departed Antwerp on 30 April, with Conrad ordered to catch up with her during her stopover in Bordeaux, the company evidently not wishing him to await her return from Africa and her next departure.)

TO MARIA BOBROWSKA

London, 6th May, 1890

Maryleczka dear,

I am sailing in an hour. As soon as the photographs are ready I shall send a letter.

The second photograph is for dear Marcia. I shall send a separate one for Aunt. Embraces and best regards for all,

Your loving,
K. N. Korzeniowski

I am sending one separately for Zunia as well.

The intimacy of tone of the next letter suggests a growing closeness between Conrad and Poradowska. Conrad had recently met with her immediate family and members of her circle during his stay in Brussels. Poradowska's widowed mother, 'Fanny' Gachet (née Marie-Françoise Jouvenel, c.1825–1904), moved in elite artistic and intellectual circles as the widow of Emile(-Léonard-Jean-Baptiste) Gachet (1809–57), a Frenchman from Lille who had settled in Brussels and made his livelihood as an archivist and historian. (He was also an editor of Rubens's letters.) Poradowska's English sister-in-law, Maud Gachet (née Chamberlin, c.1854–1921), had two children with Charles Gachet (1849–before 1921), a member of the French diplomatic corps: Jean and Alice, the latter to become an actress and teacher at London's Royal Academy of Dramatic Art. Emile Bouillot (1823–1905) – Conrad's spelling is wrong – was a Belgian painter, particularly of biblical, historical and mythological subjects, and founder of the Ecole de Dessin et de Modelage d'Ixelles (now the Ecole des Arts d'Ixelles). The 'Bishop' remains unidentified. Poradowska indicates that he was from Wola, a district of Warsaw; but the reference seems playful, and this is probably a teasing nickname for someone of ecclesiastical bent.

TO MARGUERITE PORADOWSKA

15 May 1890
Teneriffe

My dear little Aunt,

What if I were to begin by telling you I have so far avoided the fever! What if I could assure you all my letters will start with this good news! Well, we shall see! In the meanwhile I am comparatively happy, which is all one can hope for in this wicked world. We left Bordeaux on a rainy day. Dismal day, a not very cheerful departure, some haunting memories, some vague regrets, some still vaguer hopes. One doubts the future. For indeed – I ask myself – why should anyone believe in it? And, consequently, why be sad about it? A little illusion, many dreams, a rare flash of happiness followed by disillusionment, a little anger and much suffering, and then the end. Peace! That is the programme, and we must see this tragi-comedy to the end. One must play one's part in it.

The screw turns and carries me off to the unknown. Happily, there is another me who prowls through Europe, who is with you at this moment. Who will get to Poland ahead of you. Another me who moves about with great ease; who can even be in two places at once. Don't laugh! I believe it has happened. I am very serious. So don't laugh. I allow you, however, to say: 'What a fool he is!' This is a concession. Life is composed of concessions and compromises.

While on this subject, how is the Bishop? Have you compromised with the Bishop? A little with your conscience and much with your heart? Then – have you begun to live? Tell me everything when you write.

I address this letter to your mother, to whom I present my very respectful regards, as I do to your sister-in-law. I hug the children. Tell them I send them 'my love'.

I kiss your hands and commend myself to your heart.

Your very devoted
Conrad

A steamer in front of the pier at Boma – where Conrad arrived 12 June 1890 – and, *below*, a street in the 'native quarter' of the city

A trading post at Matadi and, *below*, a group of the city's colonials. Conrad arrived on 13 June: 'Made the acquaintance of Mr Roger Casement, which I should consider as a great pleasure under any circumstances and now it becomes a positive piece of luck . . . Feel considerably in doubt about the future . . . Intend avoid acquaintances as much as possible'

The Congo River downstream from Matadi known as the Cauldron of Hell owing to the violent eddies and vortexes. *Below*, the church at Matadi in 1891

Porters gathering in Matadi before leaving the city. *Below*, an ivory caravan leaving Stanley Pool for Matadi – the last pages of Conrad's diary reveal calculations made as he counted, weighed and packed ivory into casks

My compliments to Mme and M. Bouillet. Perhaps my spelling is wrong. I mean the people in the Rue Godecharles.

By the time the *Ville de Maceio* approached its destination, Conrad had picked up information from his fellow travellers – a motley assortment including adventurers, civil servants and a company of troops bound for Senegal and Dahomey (now Benin) – about conditions in the Congo, including the likelihood of falling seriously ill, which he eventually did, suffering from dysentery and fever, the latter apparently malarial. Alexandre Delcommune (1855–1922) had been appointed to lead an expedition from Matadi to the interior for the Compagnie Congolaise pour le Commerce et l'Industrie (Congo Company for Commerce and Industry), another enterprise directly under Albert Thys and created by King Leopold himself. The expedition's purpose was to explore the region's commercial possibilities and potential transportation links. The expedition did not get under way until September, well into Conrad's stay. Delcommune's brother Camille, who arrived at Matadi on 25 May, served temporarily as head of the company.

TO KAROL ZAGÓRSKI

Freetown, Sierre Leone,
22nd May, 1890.

My dearest Karol!

It is just a month today since you were scandalized by my hurried departure from Lublin. From the date and address of this letter you will see that I have had to be pretty quick, and I am only just beginning to breathe a little more calmly. If you only knew the devilish haste I had to make! From London to Brussels, and back again to London! And then again I dashed full tilt to Brussels! If you had only seen all the tin boxes and revolvers, the high boots and the tender farewells; just another handshake and just another pair of trousers! – and if you knew all the bottles of medicine and all the affectionate wishes I took away with me, you would understand in what a typhoon, cyclone, hurricane, earthquake – no! – no! – in what a universal cataclysm, in what a fantastic atmosphere of mixed shopping, business, and affecting scenes, I passed two whole weeks. But the fortnight spent at sea has allowed me to rest and I am impatiently waiting for the end of this trip. I am due to reach Boma on the 7th of next month and then leave with my caravan to go to Léopoldville. As far as I can make out from my 'lettre d'instruction' I am destined to the command of a steamboat, belonging to M. Delcommune's exploring party, which is being got ready. I like this prospect very much, but I know nothing for certain as everything is supposed to be kept secret. What makes me rather uneasy is the information that 60 per cent. of our Company's employees return to Europe before they have completed even six months' service. Fever and dysentery! There are others who are sent home in a hurry at the end of a year, so that they shouldn't die in the Congo. God forbid! It would spoil the statistics which are excellent, you see! In a word, there are only 7 per cent. who can do their three years' service. It's a fact! To tell the truth, they are French! Des nevrosés! (C'est très chic d'être nevrosé – one winks and speaks through the nose.) Yes! But a Polish nobleman, cased in British tar! What a concoction! Nous verrons! In any case I shall console myself by remembering – faithful to our national traditions – that I looked for this trouble myself.

When you see – with the help of a microscope, no doubt – the hieroglyphics of my handwriting, you will, I expect, wonder why I am writing to you? First, because it is a pleasure to talk to you; next, because, considering the distinguished personage who is penning this autograph, it ought to be a pleasure to you too. You can bequeath it to your children. Future generations will read it with admiration (and I hope with profit). In the meantime, trêve de bêtises!

I kiss my dear uncle's and aunt's hands, and your wife's too. I forget none of you, but can't write the whole list because this abominable lamp is going out.

Yours very affectionately
K. N. Korzeniowski

As Conrad's voyage drew to a close, his thoughts again turned to Poradowska, who had left Brussels to visit her late husband's relatives in Galicia.
Like Conrad himself, she was facing a transitional period, adjusting to her
widowhood. He brought with him to Africa the slowly growing manuscript of his first novel, *Almayer's Folly* (1895), whilst she continued to
work on her writings. This was another bond, although at this time she
was the established writer and he only an aspiring one.

TO MARGUERITE PORADOWSKA

10 June 1890
Libreville, Gabon

Dear little Aunt,

This being the last port of call before Boma, where my sea-voyage
ends, I am beginning this letter here at the moment of leaving so as
to continue it during the passage and end it the day of my arrival in
Boma, where of course I am going to post it.

No new events. As to feelings, also nothing new, and there is the
trouble. For, if one could unburden oneself of one's heart, one's
memory (and also – one's brain) and obtain a whole new set of
these things, life would become perfectly diverting. As this is
impossible, life is not perfectly diverting. It is abominably sad! For
example: among other things I should like to forget but cannot – I
should like to forget the memory of my charming Aunt. Naturally, it
is impossible. Consequently, I remember and am sad. Where are
you? How are you? Have you forgotten me? Have you been left
undisturbed? Are you working? That above all! Have you found the
forgetfulness and peace of work that is creative and absorbing? So,
you see! I ask myself all these questions. You have endowed my life
with new interest, new affection; I am very grateful to you for this.
Grateful for all the sweetness, for all the bitterness of this priceless
gift. I now look down two avenues cut through the thick and
chaotic jungle of noxious weeds. Where do they go? You follow one,
I the other. They diverge. Do you find a ray of sunlight, however
pale, at the end of yours? I hope so! I wish it for you! For a long time
I have no longer been interested in the goal to which my road leads.

I was going along it with my head lowered, cursing the stones. Now I am interested in another traveller; this makes me forget the petty miseries of my own path.

While awaiting the inevitable fever, I am very well. In order to make my existence even slightly bearable, I need letters, many letters. From you, among others. Do not forget what I am telling you, dear and kind little Aunt.

After my departure from Boma, there may be an extended silence. I shall be unable to write until Léopoldville. It takes twenty days to go there, on foot too! How horrible!

You will probably write to my uncle; it was your intention, I believe. It would be kind if you would give him news of me. For example, that you saw me in Brussels, that I was well in body and spirit. This will give him pleasure and make him easier about my fate. He is very fond of me, and I grow as tender as an old fool when I think of him. Forgive this weakness. When do you return to Brussels? What are your future plans? Tell me all about it in your letter and sit at your desk only when you have a strong inclination to chat with 'the absent one'. 'The absent one' will be my official name in future. I shall be very happy to know that nobody is worrying you; that you work with an untroubled free spirit. I await your new work with curiosity and impatience. You must send it to me. Agreed? I have learned that my company has a sea-going ship and probably will build others. If I could obtain the command of one, that would be much better than the river. Not only is it healthier; there is always the chance of returning to Europe at least every year. When you return to Brussels, I beg you to let me know if any ships of this sort are being built so that I can enter my request. You can learn this through M. Wauters, whereas I, in the depths of Africa, will have no news. I am sure you will do that for me.

Au revoir, dear Aunt. I love and embrace you.

C. Korzeniowski

Conrad reached Boma on about 12 June and became quickly immersed in the conditions of his new employment, leaving almost immediately for

Matadi, where he arrived on the 13th. This letter's dating is problematic since Conrad did not leave on his inland trek until Saturday 28 June (if the 'Congo Diary' is accurately dated). In any event, what he foresaw as a twenty-day tramp by foot, with porters, took more than a month. If he, in fact, wrote any letters to Poradowska or to other relatives, none survives from this period. Conditions were at times extremely challenging, and, as the 'Congo Diary' reveals, he was completely immersed in the day-to-day task of moving the caravan forward, and was under both physical and psychological stress as he adapted to the rigours of the tropical climate and to cultural and emotional isolation.

TO MARGUERITE PORADOWSKA

18 June 1890
Matadi

Thank you! Many thanks, dear Aunt, for your kind and charming letter, which met me at Boma. Only my dear little Aunt could think up such splendid surprises. Has it given me pleasure?! I have a good mind to say No in order to punish you for having asked, for having seemed to doubt it!

I leave tomorrow on foot. Not an ass here except your very humble servant. Twenty days of safari. Temperature very bearable here and health very good. I shall write as soon as possible. Now I embrace you very heartily and kiss the hand that wrote the words which made me very happy the day before yesterday. Your very loving nephew and devoted servant

Conrad

THE 'CONGO DIARY' – the name was given to this record by Conrad's friend Richard Curle – was first published shortly after Conrad's death in rather heavily abridged and edited versions in the *Blue Peter* (1925) and the *Yale Review* (1926) and as a privately printed pamphlet (1926). It was also collected in *Last Essays*, which brought together occasional pieces not published in *Notes on Life and Letters* (1921), a book of essays and reviews that Conrad himself had seen into print.

The diary, preserved by Conrad's wife, Jessie Conrad, is written in pencil in a small leather-bound notebook, and is now housed at Harvard University's Houghton Library. It covers the period 13 June to 1 August, and, apart from the opening entries about Conrad's activities at Matadi, relates his overland trek from Matadi to Nselemba, near Stanley Pool, a journey of about 230 miles. Forced to go overland because of the impassability of Livingstone Falls, Conrad faced a march through jungle and bush in hot weather. His spare, undramatic prose, which focuses briefly on incidents and individuals, remains dispassionate and documentary throughout.

Being at Matadi for almost a fortnight, at the behest of the manager of the trading post, Joseph(-Louis-Hubert) Gosse (1860–91), allowed Conrad to make the acquaintance of Roger Casement (1864–1916), then supervisor of railway construction for the Compagnie du Chemin de fer du Congo and later the British consul in the Congo Free State, whose report on Belgian colonial atrocities garnered international notice. (A controversial figure, Casement, an ardent Irish patriot, was later accused of treason, tried and hanged.) Before leaving on his trek, Conrad also encountered Arthur J. Underwood (d. 1910), local head of Hatton & Cookson, the only British company doing business on the Congo. At this time too, Conrad caught up with his arrears of correspondence, writing to close personal friends – Marguerite Poradowska ('Mar' in the entry for 24 June) and George Fountaine Weare Hope (né Hopps, 1854–1930), a sailor turned businessman, living in Stanford-le-Hope – and to business connections, the latter including James L. (Liddon) Simpson, his former employer in Australia; the secretary of the London Shipmasters' Society, Captain

A. G. (Albert George) Froud (1831 – 1901); and, seemingly, Captain Robins Purdy (1844 – 1932), originally from Great Yarmouth, but later London-based.

Accompanying Conrad on the trek as well was Prosper (Félix-Joseph) Harou (1855 – 93), a non-commissioned officer of the Société Anonyme Belge, with whom Conrad had travelled to Africa on the *Ville de Maceio* (and on the train from Brussels to Bordeaux). Harou, whose brother Victor had been with H. M. Stanley and encouraged his going to Africa, was then making his second foray to the Congo, his earlier experience having lasted from June to December 1889, a bout of dysentery forcing him to recuperate at home. He quickly fell ill yet again, and caused bother for Conrad throughout the excursion. He is recalled in *Heart of Darkness*.

During the trek Conrad met with missionaries, the American Baptist Mission Union having been active for several years in the region, as well as with fellow employees of the Société Anonyme Belge du Haut-Congo. The missionary he missed meeting at Banza Manteka on 2 July was the Revd Charles E.(Edward) Ingham (d. 1890s), of the Livingstone Inland Mission. One of the first missionaries to reach Stanley Pool (in 1881), he and his wife had translated hymns into Kikongo. (In 1887, he was temporarily relieved of his post to help transport goods from Matadi to Stanley Pool for Stanley's famed Emin Pasha expedition; he was later killed by an elephant.) When Conrad met Mrs Annie Comber (née Smith) on 27 July, she had only recently arrived at the Sutili Baptist Mission, having come out from England to marry the Revd Percy E. (Ebenezer) Comber (1862 – 92), with whom the Revd Philip Davis (d. 1895) had arrived in the Congo. (After repeated bouts of fever, Annie Comber was to die at Banana on 19 December 1890 while waiting for a homeward-bound ship.) Conrad notes that he missed meeting her companions, the Revd W. (William) Holman Bentley (1855 – 1905), later author of *Pioneering in the Congo* (1900), who had written several works on the cultures and languages of the Congo as well as translating the New Testament and some of the Old Testament into Kikongo, and his wife H. (Hendrina) Margo Kloekers (1855 – 1938; married 1885), who was actively engaged in his missionary work.

Conrad also met with company employees: on 8 July, he noted his encountering Reginald Barwick Heyn (1860 – 1902) – based at Manyanga, as the company's director of transport and responsible for overseeing railway construction, hiring labour and organising equipment – and the Paris-born Belgian Henri Jaeger (b. 1864), Heyn's adjunct, who later served as manager of the Equator and Upper Ubangi stations. The man he calls 'Heche' (entry of 27 July) was probably Antwerp-born Ernest-Albert-Louis-Adolphe Stache (1856 – 97), who had arrived in the Congo only a few months earlier and was a principal agent for the company, establishing some dozen factories on the banks of the Loulua and also engaged in exploration.

Conrad stopped recording his overland journey on 1 August, on reaching Nselemba, about 15 miles from Kinshasa, where he travelled the next day, and almost immediately began the 'Up-river Book', recounting his voyage on the Congo as a supernumerary in the *Roi des Belges*.

The last pages of the 'Congo Diary' contain highly miscellaneous (and evidently fragmentary) notes on several topics – an account of supplies, a Kikongo vocabulary, the address of a London photographic supplier and a list of books. The latter mingle works as diverse as C. M. Woodford's *A Naturalist among the Head-Hunters* (1890) and Clements R. Markham's *John Davis: Arctic Explorer and Early India Navigator* (1889), with the more surprising three-volume *The Newspaper Press: Its Origin, Progress and Present Position* (1871–2) by James Grant, and Arthur V. Palmer's essay 'A Battle Described from the Ranks', published in *The Nineteenth Century* in March 1890, perhaps in an entry made much later than the main body of the 'Congo Diary'.

The Congo Diary 1890

Arrived at Matadi on the 13th of June 1890. –

Mr Gosse chief of the station (O.K.) retaining us for some reason of his own.

Made the acquaintance of Mr Roger Casement, which I should consider as a great pleasure under any circumstances and now it becomes a positive piece of luck –

Thinks, speaks well, most intelligent and very sympathetic. –

Feel considerably in doubt about the future. Think just now that my life amongst the people (white) around here can not be very comfortable. Intend avoid acquaintances as much as possible.

Through Mr R. C. Have made the acquaint[an]$^{\underline{ce}}$ of Mr Underwood the manager of the English factory (Hatton & Cookson in Kalla Kalla) – av[era]$^{\underline{ge}}$ com[merci]$^{\underline{al}}$ – Hearty and kind. Lunched there on the 21st. –

24th Gosse and R. C. gone with a large lot of ivory down to Boma. On G. return intend to start to up the river. Have been myself busy packing ivory in casks. Idiotic employment. Health good up to now.

Wrote to Simpson, to Gov. B. to Purd to Hope, to Cap Froud, and to Mar. Prominent characteristic of the social life here: People speaking ill of each other. –

<u>Saturday</u> 28th June left Matadi with Mr Harou and a caravan of 31 men. Parted with Casement in a very friendly manner. Mr Gosse saw us off as far as the State Station. –

First halt. M'poso. 2 Danes in Comp[a]ny.

Sund: 29th. Ascent of Palaballa. Sufficiently fatiguing – Camped at 11$^{\underline{h}}$ am at Nsoke-River. Mosquitos –

Monday. 30th – to Congo da Lemba after passing black rocks long ascent. Harou giving up. Bother. Camp bad. Water far. Dirty. At night Harou better.

1st July.

Tuesday. 1st Left early in a heavy mist marching towards Lufu River. – Part route through forest on the sharp slope of a high mountain. Very long descent. Then, market place, from where short walk to the bridge (good) and Camp. V[ery] G[ood]. Bath – Clear river – Feel well Harou all right – 1st chicken. 2p.[m.]
No sunshine today –

Wednesday 2^{d} July –

Started at 5^{h}30 after a sleepless night – Country more open – Gently andulating [sic] hills. Road good in perfect order – (District of Lukungu). Great market at 9.30. Bought eggs & chickens –
Feel not well today. Heavy cold in the head. Arrived at 11^{h} at Banza Manteka – Camped on the market place. Not well enough to call on the missionary. Water scarce and bad – Camp[in]^{g} place dirty. –
2 Danes still in company.

Thursday 3^{d} July.

Left at 6 am. after a good night's rest. Crossed a low range of hills and entered a broad valley or rather plain with a break in the middle – Met an off[ic]^{er} of the State inspecting; a few minutes afterwards saw at a camp[in]^{g} place the dead body of a Backongo – Shot? Horrid smell. – Crossed a range of mountains running NW–SE. by a low pass. Another broad flat valley with a deep ravine through the centre. – Clay and gravel – Another range parallel to the first-mentioned with a chain of low foothills running close to it – Between the two came to camp on the banks of Luinzono River. Camp[in]^{g} place clean. River clear. Gov[ernmen]^{t} Zanzibari with register. Canoe. 2 Danes camp[in]^{g} on the other bank. – Health good –
General tone of landscape grey yellowish, (Dry grass) with red-dish patches (soil) and clumps of dark green vegetation scattered sparsely about – Mostly in steep gorges between the higher mountains or in ravines cutting the plain – Noticed Palma Christi – Oil palm. Very straight tall and thick trees in some places. Name not known to me – Villages quite invisible. Infer their existence from cal[a]bashes suspended to palm trees for the 'malafu'. –

Good many caravans and travellers – No women unless on the market place. –

Bird notes charming – One especially a flute-like note. Another kind of 'boom' ressembling [*sic*] the very distant baying of a hound. – Saw only pigeons and a few green parroquets; very small and not many. No birds of prey seen by me. Up to 9 am – Sky clouded and calm – Afterwards gentle breeze from the Nth generally and sky clearing – Nights damp and cool. – White mists on the hills up about half way. Water effects, very beautiful this morning. Mists generally raising before sky clears.

[*Sketch: 'Section of to day's road.' Marked on the sketch: 'Luinzono River', '3 hills', 'Banza Manteka'. Beneath the sketch: 'Distance 15 miles. General direction NNE ← SSW'.*]

Friday – 4th July. –

Left camp at 6^h am – after a very unpleasant night – Marching across a chain of hills and then in a maze of hills – at 8.15 opened out into an andulating [*sic*] plain. Took bearings of a break in the chain of mountains on the other side. Bearing <u>NNE</u> – Road passes through that. Sharp ascents up very steep hills not very high. The higher mountains recede sharply and show a low hilly country – at 9.30 market place.

At 10^h passed R. Lukanga and at 10.30 Camped on the Mpwe R.

[*Sketch*: '*To day's march – Direction <u>NNE½N</u>. ← Dist[an]<u>ce</u> <u>13 miles</u>'. Marked on sketch: 'Camp', '<u>Luinzono</u>'.]

Saw another dead body lying by the path in an attitude of meditative repose. –

In the evening 3 women of which one albino passed our camp – Horrid chalky white with pink blotches. Red eyes. Red hair. Features very negroid and ugly. –

Mosquitos. At night when the moon rose heard shouts and drumming in distant villages. Passed a bad night.

Saturday 5th July. 90.

Left at 6.15. Morning cool, even cold and very damp – Sky densely overcast. Gentle breeze from NE. Road through a narrow plain up to R. <u>Kwilu</u>. Swift flowing and deep 50 y[ar]ds wide – Passed in canoes – After[war]<u>ds</u> up and down very steep hills intersected by deep ravines – Main chain of heights running mostly NW–SE, or W and E (at times[)]. Stopped at Manyamba – Camp[in]<u>g</u> place bad – in a hollow – Water very indifferent. Tent set at 10<u>h</u> 15<u>m</u>

[*Sketch*: '*Section of to day's road NNE*' ← Dist[an]<u>ce</u> 12<u>milles</u>'. Marked on sketch: 'Camp', 'Manyamba', 'Kwilu River'.]

To day fell into a muddy puddle – Beastly. The fault of the man that carried me. After camp[in]^g went to a small stream bathed and washed clothes. – Getting jolly well sick of this fun. –

Tomorrow expect a long march to get to Nsona. 2 days from Manyanga. –

No sunshine to-day

Sunday 6th July –

Started at 5.40. – The route at first hilly then after a sharp descent traversing a broad plain. At the end of it a large market place.

At 10$^{\underline{h}}$ Sun came out. –

After leaving the market passed another plain then walking on the crest of a chain of hills passed 2 villages and at 11^h arrived at Nsona. – Village invisible –

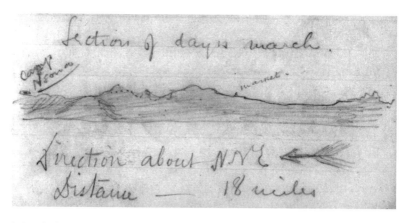

[*Sketch: 'Section of day's march'. Marked on sketch: 'Camp Nsona', 'Market'. Beneath sketch: 'Direction about NNE ← Distance – 18 miles'.*]

In this camp (Nsona –) there is a good camp[in]^g place. Shady. Water far and not very good. – This night no mosquitos owing to large fires lit all round our tent. –

Afternoon very close

Night clear and starry.

Monday – 7th July –

Left at 6$^{\underline{h}}$ after a good night's rest on the road to Inkandu which is some distance past Lukungu gov[ernmen]$^{\underline{t}}$ station. –

Route very accidented. Succession of round steep hills. At times walking along the crest of a chain of hills. –

Just before Lukunga our carriers took a wide sweep to the southward till the station bore Nth. – Walking through long grass for 1½ hours. – Crossed a broad river about 100 feet wide and 4 deep. – After another ½ hours walk through manioc plantations in good order rejoined our route to the E[astwar]$^{\underline{d}}$ of the Lukunga Sta[ti]$^{\underline{on}}$ walking along an undulating plain towards the Inkandu market on a hill. – Hot, thirsty and tired. At 11^{h} arrived on the M[ar]ket place – About 200 people. – Business brisk. No water. No camp[in]^{g} place – After remaining for one hour left in search of a resting place. –

Row with carriers – No water. At last about 1½ p.m. camped on an exposed hill side near a muddy creek. No shade. Tent on a slope. Sun heavy. Wretched.

[*Untitled sketch of day's journey. Marked on sketch: 'Camp', 'Inkandu', 'River bearing N[or]th', 'Lukunga', 'Nsona'. Beneath sketch: 'Direction NE by N. ← Distance 22 miles'.*]

Night miserably cold. –
No sleep. Mosquitos –

Tuesday 8th July

   Left at 6^h am

About ten minutes from camp left main gov[ernmen]^t path for the Manyanga track. Sky overcast. Road up and down all the time – Passing a couple of villages.

   The country presents a confused wilderness of hills, land slips on their sides showing red. Fine effect of red hill covered in places by dark green vegetation.

   ½ hour before beginning the descent got a glimpse of the Congo. – Sky clouded.

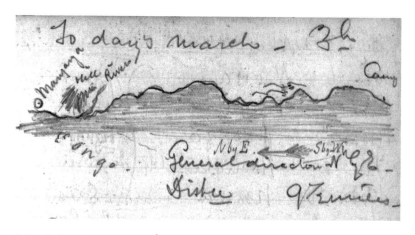

[*Sketch: 'To day's march – 3^h. Marked on sketch: 'Manyanga', 'Congo', 'Hill', 'River', 'Camp'. Beneath sketch: 'NbyE ← SbyW General direction NbyE – Dist[an]^{ce} 9½ miles'.*]

   Arrived at Manyanga at 9^h a.m.

   Received most kindly by Messr[s] Heyn & Jaeger. –

   Most comfortable and pleasant halt. –

   Stayed here till the 25. Both have been sick. – Most kindly care taken of us. Leave with sincere regret.

(Mafiela)

Frid^y 25th –	Nkenghe –	<u>left</u>
Sat. 26	Nsona	Nkendo.k
Sund. 27	Nkandu	<u>Luasi</u>
Mond 28	Nkonzo	<u>Nzungi</u> (Ngoma)
Tues. 29	Nkenghe	Inkissi
Wedn: 30	Nsona	<u>mercredi</u> = Stream
Thurs: 31.	Nkandu	Luila
Frid^y 1st Aug.	Nkonzo	Nselemba
Sat^y 2^d	Nkenghe	
Sund. 3^d	Nsona	
Mond. 4th	Nkandu	
Tues^d: 5th	Nkonzo.	
Wedn^y 6th	Nkenghe.	

<u>Friday the 25th July 1890.</u> –

Left Manyanga at 2½ p.m – with plenty of hammock carriers. H[arou] lame and not in very good form. Myself ditto but not lame. Walked as far as Mafiela and camped – 2^h

Saturday – 26th

Left very early. – Road ascending all the time. – Passed villages. Country seems thickly inhabited. At 11^h arrived at large Market place. Left at noon and camped at 1^h pm.

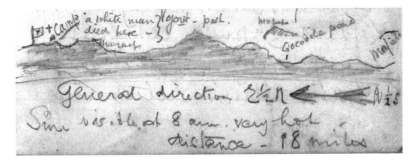

[*Untitled sketch of the day's journey. Marked: [flag], 'ϯ', 'Camp', 'a white man died here –', 'market', 'gov[ernmen]t path', 'mount', 'Crocodile pond', 'Mafiela'. 'General direction E½N ← W½S'. Sun visible at 8 am. Very hot | distance – 18 miles'.*]

Sunday, 27[th] –

Left at 8[h] am – Sent luggage carriers straight on to Luasi and went ourselves round by the Mission of Sutili.

Hospitable reception by Mrs Comber – All the missio[naries] absent. –

The looks of the whole establishment eminently civilized and very refreshing to see after the lot of tumble down hovels in which the state & Company agents are content to live – fine buildings. Position on a hill. Rather breezy. –

Left at 3[h] pm. At the first heavy ascent met M[r] Davis Miss[ionary] returning from a preaching trip. Rev. Bentley away in the South with his wife. –

This being off the road no section given – Distance traversed about 15 miles – Gen[eral] direction ENE. –

At Luasi we get on again on to the gov[ernmen][t] road. –

Camped at 4½ pm. With M[r] Heche in company. –

To day no sunshine –

Wind remarkably cold –

Gloomy day. –

Monday. 28th

Left camp at 6.30 after breakfasting with Heche –

Road at first hilly. Then walking along the ridges of hill chains with valleys on both sides. – The country more open and there is much more trees growing in large clumps in the ravines. –

Passed Nzungi and camped 11[h] on the right bank of Ngoma. A rapid little river with rocky bed. Village on a hill to the right. –

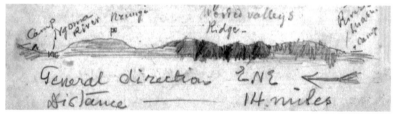

[*Untitled sketch. Marked: 'Camp', 'Ngoma River', 'Nzungi', [flag], 'Wooded valleys', 'Ridge –', 'River', 'Luasi', 'Camp'. 'General direction ENE ← Distance – 14 miles'.*]

No sunshine. Gloomy cold day. Squalls.

Tuesday – 29th
Left camp at 7[h] after a good night's rest. Continuous ascent; rather easy at first. – Crossed wooded ravines and the river Lunzadi by a very decent bridge –

At 9[h] Met M[r] Louette escorting a sick agent of the Comp[an][y] back to Matadi – Looking very well – Bad news from up the river – All the steamers disabled. One wrecked. – Country wooded – at 10.30 camped at Inkissi.

[*Untitled sketch. Marked: 'Camp', [flag], 'Inkissi River', 'Met Mr Louette', 'Lunzadi River', 'Ngoma'. 'General direction ENE ← Dist[an]ce 15 miles'.*]

Sun visible at 6.30. Very warm day. –

29[th]
Inkissi River very rapid, is about 100 yards broad – Passage in canoes. – Banks wooded very densely and valley of the river rather deep but very narrow. –

To day did not set the tent but put up in gov[ernmen][t] shimbek. Zanzibari in charge – Very obliging. – Met ripe pineapple for the first time. –

On the road to day passed a skeleton tied-up to a post. Also white man's grave – No name. Heap of stones in the form of a cross.

Health good now –

<u>Wednesday – 30th.</u>

Left at 6 am intending to camp at Kinfumu – Two hours sharp walk brought me to Nsona na Nsefe – Market – ½ hour after Harou arrived very ill with bilious attack and fever. – Laid him down in gov[ernmen]^t shimbek – Dose of Ipeca. Vomiting bile in enormous quantities. At 11^h gave him 1 gramme of quinine and lots of hot tea. Hot fit ending in heavy perspiration. At 2^h p.m. put him in hammock and started for Kinfumu – Row with carriers all the way. Harou suffering much through the jerks of the hammock. Camped at a small stream. –

At 4^h Harou better. Fever gone. –

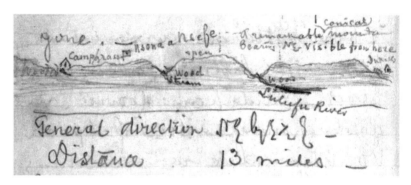

[*Untitled sketch. Marked:* 'Wooded', 'Camp/grass', [*flag*], 'Nsona [n]a Nsefe', 'Wood', 'Stream', 'Open', 'A remarkable conical mountain bearing NE visible from here', 'Wood', 'Lulufu River', 'Inkissi', 'Sward'. 'General direction NEbyE½E – Distance 13 miles –'.]

Up till noon, sky clouded and strong NW wind very chilling. From 1^{h}pm to 4^h pm sky clear and a very hot day. Expect lots of bother with carriers to-morrow – Had them all called and made a speech which they did not understand. They promise good behaviour.

<u>Thursday – 31st</u>

Left at 6^h. – Sent Harou ahead and followed in ½ an hour. – Road presents several sharp ascents and a few others easier but rather long – Notice in places sandy surface soil instead of hard clay as heretofore; think however that the layer of sand is not very thick and that the clay would be found under it. Great difficulty in carrying Harou. – Too heavy. Bother! Made two long halts to rest the carriers. Country wooded in valleys and on many of the ridges.

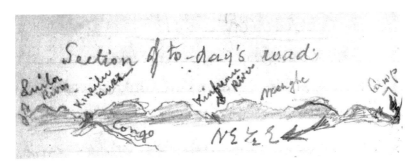

[*Sketch: 'Section of to-day's road'. Marked: 'Luila River', 'Kinzilu River', 'Kinfumu River', [flag], 'Nkenghe', 'Camp'. Below 'Kinzilu River' is 'Congo [River]' and 'NE½E ←'.*]

At 2.30 pm reached Luila at last and camped on right bank. – Breeze from SW

General direction of march about NE½E

Distance est[imate]$^{\underline{d}}$ 16 miles

Congo very narrow and rapid. Kinzilu rushing in. A short distance up from the mouth fine waterfall. –

– Sun rose red – from 9^h a.m. infernally hot day. –

Harou very little better.

Self rather seedy. Bathed.

Luila about 60 feet wide. Shallow

<u>Friday</u> – 1st of August 1890

Left at 6.30 am after a very indifferently passed night – Cold, Heavy mists – Road in long ascents and sharp dips all the way to Mfumu Mbé –

After leaving there a long and painful climb up a very steep hill; then a long descent to Mfumu Koko where a long halt was made.

Left at 12.30 pm – towards Nselemba. – Many ascents – The aspect of the country entirely changed – Wooded hills with openings. – Path almost all the afternoon thro' a forest of light trees with dense undergrowth. –

After a halt on a wooded hillside reached Nselemba at 4^h 10^m p.m.

[*Untitled sketch of the day's march. Marked: 'Camp', 'Nselemba', [flag], 'Stream', 'Mostly Wooded', 'Stream', 'Stream', 'Koko', 'Grass', 'Woods', 'Mfumu Mbé', 'Camp'.*]

Put up at gov[ernmen]^t shanty. –

Row between the carriers and a man stating himself in gov[ernmen]^t employ, about a mat. – Blows with sticks raining hard – Stopped it – Chief came with a youth about 13 suffering from gunshot wound in the head. Bullet entered about an inch above the right eyebrow and came out a little inside the roots of the hair, fairly in the middle of the brow in a line with the bridge of the nose – Bone not damaged apparently. Gave him a little glycerine to put on the wound made by the bullet on coming out.

Harou not very well. Mosquitos – Frogs – Beastly. Glad to see the end of this stupid tramp.

Feel rather seedy –

Sun rose red – Very hot day – wind Sth

General direction of march – NEbyN

Distance about 17 miles

[*There is an undefinable sketch of four conic-shaped figures underpinned by three circles – a doodle lacking a context for interpretation. This is followed by a blank leaf.*]

[A small sketch of one large and two small hills appears at the top of the page, with a column of fourteen numbers, of unknown context, adding up to 702. The following three leaves have been torn out.]

[A crossed-out list of oil cans, drums and paint tins, followed by another list with a different enumeration, indicating a corrected count as follows:]

Oil Cans –	29 –
Oil Drums	12
flattening (?)	3 *[perhaps from 'flattening', 'a paint with a matt finish' (OED); or 'flattened' (i.e. 'squeezed or beaten out' – OED) drums or cans]*
Mar[ke]^t [?] color – tins	4
Paint tins	28

[Four blank leaves follow including figures and calculations, most likely relating to dead reckoning, and probably of the location of the Torrens *(of which he was first mate in 1891). Among the various figures are readings of latitude and longitude, such as a series of calculations leading to the conclusion: 79° 33'; and 122° 17' E. / 40° 51' S, a position south of Australia. The abbreviation 'DR' on the first of the two pages most likely stands for 'Dead Reckoning'.]*

Naturalist amongst
the head hunters –
by C. M. Woodford

by Clement[s] Markham.
John Davis –

J. Grant
History of Newspaper
Press. (1871)

19 Century for March –
(Tel-el-Kebir). Serg^t Palmer

Tell	jingula
Very early	una nswe
dawn	kuma
noon	ntangwalungu
aftern[oon]	ntangwa wengele
evening	masika
me my	mono. ame

<u>Ju leka kuna</u>
Nous dormirons à
(We will sleep at)
– Aprésant – <u>wau</u> – (now)

Kana	nzila	Kwenda	kuna
Quand	chemin	aller	à

nkenge	Kwilu
nsona	Muembe nkenghe
nkandu	Nsona – ntombo [?]
nkonzo	Inkandu
Mercredi [Wednesday]	Manyanga
(nkenge –	

[*At the bottom is a sketch of bananas and a slice of seeded fruit, perhaps of the melon family.*]

Mueni – <u>Sun</u>	[diagram representing the sun]
Ngonda – <u>Moon</u>. –	[diagram of first-quarter moon]
Mbuetete – star(s).	[diagram of a star]
Ambno –	bottle.
Day.	Lumbu
after to-morrow	kiamene.
to-day	unu
morrow	mbaji mene
Do –	wanga
urgent.	watu (/wenta/go)
Walk	Diata
Reach	Luaka
He	yandi

this man	oyu
which is he	nkia muntu
Road	njila
Walk slow.	womboka
Take.	bonga = ma
Sam:	nsona
Dim	nkandu
Lundi 30.	nkonzo
Mardi	nkenge
Mercredi	nsona
Jeudi 3 –	nkandu
Vendre 4.	nkonzo
Samedi 5	nkenge
Dim 6	nsona
Lundi 7	nkandu
Mardi 8	nkonzo 11 days
Mercr 9.	Nkenge

Kodak Camera –
The Eastman Dry Plate & Film C^o
115 Oxford Street – £7.

Lukunga – M^r. Hoste. –
Banza Manteka Mr Ingham

Lankonzo

   G. Stern. Gray's Inn 62
   vepsalia salt
     Nkenghe

[*Written vertically:*]
Hierarchy
Anarchy

[*The last two pages of the notebook, dated 'Matadi. 23^d 6th 90' record calculations made as Conrad counted, weighed and packed ivory into casks. The
following initials also appear: 'J. C. K.' [Joseph Conrad Korzeniowski],*

'SAB' [*Société Anonyme Belge*] *and* 'GK' [*Georges-Antoine Klein*], *the* SAB *agent who died on the* Roi des Belges *and a possible source for Kurtz in* Heart of Darkness. *There are references to three casks,* 'cask 2' *containing* '150 p[ieces]' *with* 'poid [weight] – lbs 364' [165.11 kg]. *Calculations on the final page consist primarily of counting in groups of five* '卌'.]

THIS 'BOOK' IS A RECORD OF CONRAD'S observations made during his twenty-eight-day upriver passage in the *Roi des Belges*, which was briefly under his command during the trip. His journey began on 3 August 1890, with the departure from Kinshasa. Conrad arrived at Stanley Falls (now Boyoma Falls) on 1 September 1890. His record, which only goes as far as Bangala, about halfway up the Congo, is a technical one, with observations on navigating the river and on the topography of the region he was passing through. Ninety-three pages of the notebook contain writing; and an additional twenty-five pages are left blank, possibly with an eye to adding further material.

Like the 'Congo Diary', the 'Up-river Book' is written in pencil in a small leather-bound notebook; it is also now preserved at Harvard University's Houghton Library, having been sold by Richard Curle after the writer's death for the benefit of Conrad's widow and two sons. The notebook's pages are unnumbered, and marginalia appear with the main narrative, which is supplemented by twelve somewhat rudimentary sketches Conrad made. These line drawings describe various physical features: islands and sandbanks, channels, bends, bights and bores. The entries were apparently made not retrospectively but as he observed the features of the river and witnessed the activities on its banks. The roman numerals in the text presumably refer to charts Conrad had access to and used as he recorded his observations. (Part I's numbers run consecutively from I to XVIII, followed by a hiatus; they begin again with XXIIIA and conclude with XXVII; Part II runs consecutively from I.N. to XV.) The text remained unpublished until 1972, when a Polish scholar published his transcription in a literary journal, accompanied by a Polish translation. An Italian version has also appeared, with annotations (1978), as a supplement to a translation of *Heart of Darkness*.

Up-river Book 1890

Up-river book.
Commenced –
3.Augst 1890 –
S. S. 'Roi des Belges'

On leaving – from A After passing the two islands steer for clump –
high tree. two isl[and] points – Sandy beach

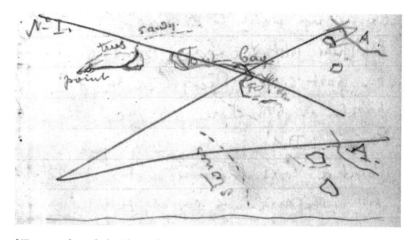

[*Two combined sketches of a sandy beach area at Stanley Pool. Marked:
four islands indicated by rectangles with an area of stones marked by a
circular broken line. Words written: 'trees', 'sandy', 'point', 'To [two?]
isl[ands] bay', 'foul [?]', 'stones', 'A', 'A' and 'No 1'.*]

No II	Steer for inside sandy point then keep out. (about East by the sun – as you approach coast breaks out into islands – B steer for Bend marked B. <u>From position C. a further point visible</u>. C – Steer for
III	sandbank II, behind hazy clumps of trees visible on a point of land.
No III–IV	No islands visible. Left bank island presents appearance of main land. Bank II covered at H[igh] W[ater]

Come up right to the bank I. Pass near islet Y. Leave Bank II – on port side – Steer for sandy patch on S[ou]th shore –

Position. D.

Point **a** looks low now.

S[ou]th side sandbank cov[ered] at H[igh] W[ater].

The opening narrows. Point <u>a</u> advancing. –

Position E.

Low land and outlying sandbanks a little to port. Steering for a little square white patch. Stick on it – Pass close to the sands – <u>Cautiously!</u>

Position F. ENE – Patch about ESE – Pass along sand shore not far from point △ Steering well in. Island X on the starboard side and generally kept ahead. On the port side (left bank) extensive and dangerous sand bank. 1½ foot (<u>Capt Koch</u>). As you proceed in point ⊙ seems closed in with Island X and apparently no passage – further on it opens again. A small grassy patch marks the end of point ⊙. High hills right ahead looming behind island X   N⁰ V. (and also IV)

Come right up to the island then steer along shore with point ⊙ a little on the port bow as from position F.a. – Coming up to a white patch after opening a small channel cutting X in two. A small island app[arent]^ly closes the passage. When nearing the end of X <u>must</u> keep close and steer into the bay 8 getting the clump of trees on the port side. Going out the highest mountain will be right ahead –   Va. V and IV.

Always keep the high mountain ahead crossing over to the left bank. To port of highest mount a low black point. Opposite a long island stretching across. The shore is wooded –   IV. V. Va

As you approach the shore the black point and the island close in together – No danger – Steering close to the mainland between the island and the grassy sandbank, towards the high mount[ain]^s. <u>Steering close to the left bank of the river all the time. Entered.</u>   V. Va.

VI

On left bank wooded point

Right valley. – 1st Reach nearly North.

2^d Reach – about NNE.

Left bank. Wooded point.

3^d Reach the same and wooded point. –

4th Reach NbyE.

Point III. Stones off.

IV Before getting abreast there is a rocky shoal ⅓ out

VI   2 hours after entering the river sighted '2 sago-trees point' not at all remarkable – Low flat at the foot of the hills. –

The appearance of point VI is bushy – Rather low. Round shape behind as per sketch.

Just before coming up to p[oin]ᵗ VI got bottom at 6 feet stones – Hauled out

Point VII called 'Sandstone P[oin]t.' with a small ledge of rock outside of it

Before closing with it – cross over to the right bank

Moored to – grassy Beach backed by trees – 25 miles from the entrance – 5ʰ30

VII   4th Augˢᵗ

This reach is about E̲

Shortly after leaving, point A opens out double in peculiar shape.

Off point VIII long stone ridge.

Point A has a small sand-spit covered at full river. –

Right below the point there is a small sandbank along the shore. – Wooding place – May get in between sandbank and the shore

After passing A point in the middle of the river there is a rocky ledge now above water – Covered at F[ull] W[ater].

River rather narrow – Steering well off the right bank

Snake tree point has a ledge of Rock lying well off – To give a wide berth

Here begins a reach about NE – (by the sun). – On the left bank many palms visible –

After passing Sn[ake] Tree point on the left bank entrance to Black River – A remark[ab]ˡᵉ clump little further on

R[iver] bank – Point C.

Off point C – cross over – On the left bank on point XI one palm rather conspicuous when coming up. –

After turning point C. You open up a remarkable point running from high mountains called point Licha

Wooding place. – (6h am) – On the right bank past point C –
Sandy beaches to be met often – On left bank a little past XI point
there is a market place. – Rocky shoals near in shore. –

(from Licha point up. –

From Licha – crossing over to right bank where there is outcrop of   VIII
rock – Small sandy beach near.

Left.6.15

Bearing – Licha   S 15° <u>W</u> ⎫   Time
              Point C –   S 25° W   ⎬   6.35 –
              Point XII.   N 48° E – ⎫   6$^{h.}$ 35^{m} | 7.15
              Point D.   N 34° E – ⎭
              Point F   N 36° E –
              Rate about 3½ miles per $\underline{h}$

VIII

After leaving Licha keep in the middle

B[earing].	T[ime].	
G. N33° E	9^{h}20^{m}	bearing from p[oin]^{t} XII.
P[oin]t XIII	8.15	opposite XII rocky cliff with ledges extending
P[oin]t XIV from P[oin]^{t} ⊗		
By NEbyNE		After point XII Indented shore with a low flat running at the foot of the hills – After passing XIII Rocky sweep – This reach is NEbyN. – Steer by the left bank 2 low points
Point H <u>at</u> 10^{h}5^{m}		with many palms in the bight an island in the middle of the bight. – Before closing with G point small S[and] B[ank] parallel to the shore – pass[age] inside (?)
<u>P[oin]^{t} XV bore</u>		good wooding place. –After passing 1st IX
NEbyN ½N		island open up a point and sight a long and
from ⊗ p[oin]^{t}		a very small island
P[oin]^{t} K bore		Island N° 2 long wooded – small islet
NNE from		N° 3 – This reach is NE by N nearly. –
Is[lan]$^{\underline{d}}$ 3		

Islet Nº 3 at 10ʰ50ᵐ	Between Is[lan]ᵈ Nº 2 and Nº 3 rocky ledges and no passage. From abreast p[oin]ᵗ H it seems as if Is[land] 3 was abreast Point XIV. The NW end of Is[lan]ᵈ 2 has a palm grove – The island lays NW–SE. All along right shore small beaches – and dead wood on most of them
IX	After passing point XIV a long stretch of low land on left bank with islands (very small). A remarkable clump of trees as per chart –
Island Nº 4 at noon	and many palm trees on the low shore
Island Nº 4 to Point M NEbyE	This stretch of low land continues for a long time with many palms – General appearance light green – Long reach with a regular sweep on the left bank. From
2ʰ30ᵐ p.m.	Island Nº 4 2½ up.

X.   This Reach is <u>NEbyN</u>.
   Directly after passing P[oin]ᵗ M – on the right shore rocky shoals extending good way out
   Afterwards same appearance
   Hills to water's edge with small sandy beaches
   Over p[oin]t XVI curious yellow path on a hill.
   Steering a little over on the right bank side. On the other side villages on slope of hill.
   After point N another p[oin]ᵗ forming a high plain. A little further ridge of rocks.

At N 3ʰ45ᵐ	Before coming to high plain P[oin]ᵗ Nº 2 there is a wooding place.

X   P[oin]ᵗ P bore. NEbyN at 4ʰ 25ᵐ from high plain p[oin]t″ Nº 2 –
   Abreast point XVII at 5ʰ10ᵐ – (length of reach 5½ ᵐ⁽ⁱˡᵉˢ⁾
   The new reach about NE½N –

Alexandre Delcommune poses with a shot hippo beside the Sankuru River. Delcommune was appointed to lead an expedition from Matadi to the interior for the Compagnie Congolaise pour le Commerce et l'Industrie, and was the brother of Camille Delcommune – 'a common ivory dealer with base instincts'. *Below*, men, women and children all gather at a market place on the caravan road

Bridge over the Lufu River, which Conrad mentions on 1 July: '. . . short walk to the bridge (good) and Camp. V[ery] G[ood]. Bath – Clear river'. *Below*, porters rest on the caravan road from Matadi to Léopoldville

Villages of the Belgian Congo. Conrad notes on Saturday 26 July: 'Passed villages. Country seems thickly inhabited. At 11$^{\underline{h}}$ arrived at large Market place. Left at noon and camped at 1^h pm'

Steamers at the port of the Société Anonyme Belge at Stanley Pool in September 1890 and, *below*, the *Roi des Belges, c.*1889, on a slipway

Abreast point XVII a long parallel ridge of rocks well off the shore –

Off Point P a long rocky ridge extending into the river (from here in one day to Ki[n]chassa down stream. 12 hours steaming).

All the time keeping over to the French shore.

Hills on left shore present a reddish appearance

All the right bank fringed with trees   X.

At the small beach near Point P at 5^h50^m – moored. –

Wooding places – Villages on the opposite bank. –

Point P.6.^{h}o^m.	Left. Cross over from the beach
End of point –	below the Point P.
Bankap bore	Here commences a reach
NEbyN from mid[d]^{le}	about <u>NE</u> –
of the river. –	After rounding P[oin]^t P. There is a
a little past	wooding place. Narrow beach.
P[oin]^t P.	
$7^{\underline{h}}45^m$ at point	From there steer a little over where there is
XVIII	a small Island not app[aren]^t. No passage –
	After that keep nearly in the middle. – All
	that shore is a low flat fringed by trees X
	backed by low hills – Bordered by reefs –
	Steer in the middle – till abreast p[oin]^t Q.
	Then a little over to the right bank –
	After p[oin]^t XVIII a[n] invisible XI.
	sandbank stretches along
from camp to	the right shore. Keep off –nearly in center –
XVIII – 6 miles	
$1^{\underline{h}}$¾	
P[oin]^t XVIII at <u>7^h45^m</u>	Bankab – NEbyN
times	Point R from m[id]$^{\underline{dle}}$ NNE.
from XVIII	On p[oin]^t Bankab two high trees – One
Reach – NEbyN½N.	broad another less spreading

XI   to p[oin]t QR.
at 9$^{\underline{h}}$ am
from XVIII to
R. 1^h 45$^{\underline{m}}$ at
say 6 miles –
NEbyN½N:

About 1 hour after passing P[oin]t XVIII –
passing the wooded false points rocks
extend out into the river P[oin]t Q bearing
about Nth and Bankab

about NNE

———————

On nearing p[oin]^t Bankab on French
shore to the Nth p[oin]^t Q small island
(N° 6) and long sandbank over which from
the middle of the river you see Ganchu
P[oin]$^{\underline{t}}$ bearing about NbyE.

Bankab P[oin]$^{\underline{t}}$
9$^{\underline{h}}$15$^{\underline{m}}$
Ganchu bore
N½W.

XI.

The islet N$^{\underline{o}}$ 6 has a few trees and a dead
palm on it. Opp[osi]te on same shore in a
Ravine small vill[ag]$^{\underline{e}}$ –Round Bank[ab]
in back curr[ent].
When rounding Bankab keep on Right side
and enter the current sweeping out of the
bight cautiously and end on nearly –
(On coming down follow the current
round the bight.)
When about the middle of the open stretch
steer right across to clear Ganchu's Point
Pass the point cautiously.
Stones – Then steer straight for P[oin]t
XIX. – Along the left shore below that
point stretches off a sand bank

P[oin]t XIX at
10$^{\underline{h}}$40$^{\underline{m}}$
P[oin]$^{\underline{t}}$ S bore N.

XI

ressembling [sic] a beach but covered at
F[ull] W[ater]. –

From p[oin]^t XIX cross over a little af[te]^r
a small beach on the opposite side by
compass about NbyW½W –
This short Reach is about NNE.
Next short Reach is about NE by N½N.
Keeping a little over on the right shore. –
On the left bank bushes growing down to

the water. Right shore low, undulating.
Wooded (coming down from S the False
XIX point would be alone visible

P[oin]t. S. – <u>at Noon</u> 12^h.
P[oin]t XX bore N½E.
Entrance of Riv[er] Kassai. NEbyN.
Point on right bank. white patch
bore N½W.
Next p[oin]t to S. N¾W.

XII.

Entrance to Kassai rather broad. On Sth side a bright beach with a
spreading dead tree above it mark the mouth.
    At the Cath[oli]^c mission moor along-side the head of the beach. –
    From P[oin]t S′ to Mission – NNE. 1$^{\underline{h}}$
    Made fast at 1^h pm.
    Pt XX. bore N 5° W

	Left the mission at 2½ –
	In the bight between the miss[ion] and
	P[oin]^t XX rocky ledges – Of[f] p[oin]t
	XX a stony ridge partially cover[e]^d at high
from XX.	water –
P[oin]^t T	Off P[oin]t XX at 3^h 20$^{\underline{m}}$ making it about
bore	2^h from the P[oin]^t S′ –
NbyE ½E	
at 3^h 20^m pm.	

XII.

	After passing P[oin]^t XX follow the left
	shore at some distance to the p[oin]t
	with the grassy slope about NNE. From
	there cross over towards point T. –
	Sandbank always covered in the bight.
off	Current easier in the middle. –
Point T	Probably there is a passage between
at 5^h 25^m	the sand and the left bank.

Point XXI bore	This reach about N.

N¾E.   (Stopped at 5ʰ45ᵐ
                        Left stopping place at 7ʰ am.

XII   On <u>Right bank</u>.
      From stopping place sighted a dark green p[oin]t – a long spit of
      sand cov[ere]ᵈ at full water with high rocks also cov[ere]ᵈ at very
      full water. –
      On <u>left shore</u> a sandb[an]k always covered extends ⅓ᵈ into the
      river.
      Got soundings below the dark green P[oin]t. bearing NbyW½W
      P[oin]t XXI bore NEbyE – <u>3f[a]th[oms] and 4f[a]th[oms]</u>
      Opening Lawson river with sandbank across the mouth and
XIII rocks stretching off. – Further along cut beach. – P[oin]t XXI gets
      indistinct on nearer approach – No danger on that side. – A small
      rocky ledge on the point
      Past Pt XXI – at –
      This reach about N by E –
      After passing P[oin]ᵗ XXI – R[i]g[h]t bank low scrubby and
      trees – Sm[all] hills – To the left higher hills with bare tops and a
      belt of forest half way up from the water's edge
      At p[oin]t U – Wooding places
      <u>Caution</u>   The landing must be approached cautiously on
                        account of stones and snags
                        Round P[oin]ᵗ U cautiously – When entering
XIII   the reach keep rather on the outer edge of the
                        current following the right shore – Sandbank on
                        left shore not visible –
      From 3 fath[oms] position the P[oin]t XXII bears NEbyE The
      middle of uncovered S[and] B[an]K bears about N½E.
      A spit with 1½ f[a]th[oms] at less than ½ full river extends
      towards U high land
      On rounding p[oin]t XXII give a wide berth. There is [*sic*] 2
XIII stony ledges – of which the outer one is cov[ere]ᵈ at full river. – This
      reach about NEbyN before passing Mission P[oin]ᵗ. You open out
      False P[oin]ᵗW which is not noticeable. Also a point on the left shore.
      Coast in perfect semicircle sand, swamp and trees – hills opened

out there. A few high thin trees dispersed in that stretch

As you near the end of the semicircle the M[issio]$^{\underline{n}}$ marked A in sketch disappears: from the same place Island N°7 – bore N¾E –

From point (Eng[lish] Mission) at Grenfell p[oin]t – at 4$^{\underline{h}}$ p. m.

When passing the dangerous sandbank called mission sands XIII keep close in with M[issi]$^{\underline{on}}$ Point and have the island either on port bow or starboard quarter till you clear M[issi]$^{\underline{on}}$ Point.

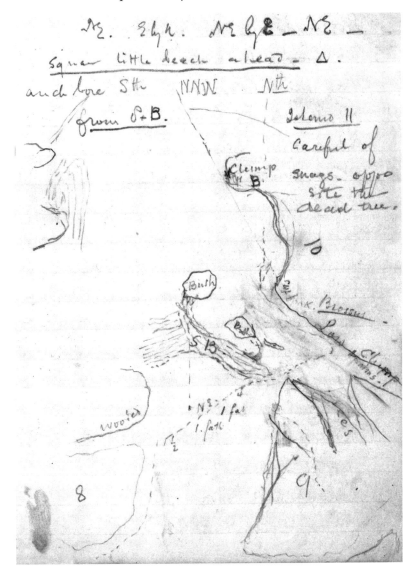

[Previous page. Sketch of Mission Point with a dotted line suggesting a channel through sand banks, snags and islands (including one designated as 'wooded'; others have 'clump B', 'palms' and 'bush') with instructions such as 'Island 11 Careful of snags opposite the dead tree'. At the top of the map are 'NE. EbyN. NEbyE – NE – Square little beach ahead – Δ and bore S[ou]th NNW N<u>th</u> from S[and] B[ank]'. Fathoms are marked 1½, 1, 1; and sections of land are numbered 8, 9, 10.]

Passage inside island 10 at full water

Passage inside small islet off 2 Palm P[oin]<u>t</u> at full water when <u>must keep</u> close inshore

	Keep close to island 12 – over a bank with 2 fath[oms] –
Koch's passage	After passing Is[lan]^d 12 steer for bush on end of the long island.

From there for bush point on the m[ai]ⁿ land follow cut bank then cross over towards Low island –

XIV　　　Sandbank right across after approaching it steer along it toward the trees on it and pass between it and the m[ai]ⁿ land (when nearing 1 f[a]th[om] to 1½ f[a]th[oms]).

Steer in middle of passage and then for XXIV p[oin]^t following the bight of the shore from p[oin]t XXIV steer between two small islands keeping over to starboard

Soundings in 1, 1½, 1 fath[om] – variable

Bolobo village. Landing place

A few minutes after passing the mission keep out a little into the river:

This reach from the mission is about NE –

Follow the right bank the courses being from NE to E till you open the bend of low shore. Then P[oin]^t of M[ai]ⁿ Land bearing NEbyE and small island bearing EbyN<u>th</u>

Steer in the bend a little watching for edge of sandbank – Leave the small island on St[arboar]^d side.

Sandbanks on both sides with spits across the course

After nearing island 12 another small island is seen to be left to
starb[oar]$^{\underline{d}}$

General direction of land from there is ENE –

After passing the island keep at mod[era]^{te} distances off

When app[roa]ch[in]^{g} long islands there is a bank with 1
f[a]th[om] at ½ full. Close in a little with the main[lan]^{d} –　　　XV

After passing steep round bank steer in with the bend

When off the swamp spit all the islands on the southern bearing
seem one land

Arrived at stopping place at 5^{h}30^{m} –　　　XVa

Village. –

    Left stopping place at 6 am –

    Steering for P[oin]t XXV keep in with the bend.

    Remarkable. Islands. –

Island bearing NNE.　　　XVI

square clump. light green follow the island 15th shore all the time
– remarkable palm –

Second small island then steer for little grassy islet –

Soundings in 1½ and 1 f[a]th[om].

Course about ENE. –

Leave grassy islet on St[arboar]^{d} hand and steer in 1½ to 2
f[a]th[oms] for Island bearing ENE N$^{\underline{o}}$ 16

    Follow the shore of island N$^{\underline{o}}$ 16 on an NE½E course –　　　XVII

Mind the snags along Island N$^{\underline{o}}$ 16.

Cross over well before getting to Roof P[oin]$^{\underline{t}}$

Cross to where higher trees begin

When nearing M[ai]^{n} Land P[oin]^{t} – you will see the open passage between Is[lan]$^{\underline{d}}$ 17 and 18

The entrance to the Oubangi is barred on the up river side by　　XVIII –
extensive sandbanks –

The opposite Congo shore forms a ½ circle from the F[ren]$^{\underline{ch}}$
mission to p[oin]t XXVI. –

When rounding P[oin]t XXVI the current is very strong. –
Rocks off the P[oin]t –

Sandbank stretching close from the N$^{\underline{th}}$ towards it always covered
but impassable at any state of the river –

XVIII   Inside the bight steer close in to guard against dangerous snags. –
Rounding the points pretty close you sight to port the commence-
ment of a long island called Flat Is[lan]$^{\underline{d}}$
Proceeding on Past the village of Pressinbi then Irebu –
Sharp bend in the shore where the mouth of the R[iver Oubangi] is.
From elbow cross over to the flat island: avoiding S[and]B[an]ks
and snags – then where a few Palms form clump cross over again
and follow main shore
  Rounding another point still follow main shore at times only 2 to
1½ fath[oms] water – Otherwise passage not intricate
  Otherwise keep generally by the line indicated on the chart. –

XXIII XXIII.A.   After leaving Irebu there is no wooding place for some time.
XXIII. and A.   Thursday. 14th Aug$^{\underline{st}}$
Left stopping place at 6. 10^{m}.
Pass outside the sm[all] islet in the first bend after leaving
The general direction since yesterday [not recorded]
Entering the next narrow reach keep on but at a little dist[an]^{ce}
from left shore – Snags –
This reach is safe across (Koch)
  A succession of canal like bends – The shore covered with dense
forest right down to water's edge.
  – The river opens suddenly disclosing more islands –

XXIV   After rounding the last P[oin]t of the narrow part the channel lies
SE – Then ahead you have 3 islands looking at first like one – As you
near the point opposite them they open out. Off that point sandbank runs over to the islands – go over it XXV –
  Then a wide bight of the main shore is entered – on the P[or]t
side many islands presenting varied aspects from different places. –
  The general direction is NE½N about

XXV –   Keep pretty well on the main shore watching for snags all along –
  On the port side extensive sandbanks – partly visible but mostly
covered at ½ F[ull] W[ater]. Both shores heavily timbered with
dense undergrowth –
  After sighting a long island and following it for some time you
enter a NbyE. reach: then you enter a narrow pass[a]^{ge} between two
islands NEbyE.

At the end of short passage islands in sight again and the river broadens out –

A broad stretch where the course is about NE½E. All islands   XXVI
seen from the broad passage are now shut together into one.

Entering another broad expansion of the river follow cautiously   XXVI
the courses set on the chart XXVI

V[i]ll[a]ge of Ikongo – Bad –

Rounding the next 2 points there is another broad stretch com-   X[X]VII
paratively free of sandb[an]ks

Steer from p[oin]^t to p[oin]^t on the main shore having always
the Islands on your P[or]t hand. –   XXVII

General direction about <u>NE</u>. –

Main shore less thickly overgrown now – Islands all heavily timbered

After passing Lower Mission Point a small bay <u>with</u> stones in it.
Beaches colored <u>red</u>.

After passing 2 more points you sight the <u>Am</u>[erican] Mission in
the bottom of a small bight

Hardly vis[i]<u>ble</u>. A big dead tree marks it exactly

II. Part
in N[or]th Lat[itu]^{de}
from Equator to Bangala –
<u>Charts in N[or]th Lat[itu]^{de}</u>
<u>Saturday – 16th Augth [*sic*]. 1890 –</u>
7^h.30^m

Left Equator – follow the bank. Short distance round the first
point pass State Station –

River narrowed by islands. App[arent]<u>ly</u> no sandbanks.

After passing the 2^d point the next reach broadens out –

Courses – NNE – NE and ENE.

After passing a point with tall trees you open out a reach about E

A low point of land without trees bearing east marks the
appr[oa]<u>ch</u> of Berouki R[iver].

The other bank of the Berouki is covered with forest growth –   I.N.

Two sm[all] islands mark the entrance of the south arm of the delta –

Steering about NE close to two small islands to port of you you app[roa]^{ch} the point of the second arm of the Berouki delta –

Steer close to it pass[a]^g[e] over 3 f[a]th[oms]: the next reach being NbyW very nearly.

Soon another branch of the delta is passed. Very narrow.

The NbyW reach ends at a low point after pass[in]^g a sm[all] clearing and a one limbed tree – Pass small river

II N. The next reach opens on about the same width; two small islands facing the bend. Direction Nth

II.N. River perhaps a little wider in this reach – The same appearance of the banks – Dense growth of bushes and not very tall trees of a dark green tint. – On the port side S[and]-B[ank] visible before reach. Point. After passing the point a straight reach due North – not very long.

⅔^{ds} up pass over the S[and]-B[ank] – Sound[in]^{gs} in 2.1. fath[oms] & 4 feet. Steer right in shore minding the snags – <u>Snags</u> to be looked out for all the way here.

Rounding the point by a fine large tree & then 2 palms enter a short reach N.b[y].E –

After a point another long reach N.b[y].E. Some small islands open out on the port side –

II N (A). Long reach to a curved point. Great quantity of dangerous snags along the starb[oar]^d shore – Follow the slight bend of the shore with caution –

The middle of the channel is a S[and]-B[ank] – always covered.

The more northerly of the 2 islands has its lower end bare of trees covered with grass a light green low bushes. Then a low flat and the upper end is timbered with light trees of a darker green tint

A long sandbank unc[overe]^d at ½ Full [Water] stretches in to the S[ou]th[war]^d. No passage inside the islands –

II N (A). After rounding the point a broad reach opens out towards NNE.

On the port side some small islands. – Starboard shore makes a great sweep to the next point –

The middle of this expansion of the river is fouled by extensive sands always covered (Koch).

Follow the bend of the shore keeping pretty well in but not to brush the bank.

Both shores uniform dark green forest. When nearing the limit point of the reach you will close with some sm[all] islands – Leave them to port. S[and] B[ank] between the islands and the point – Keeping to starboard you get over it in 2.1 fath[oms].   III. N.

Broad bend follows.

The direction of the short reach being NNE –

In the bend itself extensive sandbank to be left to port side – Patches on this bank uncovered at ½ F[ull] water. –

The channel is pretty wide; there is no necessity in shaving the starboard bank to[o] close –

After this a straight long reach on N½E bearing

Keep nearly in the middle but more to starboard – St[arboar]$^{\underline{d}}$ side islands divided by very narrow channels on port app[a]r[en]^{tly} III N one island only –

Usual app[earan]$^{\underline{ce}}$ of dense vegetation dow[n] to water's edge. Nth end sm[all] S[and] B[an]k 2 f[a]th[oms] at the Nth end sharp bend and then broad sweep – NbyE to NEbyN and N. –

To starb[oar]$^{\underline{d}}$ wide branch dividing islands before mentionned [sic] from m[ai]^{n} land.

Next reach NNE nearly – follow the starb[oar]$^{\underline{d}}$ side now M[ai]^{n} IV N L[an]$^{\underline{d}}$ river broad – same app[earan]$^{\underline{ce}}$ on Starb[oar]^{d} side past a little narrow branch opening island again.

This reach ends like the last by a straight shore across its upper end where there is a [word missing] of triangular expansion.   IV N

Next reach nearly North –

–After passing the limit point reach nearly north. –

A small double island green on the Starb[oar]$^{\underline{d}}$ side.

After this first more islands open up with pretty broad channels between, through which the back shore can be seen – River very broad   V. N. here. All the islands are laying on a line of bearing about NbyE from the last point. – Point ahead on a bearing ½ a point more northerly

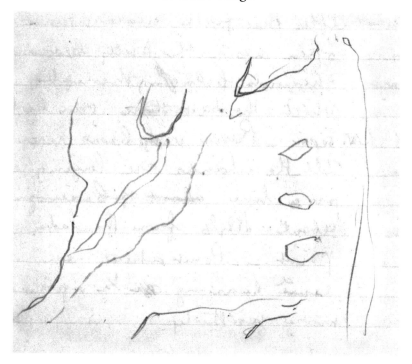

[*Sketch of the river showing large and small islands with a line marking the channel.*]

V. N. – Many large snags along the shores of the islands. –
Bush & trees to the water's edge –
After passing a narrow island take the channel where there is a small islet with a conspicuous tree in the middle of it
This channel is at first NE then gradually sweeps up to NbyE. and narrows greatly.
After coming out of it you enter a broad expanse with an islet about East and two larger islands with passage between about NNE

[*A sketch representing a reach of the river with the channel marked through several islands with the directions 'NE' and 'NNE' and the words 'big tree' written at the upper end of the sketch.*]

V N. This expanse is bounded to the Eastward by the M[ai]^n Land.

Heavy sandb[an]ks show between the further Northern and the upper eastern islands

The passage is narrow mostly NNE with a slight easterly bend on its upper end nearly NEbyN – : The main land is seen right across when coming out to the N[orthw]^{ard}

Passage clear.

VI N. M[ai]^n Land runs nearly N and S. Almost oppo[si]^{te} the Is[lan]^d Pass[a]^{ge} there is a wooding place.

Rounding the Nth point of the first straight stretch there is a L[an]^d elbow and then again a straight Nth stretch.

To Port there is 3 islands on the bend and another long island further up with some more behind it.

On M[ai]^n Shore after passing a dead stem with a few palms growing near it there is a point with a rocky ledge off it

VI N. The northern expansion of this expansion is perceived with islets and islands. The course is between these and the M[ai]^n L[an]^d. – Off the m[ai]^n shore there are rocky ledges under water in several places.

Rocks when the little N[orth]^{ern} islet bears North going along the shore. Many villages on this shore

Leaving all the islands on the Portside cross the mouth of the Loulanga R[iver] and steer along M[ai]n shore the reach lying about NbyW½W. –

It presents a narrow appearance.

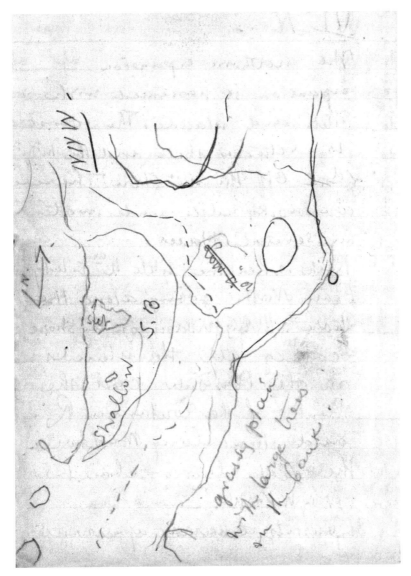

[*The first of seven continuing sketches of the Lulanga river passage. A sketch of a reach of the Congo with the directions 'N' and 'NNW'. The river channel is marked between a 'shallow S[and] B[ank]' on the port side, sketches of islands and a starboard shore marked 'grassy plain with large trees on the bank'.*]

Loulanga – R[iver] –
and French Factory –
Direction <u>NE</u> – first reach –

Entering, islet to port – Keep mod[era]^{te} dist[ance] from star[boar]<u>d</u> shore

River turns northerly –

To starb[oar]<u>d</u> Low circular island – passage round – In this back channel is the factory

Approaching landing mind the stones – High bank make fast to a tree there – small, bad land[in]^g place –

Arr[ived] at F[rench] F[actory] 8^h 15^m

VII N   Left the F[rench] F[actory] 12^h 45^m

(The back island passage through <u>Lulanga</u>).

Leaving the F[ren]^{ch} F[acto]^{ry} steer NNE when clear of round islet facing it and then NNW to enter the narrow channel between two wooded Is[lan]<u>ds</u>. Lulanga left on the starb[oar]^d side. Extensive sandbanks to port of you. Pass over in 2 fath[oms] or perhaps 9 feet at ½ full water

–The first reach – narrow – about N.b[y].W.

Keep in the middle.

A short bend Nb[y]E.

✝ Nth VII. The back passage

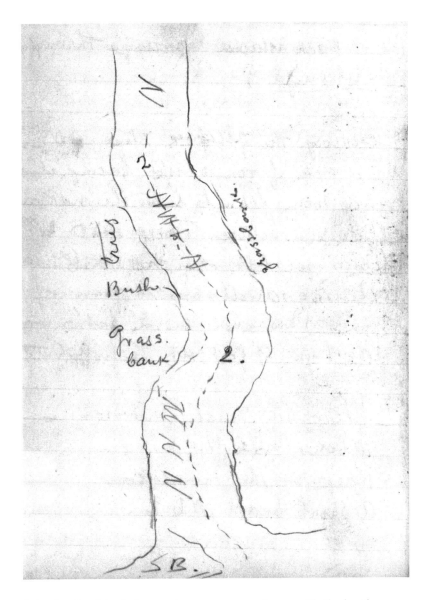

[*The sketch of the Lulanga river passage continues with the boat's course designated by a broken line marked 'NNW', 'NWbyN' and 'N', with two soundings in fathoms of 2 and 2. The port side is marked 'S[and] B[ank]', 'grass bank', 'Bush' and 'trees'; the starboard bank is marked 'grassbank'.*]

VII   The next reach is about NWbyN –

A straight due North –

A long bend. Come over to P[or]t side – snags almost in the middle of passage. –

A reach due Nth.

Another stretch NbyE –

Pass channel, to starb[oar]^d leading to Baringu – sand beach facing it stretch towards NbyW Water shallows to 9 & 7 feet

[*Three consecutive pages continue the sketch of the Lulanga river passage. The dotted line representing the route of the* Roi des Belges *is marked 'N', 'N', 'Nb[y]E', 'Nb[y]W', 'NE', 'NNE', 'NE', 'NbyE' and 'NNE'. The port side is marked 'grassb[an]k', 'Bush', 'Sm[all] beach', 'Grass', 'grass'; the starboard side is marked 'Snags', 'To Baringu', 'Grass', 'Swampy', 'Swamp grass' and 'Highbushed point'. Time required to negotiate passage: '2^h 30^m'.*]

Grass
Swampy

To Baringa

Sulcach

Bush

Grass Gra

Snags

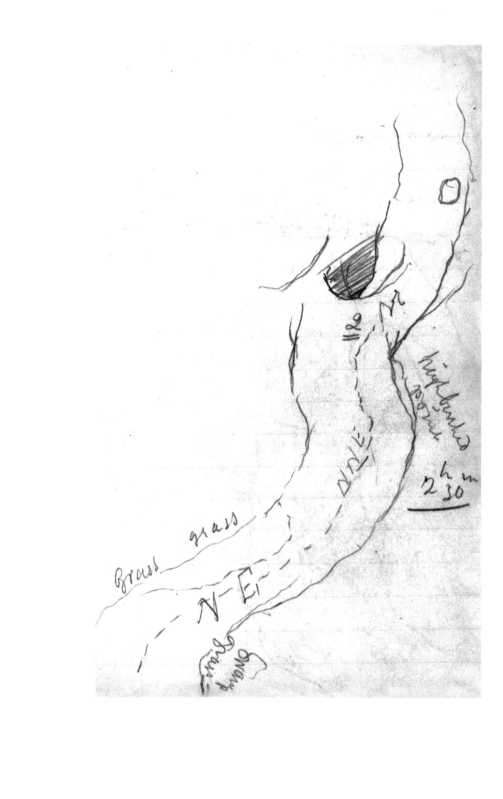

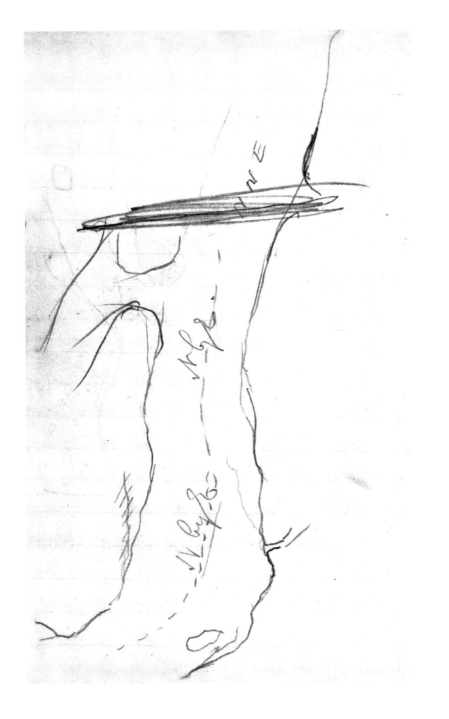

VI –   A Reach to NE follows. – grassy banks – off port bank sand shallows –

After rounding that point channels branch off – follow the more easterly small islet in it.

A long straight about NbyE½E

Passage broadens out with islands coming in sight

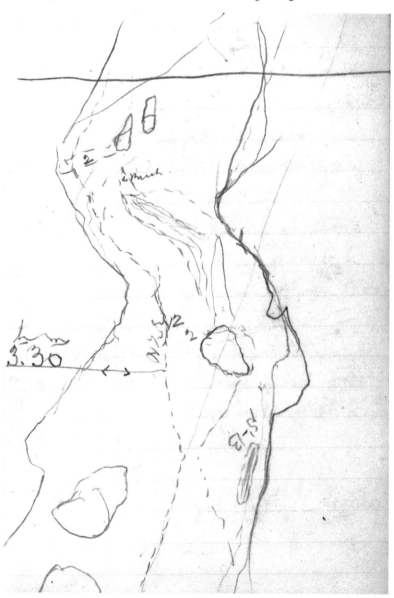

[Opposite. The penultimate sketch of the Lulanga passage, with a dotted line indicating the channel around several islands drawn in mid-stream. Time designated on the port side with arrows pointing to a small island in the centre of the river indicate '3.$^{\underline{h}}$ 30$^{\underline{m}}$' to reach that point. A 'S[and]- B[ank]' enters from the starboard side. Direction is 'N½E'; and river depth is indicated by three soundings in fathoms – 2, 2 and 2.]

Steering for a small island bearing Nth leave it on St[arboar]$^{\underline{d}}$ side –

Towards the upper end of it cross over to port avoiding snags follow the Port shore. –

In the elbow must go close in to avoid extensive S[and]B[an]k stretching right in from the island –

Before passing the two small islets get soundings in 2 fath[oms] and less. – Keep well in shore. Mind the snags –

A Broad straight NbyE nearly

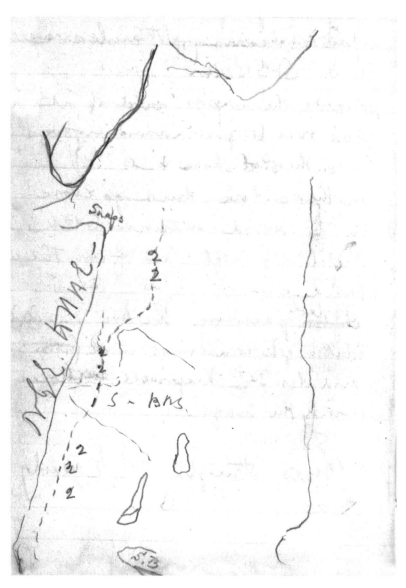

[The final sketch of the Lulanga passage. The channel is marked 'NbyE to NNE'. On the port side is marked 'Snags'. Within the river banks two small islands are sketched, and the words 'S[and] B[ank]' and 'S[and]-B[an]ks' are written, including the fathom markings 2, 2, 2, 1, 1, 2, 2, 2 and 2.]

When following it must keep close over to port avoiding how- VII
ever sunken trees –

Passing over tails of the great sandb[an]k with less than one
fath[om] up to 2 fath[oms] – soundings.

Arriving at the end of this straight cross over on a NE course and
enter the main route up the river

End of Lulanga Pass[age]

Main River [*An elongated arrow points NNE.*]

Long NE½N reach; pretty straight – Island to port in a bend VII N
of the shore – Off it 2 S[and]B[an]ks on opposite shore with 2
fath[oms] at ½ full. Steering along the starb[oar]ᵈ bank many snags
stranded well off the shore –

The point closing this reach on the Port Side has a high tree on it

After passing this there is a broad straight channel at the end of
which a point is seen. –

The Broad channel

runs NbyW[ester]ˡʸ –
Sandbanks. – Take the narrow channel
Directly inside, camp[in]ᵍ place. Indifferent wood –
A narrow reach about NEbyN –   VIII. N.
Left camp at south end of it at 6ʰ a.m.
Curve to the NNE and a little broader reach.

This reach expands in a NEbyE direction – to Port several VIII N
islands and a small islet bushy on one end, low on the other – follow
the M[ai]ⁿ Land on the Starb[oar]ᵈ side – Great many snags lining
the shore

On the Port side probably shallow water (K[och]).

At the end of this broad long stretch appear 2 islands –

The little islet to port has a long S[and]-B[an]k on its southern end

The main shore runs North-Easterly.   VIII N.

The next point to port after pass[in]ᵍ the islet has an extensive

S[and]-B[ank] uncovered in places at ½ F[ull water] stretching away along shore to next sm[all] island – from here an island appears in the middle of river beari[n]^g <u>NNE</u>.

Steering nearly for it after passing second islet to port the river opens out to starboard into islands laying NE&SW nearly or little more Easterly

VIII N –   Steer for the middle island about NbyE½E. Then into the broad reach on its port side leaving it to starb[oar]$^{\underline{d}}$

Taking this route the M[ai]^n Land of the right bank is left and course taken to Left or north bank.

(This is not the usual course not safe to follow at less than ½ full water).

IX N.   – Keep a little nearer to the middle island than to the islands on your Port side

IX N   Proceeding cautiously must feel your way in 12 to 8 feet water. The shore on the port side is the north Bank of the river. –

Snags along <u>but</u> not much off. After passing two little islands you sight a dead trunk of a tree and villages begin. – In many places cut bank. – Excellent wooding places up to the point and in the great bend – (10^{h}50)

Left 11.30

Rounding the 1st point after the dead tree you open the 2^d point bearing a$^{\underline{b[ou]t}}$ NE where this reach ends – To starb[oar]$^{\underline{d}}$ several

IX N   islands of which two are prominent. – Land backing them in a semicircle at a great distance – M[ain]^n Land on the Sth Bank not visible. –

The river very broad here.

Follow close in the bend as there is a large sandbank between the island and the main shore.

Nearing the P[oin]t sounding in 12 to 10 feet (at ½ F[ull] W[ater]).

Mind a very bad snag nearly off the point

After a bit of straight Shore and a small poin[t] ab[ou]^t ENE open out

X.N.   2 small islets come in sight. – Steer along the m[ai]^n shore. When pass[in]^g the islets much caution and good look out – Sandbanks.

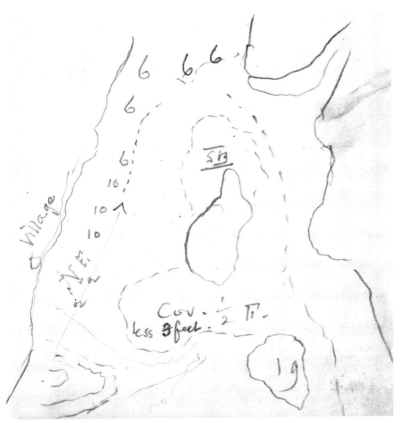

[*A sketch of the river, showing two islands mid-stream with a 'S[and]B[ank]' extending from the northernmost, and the caption below the island 'Cov[ered] ½ F[ull water] less 3 feet'. A 'NE' course is marked with soundings in feet: 10, 10, 10, 6, 6, 6, 6 and 6. 'Village' is recorded on the port side.*]

[*A sketch that has been erased and is indecipherable appears here.*]

Following the bend – When approaching the P[or]ᵗ SandB[an]k X – N – extends from islet to st[arboar]ᵈ. A snag stranded on outer edge – Pass between the shore and the snag. Another [Sand]–B[an]k on the point and snags off it. Must steer very close to the bank which is steep to –

River expands broadly here – The general direction of the main shore to the end of the expansion is ENE nearly. –

XI N   For some considerable distance the starb[oar]$^{\underline{d}}$ shore is low & grassy. After rounding the shutting in point leave the broad reach and follow the main land by a narrower channel laying about NEbyN and turning towards the NE or more easterly still. Coming out of this channel again into the broad part a great number of islands come in sight.

Steer carefully amongst sand bank watching for the edges –

– Cross over to the island and back to where 2^{d} village down is. At big clearing cross over again and enter another back passage – Sound[in]g$^{\underline{s}}$ in 10 to 6 feet. – Many snags and some of them right

XII.   in the fairway. –

Between a long low island and the main sandb[an]ks across with less than 6 feet water over them.

The passage rather intricate from islet N° 19. –

The North[er]$^{\underline{n}}$ end of that pass[a]$^{\underline{ge}}$ has a S[and]–B[an]k with 10–6 feet of water at ½ F[ull] W[ater].

Coming out of it you follow a broad stretch on a NEbyE½E course (about) and then keep off the broad channel to the NE

XII N   between the M[ai]^{n} Land and an island –

Passage narrow – where it broadens 2 islets in the bend. One of them has a thin tall dead tree with one green branch on it. It looks like a flagstaff with a bough tied up to it at right angles

Steering in always keep closer to the main shore. – Good many nasty snags all along

After passing the second of the 2 islets you may notice a third –

XIIA. N.   Small – The main shore runs NEbyE. on the Starb[oar]^{d} side many islands close together form an almost contin[u]ous shore. –

The channel is not deep from 10 to 6 feet of water some little distance up after passing the 2^{d} of two islets.

After that no soundings in <u>12</u> feet. –

Several small islets on the starb[oar]^{d} side –

XIIA N.   On the islands on the starb[oar]$^{\underline{d}}$ side good many dead palms

[An indistinct sketch – two square figures presumably representing islands in an enclosed U-shaped image – perhaps images of the two islets referred to above.]

Further on a sandbank right across – <u>6 – 10 feet</u>
At large clearing stopped. Firewood – snags –
Left at 6ʰ 30ᵐ   XIII
A straight reach NE½N.
When approaching the P[oin]t (to Port) ending the straight steer over to the other side to avoid sandbank
On starb[oar]ᵈ side small islets in the bights of the shore which is composed of long islands overlapping each other and appearing   XIII N
like one land when steaming up the river. –
Round in back again in 9 feet of water. –
Following the main shore care should be taken to avoid snags which are stranded right along it in great quantities.
<u>2d reach</u> before coming to end of it cross over to the island 20 –
Right close in to the upp[e]ʳ end – in 9 to 5 feet –
Sandbank off the main shore –
Pass close point on starb[oar]ᵈ side and steer to leave next island   XIII N
on starb[oar]ᵈ side <u>nearly</u> in midchannel. – Sandbank along the M[ai]ⁿ shore – Cross over to upper end of vill[a]ᵍᵉ clearing. –
Follow the shore – Opposite sm[a]ll beach in isl[an]ᵈ to starᵇ[ᵒᵃʳᵈ] sound[in]ᵍˢ 9 feet –
After passing this, steer off the M[ai]ⁿ shore and steer across in 9 to 5 feet to leave the small islet to port. Keep nearly in the middle when entering the pass[a]ᵍᵉ
Then steer rather over to starb[oar]ᵈ shore (big island) <u>Snags</u> –
Coming out of the back channel you sight a very [word missing] clearing bearing Nᵗʰ. – Steer a little below it passing over 10 feet   XIII N.
sound[in]ᵍˢ – When nearing the bank water deepens
Follow the cut bank pretty close – Safe. no snags there. –
Half round reach follows in a EbyN direction. Forest. Snags again. Keep a little off. – a very small creek hardly noticeable before coming to the closing P[oin]t on P[or]ᵗ side <u>sound[in]gs</u> <u>10 feet.</u>

Another bend where you keep nearly in the middle <u>10 feet</u>
<u>s[oun]d[in]gs</u> in one place –

This bend terminates in a NE direction.

XIV   There is now a double channel – one broad about EbyN another
narrow nearly NE –

Leave the island to star<u>b[oard]</u> and follow its inner shore to take
the narrow p[assa]<u>ge</u> Sound[in]<u>gs</u> 9. to 5 feet

This passage is between the M[ai]ⁿ Land on portside and 2
islands on starb[oar]<u>d</u> where the 1st Is[lan]<u>d</u> finishes there is a sandbank –

Steering close in to the islands in s[ou]nd[ing]s 10 to 5 feet –
Then over to M[ai]ⁿ shore and back again – All the way about 7 feet
of water. Less in places

After leaving this narrow passage and rounding the point another
XIV   similar passage presents itself – Keep nearly in the middle where <u>7</u>
<u>to 9 feet water</u> are obtained at ½ F[ull] W[ater]. –

Another narrow passage presenting the same features only a little narrower – About 10 feet of water – Passage ends on an Eastern
bearing. –

Coming out of this last the main stream is entered – River
XV   broadens. This is the upper end of the northern bank passage

FAMILY NEWS AGAIN OCCUPIED CONRAD, distant from Europe. Tadeusz Bobrowski's planned visit to Radom and Lublin was, as he informed Conrad in a letter of 10 July, to have occupied three weeks, beginning in early August and extending for much of the rest of the month. Maria Bobrowska, who married on 3 July, was adapting to both her changed circumstances and a new home. She seems to have established a warm friendship with her cousin, but their correspondence either soon petered out or is lost. Conrad's plans for a prolonged stay in the Congo began to alter the longer he remained, and the possible year mentioned here is evidence of considerable optimism, especially in light of his next letter, which vividly expresses disenchantment about everything to do with his situation.

TO MARIA TYSZKOWA

Kinshasa,
Stanley Pool,
Congo.
24th September, 1890.

My dear Maryleczka,

Your letter and the photograph reached me today and I hasten to write and explain to you the long interruption in our correspondence.

I have been on the river Congo, some 2,000 versts from the coast where the post office is, so I could neither send nor get news from Europe. I was pleased to get your letter although at the same time it saddened me slightly. I have lived long enough to realize that life is full of griefs and sorrows which no one can escape, nevertheless I cannot help feeling sad at the thought that people whom I love must suffer, and are suffering. It is nonetheless pleasing to get a proof of the trust you place in me by writing openly about your worries. Indeed, I do not deserve to have a place in your hearts – for I am practically a stranger to you – nevertheless the affectionate words you have written are most precious to me. I shall carefully preserve them in my heart, and the photograph will be in my album so that I can glance each day at my dear little sister.

Now that you are married and your desires fulfilled my wish for you both is that your lives will be nothing but sunshine with no clouds in the sky. Please, assure your husband of my deep esteem, and of the very friendly feelings I have for him. I accept your invitation with gratitude and I promise to devote as much time as possible to my good lady sister. I trust that Aunt's health will improve steadily now that all the unpleasant contacts are left behind. I have a letter from Uncle Tadeusz, who intended to visit you in August. He is probably back home by now.

I am very busy with all the preparations for a new expedition to the River Kassai. In a few days I shall probably be leaving Kinshasa again for a few months, possibly even for a year or longer. Thus you must not be surprised if you get no sign of life from me for a long time.

My love to dear Zuzia and my apologies for not having written to her. Please send me her exact address – and your new one as well. I kiss dear Aunt's hands. I commend myself to your thoughts and especially to your heart, dear Maryleczka.

Do not forget about me amidst all the new events in your life. I embrace you most warmly.

Your always loving brother,
K. N. Korzeniowski

As a letter of 28 October to Conrad from his uncle Tadeusz Bobrowski indicates, Poradowska, still in Lublin with the Zagórskis, planned to remain with them until Christmas. (Unless she had been recently away for a short trip, Conrad's comment that she might soon see the Zagórskis seems to stem from a misunderstanding.) The reference to 'the Academy' is unclear, the word open to several meanings in French; possibly Poradowska had been looking for some short-term employment in Lublin, or this may have to do with a learned society in Belgium. The atmosphere in

The steamer *Roi des Belges* in 1889. Conrad would describe a similar ship in 'An Outpost of Progress' as resembling 'an enormous sardine box with a flat-roofed shed erected on it'

The *Roi des Belges* on the Sankuru River and, *below*, being visited by the members of the village of Mutchié on the Kasai River, both tributaries of the Congo

The steamer workshops at Bolobo in a photograph taken by the Reverend George Grenfell – Conrad mentions, in the 'Up-river Book', passing 'From point (Eng[lish] Mission) at Grenfell p[oin]t – at 4^{h} p. m.' *Below*, the bank of the river near Irebu

Villagers from a forest tribe view the passing of the *Roi des Belges* from the riverbank, and, *below*, the dense forests of the Congo

Lublin might have been somewhat oppressive, as Gabriela Zagórska ('Aunt Gaba') had become partly paralysed. Marcelina Ołdakowska and her daughter Maria ('Marysieńka') were more distant relatives, the sister and niece of Aleksander Poradowski. Dwelling on his relatives' lives might have provided a welcome distraction from his immediate situation: Conrad's dislike of Delcommune was returned in full. It was now clear that he could look forward to no advancement in the Société Anonyme Belge, to which he was tied by a three-year contract. His health, however, already poor on the trip upriver, continued to plague him. According to the fragmentary company records, he was back in Matadi on 16 November; and, having obtained a release from his contract on the basis of a medical certificate, he left for Europe on 4 December.

TO MARGUERITE PORADOWSKA

26 September 1890
Kinshasa

Dearest and best of Aunts!

I received your three letters together on my return from Stanley Falls, where I went as a supernumerary on board the vessel *Roi des Belges* in order to learn about the river. I learn with joy of your success at the Academy, which, of course, I never doubted. I cannot find words sufficiently strong to make you understand the pleasure your charming (and above all kind) letters have given me. They were as a ray of sunshine piercing through the grey clouds of a dreary winter day; for my days here are dreary. No use deluding oneself! Decidedly I regret having come here. I even regret it bitterly. With all of a man's egoism, I am going to speak of myself. I cannot stop myself. Before whom can I ease my heart if not before you?! In speaking to you, I am certain of being understood down to the merest hint. Your heart will divine my thoughts more quickly than I can express them.

Everything here is repellent to me. Men and things, but men above all. And I am repellent to them, also. From the manager in Africa who has taken the trouble to tell one and all that I offend him supremely, down to the lowest mechanic, they all have the gift of irritating my nerves – so that I am not as agreeable to them perhaps as I should be. The manager is a common ivory dealer with base instincts who considers himself a merchant although he is only a kind of African shop-keeper. His name is Delcommune. He detests the English, and out here I am naturally regarded as such. I cannot hope for either promotion or salary increases while he is here. Besides, he has said that promises made in Europe carry no weight here if they are not in the contract. Those made to me by M. Wauters are not. In addition, I cannot look forward to anything because I don't have a ship to command. The new boat will not be completed until June of next year, perhaps. Meanwhile, my position here is unclear and I am troubled by that. So there you are! As crowning joy, my health is far from good. *Keep it a secret for me –* but the truth is that in going up the river I suffered from fever four times in two months, and then at the Falls (which is its home territory), I suffered an attack of dysentery lasting five days. I feel somewhat weak physically and not a little demoralized; and then, really, I believe that I feel homesick for the sea, the desire to look again on the level expanse of salt water which has so often lulled me, which has smiled at me so frequently under the sparkling sunshine of a lovely day, which many times too has hurled the threat of death in my face with a swirl of white foam whipped by the wind under the dark December sky. I regret all that. But what I regret even more is having tied myself down for three years. The truth is that it is scarcely probable I shall see them through. Either someone in authority will pick a groundless quarrel in order to send me back (and, really, I sometimes find myself wishing for it), or I shall be sent back to Europe by a new attack of dysentery, unless it consigns me to the other world, which would be a final solution to all my distress! And for four pages I have been speaking of myself! I have not told you with what pleasure I have read your descriptions of men and things at home. Indeed, while reading your dear letters I have forgotten Africa, the Congo, the black savages and the white slaves (of whom I am one) who inhabit it. For one hour I have been happy. Know that it is not a small thing (nor an easy thing) to make a human being happy for an *entire hour*. You can be proud of having

succeeded. And so my heart goes out to you with a burst of gratitude and the most sincere and most profound affection. When will
we meet again? Alas, meeting leads to parting – and the more one
meets, the more painful the separations become. Such is Fate.

Seeking a practical remedy to the disagreeable situation which I
have made for myself, I conceived of a little plan – still up in the air
– in which you could perhaps help me. It appears that this company,
or another affiliated with it, will have some ocean-going vessels (or
even has one already). Probably that great (or fat?) banker who
rules the roost where we are concerned will have a large interest in
the other company. If someone could submit my name for the command of one of their ships (whose home port will be Antwerp) I
would be able to get away for a day or two in Brussels when you are
there. That would be ideal! If they wanted to call me home to take
command, I would naturally pay the cost of coming back myself.
This is perhaps not a very practicable idea, but if you return to Brussels in the winter, you could learn through M. Wauters what the
chances are. Isn't that so, dear little Aunt?

I am going to send this care of the Princess (whom I love because
she loves you). Soon, probably, you will see poor, dear Aunt Gaba,
and that dear and good Charles Zagórski family with their charming little daughters. I envy you! Tell them that I love them all and
that I ask a little something in return. Mlle Marysieńka has probably forgotten the promise she made me about her photograph. I am
ever her devoted cousin and servant. I dare not say 'admirer' for fear
of my Aunt Ołdakowska, to whom I wish to be remembered with
affection. I urge you by all the gods to keep secret from *everybody*
the state of my health, or else my uncle will certainly hear of it. I
must finish. I leave within an hour for Bamou, by canoe, to select
trees and have them felled for building operations at the station
here. I shall remain encamped in the forest for two or three weeks,
unless ill. I like the prospect well enough. I can doubtless have a
shot or two at some buffaloes or elephants. I embrace you most
warmly. I shall write a long letter by the next mail.

Your affectionate nephew
J.C.K.

ACTING IN EFFECT AS HIS LITERARY AGENT, Conrad's first publisher Thomas Fisher Unwin (1848–1935) carefully nurtured his author's interests in seeking to place his early short stories for serialisation. The story Conrad intended for *Cosmopolis*, an international and multilingual magazine addressed to an elite and cosmopolitan readership, was 'An Outpost of Progress'. This choice was a canny one, for Unwin's firm printed the magazine, which was distributed in England and on the Continent, and featured a medley of articles on international political affairs as well as coverage of the arts and a smattering of original fiction. Edward Garnett (1868–1937), who had worked for Unwin as a publisher's reader and become a close friend and mentor of Conrad, was the story's dedicatee. Unwin's wife, Jane Cobden-Unwin (1851–1947), whom Conrad greets in his postscript, was the daughter of Richard Cobden, a statesman and social reformer, and herself involved in liberal political issues, including, notably, women's suffrage.

TO T. FISHER UNWIN

22^{d} July. 96.
Ile Grande
par *Lannion*

Dear Mr Unwin.

Thanks for Your unwearied endeavours to place my story. I am very much touched but suspect that you must have about enough of me and of my 'masterpieces'.

The acceptance of my story would have given me pleasure. But its refusal is not without its compensations – for it is exactly what I did foresee. It shows me that I have judged the work rightly. I am not ashamed of it for all that. Bad or good I cannot be ashamed of what is produced in perfect single mindedness – I cannot be ashamed of those things that are like fragments of my innermost being produced for the public gaze.

But I must live. I don't care much where I appear since the acceptance of such stories is not based upon their artistic worth. It is probably right that it should be so. But in that case there is no particular
gratification in being accepted *here* rather than *there*. – If the 'Savoy'
thing asks for my work – why not give it to them? I understand they
pay tolerably well (2g[uinea]s per page?). The only thing I wish is
that your right to reproduce in a volume should be perfectly clear.
You said you would – yourself. And it has been a great pleasure for
me to hear it. And I feel that the stories will be worth[y] of your
imprint – even if stones are cast at them. But I should like to sell
them. If you think I am greedy then consider I am greedy for very
little after all. And if you knew the wear and tear of my writing you
would understand my desire for some return. I writhe in doubt over
every line. – I ask myself – is it right? – is it true? – do I feel it so? – do
I express all my feeling? And I ask it at every sentence – I perspire in
incertitude over every word! – Perhaps you will smile over all this
fuss. But I am sure You will not smile unkindly. After all it is my
work. The only lasting thing in the world. People die – affections die
– all passes – but a man's work remains with him to the last.

– You will soon receive a story for the *Cosmo*. I suspect that they
won't take it after all. I send it to Garnett for the reason that it refers
(in its execution) to a certain discussion we had on matters of art
and I should like to know whether I have succeeded in achieving my
purpose – my artistic purpose. The effect produced on him will tell
me that.

– It is a story of the Congo. There is no love interest in it and no
woman – only incidentally. The exact locality is not mentioned. All
the bitterness of those days, all my puzzled wonder as to the meaning of all I saw – all my indignation at masquerading philanthropy –
have been with me again, while I wrote. The story is simple – there is
hardly any description. The most common incidents are related –
the life in a lonely station on the Kassai. I have divested myself of
everything but pity – and some scorn – while putting down the
insignificant events that bring on the catastrophe. Upon my word I
think it is a good story – and not so gloomy – not fanciful – alas! I
think it interesting – some may find it a bore! If the *Cosmo* won't take

it (it is as long as the other) I shall put it by. A day may come for it. I wonder you find time to read my letters! Thanks once more. Yours very faithfully

Jph Conrad

My most respectful and affct^nte regards, Mrs Unwin. I ought to thank you for the Cobden number of the Dly News. I was immensely pleased to be remembered in that way.

IN THE 'AUTHOR'S NOTE' he later provided to a collection of stories that reprinted 'An Outpost of Progress', Conrad characterised this tale as 'the lightest part of the loot I carried off from Central Africa'. The heavier part consisted of *Heart of Darkness*, and, still more importantly, he arrived back in Europe with an altered view of life.

He wrote this story – only his second and originally called 'A Victim of Progress' and then 'Two Victims of Progress' – on his honeymoon in Brittany in July 1896, taking about three weeks to compose a first draft, written 'with pleasure if with difficulty' (letter to Edward Garnett, 5 August 1896). He worked on it further in the typescript that his wife prepared. The manuscript survived, finally finding its way into the Beinecke Rare Book and Manuscript Library at Yale University; the typescripts have perished.

The story first appeared in *Cosmopolis* in its issues of June and July 1897. Its division into two parts, Conrad felt, ruined the story, and he protested vigorously but without avail against his editor's decision. It was, however, much too long to appear as the author wished, and it appeared in this format until 2012, when the Cambridge Edition critical text finally paid heed to the author's express wishes. That restored version is printed below.

Conrad hinted to his first biographer that the story was based on an anecdote Prosper Harou (see introductory note to the 'Congo Diary') had told him. Conrad's two hapless vagabonds bear the names of people he had met in the Congo: Carlier (1851–1930), who was given command over the *Florida*, which had been promised to Conrad, and Alphonse Kayaerts (1852–?), who did indeed, as does his namesake in the story, work in Belgium's Poste et Télégraphe service, and who travelled with Conrad in the *Roi des Belges*. Gobila also borrows the name of an actual person, a Bateke chief who exercised authority on the Congo's left bank near what is now Brazzaville. He had some eighty wives and innumerable slaves. H. M. Stanley had met him, and several other travellers mention him in their accounts of the Congo. The managing director of the Great Civilising Company at the end of the story is an allusion to Camille Delcommune of the Société Anonyme Belge. Writing to his publisher, Conrad identified the story's scene as 'a lonely station on the Kassai' (letter to T. Fisher Unwin, 22 July 1896), the Congo's chief southern tributary; but the story leaves the specific locality vague.

An Outpost of Progress

To Edward Garnett

There were two white men in charge of the trading station. Kayerts, the chief, was short and fat. Carlier, the assistant, was tall with a large head and a very broad trunk perched upon a long pair of thin legs. The third man on the staff was a Sierra-Leone nigger who maintained that his name was Henry Price. However for some reason or other the natives down the river had given him the name of Makola and it stuck to him through all his wanderings about the country. He spoke English and French with a warbling accent, wrote a beautiful hand, understood book-keeping and cherished in his innermost heart the worship of evil spirits. His wife was a negress from Loanda, very large and very noisy. Three children rolled about in sunshine before the door of his low shed-like dwelling. Makola, taciturn and impenetrable, despised the two white men. He had charge of a small clay storehouse with a dried-grass roof and pretended to keep a correct account of beads, cotton cloths, red kerchiefs, brass wire, and other trade goods it contained. Besides the storehouse and Makola's hut there was only one large building in the cleared ground of the station. It was built neatly of reeds with a verandah on all the four sides. There were three rooms in it. The one in the middle was the living room and had two rough tables and a few stools in it. The other two were the bedrooms for the white men. Each had a bedstead and a mosquito net for all furniture. The plank floor was littered with the belongings of the white men – open half empty boxes, torn wearing apparel, old boots – all the things dirty, and all the things broken that accumulate mysteriously round untidy men. There was also another dwelling place some distance away from the buildings. In it under a tall cross much out of the perpendicular slept the man who had seen the beginning of all this, who had planned and had watched the construction of this outpost of progress. He had been at home an unsuccessful painter who, weary of pursuing fame on an empty stomach, had gone out there – through high protections. He had been the first chief of that station. Makola had watched the energetic artist die of fever in the just finished house with his usual kind of 'I told-you-so' indifference. Then for a time he dwelt alone with his family, his account books and the Evil Spirit that rules the lands under the equator. He got on very well with his god. Perhaps he had propitiated him by a promise of more white men to play with by and by. At any rate the Director of the Great Trading Company, coming up in a steamer that resembled an enormous sardine box with a flat-roofed shed erected on it, found the station in good order and Makola as usual quietly diligent. The Director had the cross put up over the first agent's grave and appointed Kayerts to the post. Carlier was told off as second in charge. The Director was a man ruthless and efficient, who at times, but very imperceptibly, indulged in grim humour. He made a speech to Kayerts and Carlier pointing out to them the promising aspect of their station. The nearest trading post was about three hundred miles away. It was an exceptional opportunity for them to distinguish themselves and to earn percentages on the trade. This appointment was a favour done to beginners. Kayerts was moved almost to tears by his Director's kindness. He would – he said – by doing his best try to justify the flattering confidence etc. etc. Kayerts had been in the Administration of the Telegraphs and knew how to express himself correctly. Carlier, an ex-non-commissioned officer of cavalry in an army guaranteed from harm by several European Powers, was less impressed; if there were commissions to get, so much the better; and trailing a sulky glance over the river, the forests, the impenetrable bush that seemed to cut off the station from the rest of the world, he muttered between his teeth: 'We shall see, very soon.'

Next day, some bales of cotton goods and a few cases of provisions having been thrown on shore, the sardine-box steamer went off not to return for another six months. On the deck the Director touched his cap to the two agents who stood on the bank waving their hats, and turning to an old servant of the Company on his passage to headquarters said: 'Look at those two imbeciles. They must be mad at home to send me such specimens. I told those fellows to plant a vegetable garden, build new storehouses and fences and construct a landing stage. I bet nothing will be done. They won't know how to begin. I always thought the station on this river useless – and they just fit the station!'

'They will form themselves there,' said the old stager with a quiet smile.

'At any rate, I am rid of them for six months,' retorted the Director.

The two men watched the steamer round the bend, then ascending arm in arm the slope of the bank returned to the station. They had been in this vast and dark country only a very short time and as yet always in the midst of other white men, under the eye and guidance of their superiors. And now, dull as they were to the subtle influence of surroundings, they felt themselves very much alone – when suddenly left unassisted to face the wilderness, a wilderness rendered more strange, more incomprehensible by the mysterious glimpses of the vigorous life it contained. They were two perfectly insignificant and incapable individuals whose existence is only rendered possible through the high organization of the civilized crowds. Few men realize that their life, the very essence of their character, their capabilities and their audacities are only the expression of their belief in the safety of their surroundings. The courage, the composure, the confidence, the emotions and principles, every great and every insignificant thought belongs not to the individual but to the crowd – to the crowd that believes blindly in the irresistible force of its institutions and of its morals, in the power of its police and of its opinion. But the contact with pure unmitigated savagery, with primitive nature and primitive man, brings sudden and profound trouble into the heart. To the sentiment of being alone of one's kind, to the clear perception of the loneliness – of one's thoughts, of one's sensations – to the negation of the habitual, which is safe, there is added the affirmation of the unusual, which is dangerous, a suggestion of things vague, uncontrollable and repulsive, whose discomposing intrusion excites the imagination and tries the civilized nerves of the foolish and the wise alike.

Kayerts and Carlier walked arm in arm – drawing close to one another as children do in the dark; and they had the same not altogether unpleasant sense of danger which one half suspects to be imaginary. They chatted persistently in familiar tones. 'Our station is prettily situated,' said one. The other assented with enthusiasm, enlarging volubly on the beauties of the situation. Then they passed near the grave. 'Poor devil,' said Kayerts. – 'He died of fever – didn't he?' muttered Carlier stopping short. – 'Why,' retorted Kayerts with indignation – 'I've been told that the fellow exposed himself reck-lessly to the sun. The climate here – everybody says – is not at all worse than at home – as long as you keep out of the sun. Do you hear that, Carlier? I am chief here and my orders are that you should not expose yourself to the sun!' He assumed his superiority jocularly but his meaning was serious. The idea that he would per-haps have to bury Carlier and remain alone gave him an inward shiver. He felt suddenly that this Carlier was more precious to him here in the centre of Africa than a brother could be anywhere else. Carlier, entering into the spirit of the thing, made a military salute and answered in a brisk tone, 'Your orders shall be attended to, chief!' – Then he burst out laughing, slapped Kayerts on the back and shouted, 'We shall let life run easily here! Just sit still and gather in the ivory those savages will bring. This country has its good points after all!' They both laughed loudly while Carlier thought: that poor Kayerts – he is so fat and unhealthy. It would be awful if I had to bury him here. He is a man I respect . . . Before they reached the verandah of their house they called one another 'my dear fellow'.

The first day they were very active – pottering about with ham-mers and nails and red calico, to put up curtains, make their house habitable and pretty; resolved to settle down comfortably to their new life. For them an impossible task. To grapple effectually with even purely material problems requires more serenity of mind and more lofty courage than people generally imagine. No two beings could have been more unfitted for such a struggle. Society – not from any tenderness but because of its strange needs – had taken care of those two men, forbidding them all independent thought, all initiative, all departure from routine – and forbidding it under pain of death. They could only live on condition of being machines. And now, released from the fostering care of men with pens behind the ears or of men with gold lace on the sleeves, they were like those lifelong prisoners who, liberated after many years, do not know what use to make of their freedom. They did not know what use to make of their faculties being both through want of practice incapable of independent thought.

At the end of two months Kayerts often would say: 'If it was not for my Mélie you wouldn't catch me here.' Mélie was his daughter. He had thrown up his post in the Administration of the Telegraphs, though he had been for seventeen years perfectly happy there, to earn a dowry for his girl. His wife was dead and the child was being brought up by his sisters. He regretted the streets, the pavements, the cafés, his friends of many years: all the things he used to see day after day, all the thoughts suggested by familiar things – the thoughts effortless, monotonous and soothing of a government clerk; he regretted all the gossip, the small enmities, the mild venom and the little jokes of government offices. – 'If I had had a decent brother in law,' Carlier would remark, 'a fellow with a heart, I would not be here.' He had left the army and had made himself so obnoxious to his family by his laziness and impudence that an exasperated brother in law had made superhuman efforts to procure him an appointment in the Company as a second class agent. Having not a penny in the world he was compelled to accept this means of livelihood as soon as it became quite clear to him that there was nothing more to squeeze out of his relations. He, like Kayerts, regretted his old life. He regretted the clink of sabre and spurs on a fine afternoon, the barrack-room witticisms – the girls of garrison towns; but besides he had also a sense of grievance. He was evidently a much ill-used man. This made him moody, at times. But the two men got on well together in the fellowship of their stupidity and laziness. Together they did nothing – absolutely nothing – and enjoyed the sense of the idleness for which they were paid. And in time they came to feel something resembling affection for one another.

They lived like blind men in a large room, aware only of what came in contact with them (and of that only imperfectly) but unable to see the general aspect of things. The river, the forest, all the great land throbbing with life were like a great emptiness.

Even the brilliant sunshine disclosed nothing intelligible. Things appeared and disappeared before their eyes in an unconnected and aimless kind of way. The river seemed to come from nowhere and flow nowhither. It flowed through a void. Out of that void at times came canoes, and men with spears in their hands would suddenly crowd the yard of the station. They were naked, glossy black, ornamented with snowy shells and glistening brass wire, perfect of limb. They made an uncouth babbling noise when they spoke, moved in a stately manner and sent quick wild glances out of their startled never-resting eyes. Those warriors would squat in long rows four or more deep before the verandah while their chiefs bargained for hours with Makola over an elephant tusk. Kayerts sat on his chair and looked down on the proceedings, understanding nothing. He stared at them with his round blue eyes – called out to Carlier: 'Here! look, look at that fellow there . . . and that other one to the left. Did you ever see such a face? Oh the funny brute!' Carlier, smoking native tobacco in a short wooden pipe, would swagger up twirling his moustaches and, surveying the warriors with haughty indulgence, would say:

'Fine animals. Brought any bone? Yes? Isn't any too soon. Look at the muscles of that fellow . . . third from the end. I wouldn't care to get a punch on the nose from him. Fine arms – but legs no good below the knee. Couldn't make cavalry-men of them.' . . . And after glancing down complacently at his own shanks he always concluded: 'Pah! Don't they stink! You, Makola! Take that herd over to the fetish (the storehouse was in every station called the fetish, perhaps because of the spirit of civilization it contained) and give them up some of the rubbish you keep there. I'd rather see it full of bone than full of rags.'

Kayerts approved:

'Yes! Yes. Go and finish that palaver over there, Mr Makola. I will come round when you are ready to weigh the tusk. We must be careful.' . . . Then turning to his companion: 'This is the tribe that lives down the river – they are rather aromatic. I remember – they had been once before here . . . D'ye hear that row? What a fellow has got to put up with in this dog of a country! . . . My head is split.'

Such profitable visits were rare. For days the two pioneers of trade and progress would look on their empty courtyard in the vibrating brilliance of vertical sunshine. Below the high bank the silent river flowed on glittering and steady. On the sands in the middle of the stream hippos and alligators sunned themselves side by side. And stretching away in all directions, surrounding the insignificant cleared spot of the trading-post, immense forests hiding fateful complications of fantastic life, lay in the eloquent silence of mute greatness. The two men understood nothing, cared for nothing but for the passage of days that separated them from the steamer's return. Their predecessor had left some torn books. They took up these wrecks of novels and, as they had never read anything of the kind before, they were surprised and amused. Then during long days there were interminable and silly discussions about plots and personages. In the centre of Africa they made the acquaintance of Richelieu and of d'Artagnan, of Hawk's eye and of Father Goriot and of many other people. All these imaginary personages became subjects for gossip as if they had been living friends. They discounted their virtues, suspected their motives, decried their successes, were scandalized at their duplicity or were doubtful about their courage. The accounts of crimes filled them with indignation while tender or pathetic passages moved them deeply. Carlier cleared his throat and said in a soldierly voice, 'What nonsense!' Kayerts, his round eyes suffused with tears, his fat cheeks quivering, rubbed his bald head and declared: 'This is a splendid book. I had no idea there were such clever fellows in the world.' They also found some old copies of a home paper. That print discussed – what it was pleased to call – 'our colonial expansion' in high flown language. It spoke much of the rights and duties of civilization – of the sacredness of the civilizing work, and extolled the merits of those who went about bringing light and faith and commerce to the dark places of the earth. Carlier and Kayerts read, wondered and began to think better of themselves. Carlier said one evening waving his hand about, 'In a hundred years there will be perhaps a town here. Quays and warehouses and barracks . . . and . . . and . . . billiard rooms. Civilization, my boy, and virtue . . . and all. And then, chaps will read that two good fellows, Kayerts and Carlier, were the first civilized men to live at this very spot.' – Kayerts nodded, 'Yes, it is a consolation to think of that.' They seemed to forget their dead predecessor; but early one day Carlier walked out and replanted the cross firmly. – 'It used to make me squint whenever I went that way' – he explained to Kayerts over the morning coffee – 'It made me squint leaning over so much. So I just planted it upright. And solid, I promise you. I suspended myself with both hands to the cross-piece. Not a move. Oh, I did that properly.'

At times Gobila came to see them. Gobila was the chief of the neighbouring villages. He was a grey-headed savage, thin and black, with a white cloth round his loins and a mangy panther skin hanging over his back. He came up with long strides of his skeleton legs swinging a staff as tall as himself and, entering the common room of the station, would squat on his heels to the left of the door. There he sat watching Kayerts and now and then making a speech which the other did not understand. Kayerts, without interrupting his occupation, would from time to time say in a friendly manner: 'How goes it, you old image?' and they would smile at one another. The two whites had a liking for that old and incomprehensible creature and called him Father Gobila. Gobila's manner was paternal and he seemed really to love all white men. They all appeared to him very young, indistinguishably alike (except for stature) and he knew that they were all brothers and also immortal. The death of the artist – who was the first white man whom he knew intimately – did not disturb this belief because he was firmly convinced that the white stranger had pretended to die and got himself buried for some mysterious purpose of his own into which it was useless to inquire. Perhaps it was his way of going home to his own country. At any rate these were his brothers – and he transferred his absurd affection to them. They returned it in a way. Carlier slapped him on the back and recklessly struck off matches for his amusement. Kayerts was always ready to let him have a sniff at the ammonia bottle. In short they behaved just like that other white creature that had hidden itself in a hole in the ground. Gobila considered them attentively. Perhaps they were the same being with the other – or one of them was. He couldn't decide – clear up that mystery; but he remained always very friendly. In consequence of that friendship the women of Gobila's village walked in single file through the reedy grass bringing every morning to the station fowls, and sweet potatoes and palm wine and sometimes a goat. The company never provisions the stations fully and the agents required these local supplies to live. They had them through the good-will of Gobila and lived well. Now and then one of them had a bout of fever and the other nursed him with gentle devotion. They did not think much of it. It left them weaker and their appearance changed for the worse. Carlier was hollow-eyed and irritable. Kayerts showed a drawn flabby face above the rotundity of his stomach which gave him a weird aspect. But being constantly together they did not notice the change that took place gradually in their appearance and also in their disposition.

Five months passed in that way.

Then, one morning, as Kayerts and Carlier lounging in their chairs under the verandah talked about the approaching visit of the steamer, a knot of armed men came out of the forest and advanced towards the station. They were strangers to that part of the country. They were tall, slight, draped classically from neck to heel in blue fringed cloths and carried percussion muskets over their bare right shoulders. Makola showed signs of excitement and ran out of the store (where he spent all his days) to meet these visitors. They came into the courtyard and looked about them with steady, scornful glances. Their leader, a powerful and determined-looking negro with bloodshot eyes, stood in front of the verandah and made a long speech. He gesticulated much and ceased very suddenly.

There was something in his intonation, in the sounds of the long sentences he used, that startled the two whites. It was like a reminiscence of something not exactly familiar and yet resembling the speech of civilized men. It sounded like one of those impossible languages which sometimes we hear in our dreams.

'What lingo is that?' said the amazed Carlier. 'In the first moment I fancied the fellow was going to speak French. Anyway it is a different kind of gibberish to what we ever heard.'

'Yes,' replied Kayerts. 'Hey, Makola, what does he say? where do they come from? who are they?'

But Makola, who seemed to be standing on hot bricks, answered hurriedly: 'I don't know. They come from very far. Perhaps Mrs Price will understand. They are perhaps bad men.'

The leader after waiting for a while said something sharply to Makola, who shook his head. Then the man after looking round noticed Makola's hut and walked over there. The next moment Mrs Makola was heard speaking with great volubility. The other strangers – they were six in all – strolled about with an air of ease, put their heads through the door of the store room, congregated round the grave, pointed understandingly at the cross and generally made themselves at home.

'I don't like those chaps . . . and, I say, Kayerts, they must be from the coast, they've got firearms,' observed the sagacious Carlier.

Kayerts also did not like those chaps. They both for the first time became aware that they lived in conditions where the unusual may be dangerous – and that there was no power on earth outside of themselves to stand between them and the unusual. They became uneasy, went in and loaded their revolvers. Kayerts said: 'We must order Makola to tell them to go away before dark.'

The strangers left in the afternoon after eating a meal prepared for them by Mrs Makola. The immense woman was excited and talked much with the visitors. She rattled away shrilly, pointing here and pointing there at the forests and at the river. Makola sat apart and watched. At times he got up and whispered to his wife. He accompanied the strangers across the ravine at the back of the station-ground and returned slowly looking very thoughtful. When questioned by the white men he was very strange, seemed not to understand, seemed to have forgotten French – seemed to have forgotten how to speak altogether. Kayerts and Carlier agreed that the nigger had had too much palm wine. There was some talk about keeping a watch in turn but in the evening everything seemed so quiet and peaceful that they retired as usual. All night they were disturbed by a lot of drumming in the villages. A deep rapid roll near by would be followed by another far off – then all ceased. Soon, short appeals would rattle out here and there, then all mingle together, increase, become vigorous and sustained; would spread out over the forest, roll through the night, unbroken and ceaseless, near and far, as if the whole land had been one immense drum booming out steadily an appeal to heaven. And through the deep and tremendous noise sudden yells that resembled snatches of songs from a madhouse darted shrill and high in discordant jets of sound which seemed to rush far above the earth and drive all peace from under the stars.

Carlier and Kayerts slept badly. They both thought they had heard shots fired during the night – but they could not agree as to the direction. In the morning Makola was gone somewhere. He returned about noon with one of yesterday's strangers and eluded all Kayerts' attempts to close with him. Had become deaf apparently. Kayerts wondered. Carlier, who had been fishing off the bank, came back and remarked while he showed his catch, 'The niggers seem to be in a deuce of a stir. I wonder what's up. I saw about fifteen canoes cross the river during the two hours I was there fishing.' Kayerts, worried, said: 'Isn't this Makola very queer to-day?' Carlier advised, 'Keep all our men together in case of some trouble.'

There were ten station men who had been left by the Director. Those fellows, having engaged themselves to the Company for six months (without having any idea of a month in particular and only a very faint notion of time in general), had been serving the cause of progress for upwards of two years. Belonging to a tribe from a very distant part of this land of darkness and sorrow, they did not run away, naturally supposing that as wandering strangers they would be killed by the inhabitants of the country. In which they were right. They lived in straw huts on the slope of a ravine overgrown with reedy grass, just behind the station buildings. They were not happy, regretting the festive incantations, the sorceries, the human sacrifices of their own land, where they also had parents, brothers, sisters, admired chiefs, respected magicians, loved friends, and other ties supposed generally to be human. Besides, the rice rations served out by the Company did not agree with them, being a food unknown to their land and to which they could not get used. Consequently they were unhealthy and miserable. Had they been of any other tribe they would have made up their minds to die – for nothing is easier to certain savages than suicide – and so have escaped from the puzzling difficulties of existence. But belonging, as they did, to a warlike tribe with filed teeth, they had more grit and went on stupidly living through disease and sorrow. They did very little work and had lost their splendid physique. Carlier and Kayerts doctored them assiduously without being able to bring them back into condition again. They were mustered every morning and told off to different tasks – grass cutting, fence building, tree felling etc. etc. – which no power on earth could induce them to execute efficiently. The two whites had practically very little control over them.

In the afternoon Makola came over to the big house and found Kayerts watching three heavy columns of smoke rising above the forests. 'What is that?' asked Kayerts. 'Some villages burn,' answered Makola, who seemed to have regained his wits. Then he said abruptly: 'We have got very little ivory. Bad six months trading. Do you like get a little more ivory?'

'Yes,' said Kayerts eagerly. He thought of percentages, which were low.

'Those men who came yesterday are traders from Loanda who have got more ivory than they can carry home. Shall I buy? I know their camp.'

'Certainly,' said Kayerts. 'What are those traders?'

'Bad fellows,' said Makola indifferently. 'They fight with people and catch women and children. They are bad men and have got guns. There is a great disturbance in the country. Do you want ivory?'

'Yes,' said Kayerts. Makola said nothing for a while. Then: 'Those workmen of ours are no good at all,' he muttered looking round. 'Station in very bad order, sir. Director will growl. Better get a fine lot of ivory – then he say nothing.'

'I can't help it; the men won't work,' said Kayerts. 'When will you get that ivory?'

'Very soon,' said Makola. 'Perhaps to-night. You leave it to me, and keep indoors, sir. I think you had better give some palm wine to our men to make a dance this evening. Enjoy themselves.

Work better to-morrow. There's plenty palm wine – gone a little sour' . . .

Kayerts said yes and Makola with his own hands carried the big calabashes to the door of his hut. They stood there till the evening and Mrs Makola looked into every one. The men got them at sunset. When Kayerts and Carlier retired a big bonfire was flaring before the men's huts. They could hear their shouts and drumming. Some men from Gobila's village had joined the station hands and the entertainment was a great success.

In the middle of the night Carlier, waking suddenly, heard a man shout loudly; then a shot was fired. Only one. Carlier ran out and met Kayerts on the verandah. They were both startled. As they went across the yard to call Makola they saw shadows moving in the night. One of them cried, 'Don't shoot. It's me – Price.' Then Makola appeared close to them. 'Go back! go back, please,' he urged. 'You spoil all.' – 'There are strange men about,' said Carlier. 'Never mind – I know,' said Makola. Then he whispered, 'All right. Bring ivory. Say nothing. I know my business.' The two white men reluctantly went back to the house but did not sleep. They heard footsteps, whispers, some groans. It seemed as if a lot of men came in, dumped heavy things on the ground – squabbled a long time – then went away. They lay on their hard beds and thought: this Makola is invaluable. In the morning Carlier came out very sleepy and pulled at the cord of the big bell. The station hands mustered every morning to the sound of the bell. That morning nobody came. Kayerts turned out also yawning. Across the yard they saw Makola come out of his hut, a tin basin of soapy water in his hand. Makola, a civilized nigger, was very neat in his person. He threw the soapsuds skilfully over a wretched little yellow cur he had, then turning his face to the agents' house he shouted from the distance: 'All the men gone, last night!'

They heard him plainly but in their surprise they both yelled out together: 'What!' Then they stared at one another. 'We are in a proper fix now,' growled Carlier. – 'It's incredible!' muttered Kayerts. – 'I will go to the huts and see,' said Carlier striding off. Makola coming up found Kayerts standing alone.

'I can hardly believe it' – said Kayerts tearfully, 'We took care of them as if they had been our children.'

'They went with the coast people,' said Makola after a moment of hesitation.

'What do I care with whom they went – the ungrateful brutes!' exclaimed the other. Then with sudden suspicion and looking hard at Makola he added: 'What do you know about it?'

Makola moved his shoulders, looking down on the ground. 'What do I know? I think only . . . Will you come and look at the ivory I've got there? It is a fine lot. You never saw such.'

He moved towards the store. Kayerts followed him mechanically, thinking about the incredible desertion of the men. On the ground before the door of the fetish lay six splendid tusks.

'What did you give for it?' asked Kayerts after surveying the lot with satisfaction.

'No regular trade,' said Makola. 'They brought the ivory and gave it to me. I told them to take what they most wanted in the station. It is a beautiful lot. No station can show such tusks. Those traders wanted carriers badly – and our men were no good here . . . No trade – no entry in books – all correct' . . .

Kayerts nearly burst with indignation. 'Why!' he shouted, 'I believe you have sold our men for these tusks!' . . . Makola stood impassive and silent . . . 'I . . . I . . . will . . . I . . .' stuttered Kayerts . . . 'You fiend!' he yelled out.

'I did the best for you and the Company,' said Makola imperturbably – 'Why you shout so much? Look at this tusk.'

'I dismiss you! I will report you . . . I won't look at the tusk. I forbid you to touch them. I order you to throw them into the river. You! . . . you! . . .'

'You very red Mr Kayerts . . . If you are so irritable in the sun you will get fever and die . . . like the first chief,' pronounced Makola impressively.

They stood still contemplating one another with intense eyes as if they had been looking with effort across immense distances. Kayerts shivered. Makola had meant no more than he said but his words seemed to Kayerts full of ominous menace. He turned sharply and went away to the house; Makola retired into the bosom of his family; and the tusks left lying before the store looked very large and valuable in the sunshine.

Carlier came back on the verandah. 'They're all gone, hey?' asked Kayerts from the far end of the common room in a muffled voice. 'You did not find anybody?' – 'Oh, yes,' said Carlier, 'I found one of Gobila's people lying dead before the huts – shot through the body. We heard that shot last night.' – Kayerts came out quickly. He found his companion staring grimly over the yard at the tusks, away by the store. They both sat in silence for a while. Then Kayerts related his conversation with Makola. Carlier said nothing. At the midday meal they ate very little. They hardly exchanged a word that day. A great silence seemed to lay heavily over the station and press on their lips. Makola did not open the store. He spent the day playing with his children. He lay full length on a mat outside his door and the youngsters sat on his chest and clambered all over him. It was a touching picture. Mrs Makola was busy cooking all day as usual. The white men made a somewhat better meal in the evening. Afterwards Carlier, smoking his pipe, strolled over to the store; he stood a long time over the tusks; touched one or two with his foot, even tried to lift the largest one by its small end. He came back to his chief, who had not stirred from the verandah, threw himself in the chair and said:

'I can see it. They were pounced upon while they slept heavily after drinking all that palm wine you've allowed Makola to give them. A put up job. See? The worst is some of Gobila's people were there and got carried off too, no doubt. The least drunk woke up and got shot for his sobriety. This is a funny country. What will you do – now?'

'We can't touch it, of course,' said Kayerts.

'Of course not,' assented Carlier.

'Slavery is an awful thing,' stammered out Kayerts in an unsteady voice.

'Frightful . . . the sufferings . . .' grunted Carlier with conviction.

They believed their words. Everybody shows a respectful deference to certain sounds that he and his fellows can make. But about feelings people really know nothing. We talk with indignation, or enthusiasm, we talk about oppression, cruelty, crime, devotion, self-sacrifice, virtue – and we know nothing real beyond the words. Nobody knows what suffering or sacrifice mean – except, perhaps, the victims of the mysterious purpose of these illusions.

Next morning they saw Makola very busy setting up in the yard the big scales used for weighing ivory. By and bye Carlier said: 'What's that filthy scoundrel up to?' and lounged out into the yard. Kayerts followed. They stood by, watching. Makola took no notice. When the balance was swung true, he tried to lift a tusk into the scale.

It was too heavy. He looked up helplessly without a word, and for a minute they stood around that balance as mute and still as three statues. Suddenly Carlier said: 'Catch hold of the other end, Makola – you beast!' and together they swung the tusk up. Kayerts trembled in every limb. He muttered: 'I say! O! I say!' and putting his hand in his pocket found there a dirty bit of paper and the stump of a pencil. He turned his back on the others as if about to do something tricky and noted stealthily the weights which Carlier shouted out to him with unnecessary loudness. When all was over Makola whispered as if to himself: 'The sun's very strong here for the tusks.' Carlier said to Kayerts in a careless tone: 'I say, chief, I might just as well give him a lift with this lot into the store.'

As they were going back to the house Kayerts observed with a sigh: 'It had to be done.' And Carlier said: 'It's deplorable but the men being Company's men, the ivory is Company's ivory. We must look after it.' – 'I will report to the Director of course' – said Kayerts. 'Of course – let him decide,' approved Carlier.

At midday they made a hearty meal. Kayerts sighed from time to time. Whenever they mentioned Makola's name they always added to it an opprobrious epithet. It eased their consciences. Makola gave himself a half-holiday and bathed his children in the river. No one from Gobila's villages came near the station that day. No one came the next day . . . and the next . . . nor for a whole week. Gobila's people might have been all dead and buried for any sign of life they gave. But they were only mourning for those they had lost by the witchcraft of white men who had brought wicked people into their country. The wicked people were gone, but fear remained. Fear always remains. A man may destroy everything within himself: love and hate, and belief – and even doubt; but as long as he clings to life he cannot destroy fear; the fear, subtle, indestructible and terrible, that pervades his being, that tinges his thoughts, that lurks in his heart, that watches on his lips the struggle of his last breath.

In his fear the mild, old Gobila offered extra human sacrifices to all the evil spirits that had taken possession of his white friends. His heart was heavy. Some warriors spoke about burning and killing but the cautious old savage dissuaded them. Who could foresee the woe those mysterious creatures – if irritated – might bring? They should be left alone. Perhaps in time they would disappear into the earth as the first one had disappeared. His people must keep away from them and hope for the best.

Kayerts and Carlier did not disappear but remained above on this earth that, somehow, they fancied, had become bigger and very empty. It was not the absolute and dumb solitude of the post that impressed them so much as an inarticulate feeling that something from within them was gone, something that worked for their safety and had kept the wilderness from interfering with their hearts. The images of home, the memory of people like them, of men that thought and felt as they used to think and feel receded into distances made indistinct by the glare of unclouded sunshine. And out of the great silence of the surrounding wilderness its very hopelessness and savagery seemed to approach them nearer, to draw them gently, to look upon them, to envelop them with a solicitude irresistible, familiar and disgusting.

Days lengthened into weeks, then into months. Gobila's people drummed and yelled to every new moon as of yore but kept away from the station. Makola and Carlier tried once in a canoe to open communications but were received with a shower of arrows and had to fly back to the station for dear life. That attempt set the country up and down the river into an uproar that could be very distinctly heard for days. The steamer was late. At first they spoke of the delay jauntily, then anxiously, then gloomily. The matter was becoming serious. Stores were running short. Carlier cast his lines off the bank but the river was low and the fish kept out in the stream. They dared not stroll far away from the station to shoot. Moreover there was no game in the impenetrable forest. Once Carlier shot a hippo in the river. They had no boat to secure it and it sank. When it floated up it drifted away and Gobila's people secured the carcass. It was the occasion for a national holiday, but Carlier had a fit of rage over it, and talked about the necessity of exterminating all the niggers before the country could be habitable. Kayerts mooned about silently – spent hours looking at the portrait of his Mélie. It represented a little girl with long bleached tresses and a rather sour face. His legs were much swollen and he could hardly walk. Carlier, undermined by fever, could not swagger any more but kept tottering about, still with a devil-may-care air, as became a man who remembered his crack regiment. He had become hoarse, sarcastic and inclined to say unpleasant things. He called it: 'being frank with you'. They had long ago reckoned their percentages on trade including in them that last deal of 'this infamous Makola'. They had also concluded not to say anything about it. Kayerts hesitated at first. Was afraid of the Director.

'He has seen worse things done on the quiet,' maintained Carlier with a hoarse laugh. 'Trust him! He won't thank you if you blab. He is no better than you or me. Who will talk if we hold our tongue? There is nobody here.'

That was the root of the trouble! There was nobody there; and being left there alone with their weakness they became daily more like a pair of accomplices, than like a couple of devoted friends. They had heard nothing from home for eight months. Every evening they said, 'To-morrow we shall see the steamer.' But one of the Company's steamers had been wrecked and the Director was busy with the other, relieving very distant and important stations on the main river. He thought that the useless station and the useless men could wait. Meantime Kayerts and Carlier lived on rice boiled without salt and cursed the Company, all Africa, and the day they were born.

One must have lived on such diet to discover what ghastly trouble the necessity of swallowing one's food may become. There was literally nothing else in the station but rice and coffee. They drank the coffee without sugar. The last fifteen lumps Kayerts had solemnly locked away in his box together with a half-bottle of Cognac; 'in case of sickness,' he explained. Carlier approved. 'When one is sick' – he said – 'any little extra like that is cheering.'

They waited. Rank grass began to sprout over the courtyard. The bell never rang now. Days passed silent, exasperating and slow. When the two men spoke, they snarled; and their silences were bitter as if tinged by the bitterness of their thoughts.

One day after a lunch of boiled rice, Carlier put down his cup untasted and said: 'Hang it all! Let's have a decent cup of coffee for once. Bring out that sugar, Kayerts!'

'For the sick,' muttered Kayerts without looking up.

'For the sick,' mocked Carlier. 'Bosh! Well! I am sick.'

'You are no more sick than I am, and I go without,' said Kayerts in a peaceful tone.

'Come! Out with that sugar you stingy old slave-dealer.'

Kayerts looked up quickly. Carlier was smiling with marked insolence. And suddenly it seemed to Kayerts that he had never seen that man before. Who was he? He knew nothing about him. What was he capable of? There was a surprising flash of violent emotion within him as if in the presence of something undreamt of, dangerous and final. But he managed to pronounce with composure.

'That joke is in very bad taste. Don't repeat it.'

'Joke!' said Carlier, hitching himself forward on his seat. 'I am hungry, I am sick, I don't joke. I hate hypocrites. You are a hypocrite. You are a slave-dealer, I am a slave-dealer – there's nothing but slave-dealers in this cursed country. I mean to have sugar in my coffee to-day, anyhow!'

'I forbid you to speak to me in that way,' said Kayerts with a fair show of resolution.

'You! . . . what?' shouted Carlier jumping up.

Kayerts stood up also. 'I am your chief,' he began, trying to master the shakiness of his voice.

'What?' yelled the other. 'Who's chief? There's no chief here.

There's nothing here. There's nothing but you and I. Fetch the sugar – you pot-bellied ass.'

'Hold your tongue. Go out of this room,' screamed Kayerts. 'I dismiss you – you scoundrel!'

Carlier swung a stool. All at once he looked dangerously in earnest.

'You flabby, good-for-nothing civilian . . . take that!' he howled.

Kayerts dropped under the table, and the stool struck the grass inner wall of the room. Then as Carlier was trying to upset the table Kayerts in desperation made a blind rush, head low, like a cornered pig would do, and overturning his friend bolted along the verandah and into his room. He locked the door, snatched his revolver and stood panting. In less than a minute Carlier was kicking at the door furiously, howling, 'If you don't bring out that sugar I will shoot you at sight like a dog. Now then . . . One . . . two . . . three . . . You won't? . . . I will show you who's the master.'

Kayerts thought the door would fall in, and scrambled through the square hole that served for a window in his room. There was then the whole breadth of the house between them. But the other was apparently not strong enough to break in the door and Kayerts heard him running round. Then he also began to run laboriously on his swollen legs. He ran as quick as he could, grasping the revolver, and unable yet to understand what was happening to him. He saw in succession Makola's house, the store, the river, the ravine and the low bushes – and he saw all those things again as he ran for the second time round the house. Then again they flashed past him . . . That morning he could not have walked a yard without a groan.

And now he ran. He ran fast enough to keep out of sight of the other man.

Then, weak and desperate, he thought: Before I finish the next round I will die – he heard the other man stumble heavily, then stop. He stopped also. He had the back and Carlier the front of the house as before. He heard him drop into a chair cursing, and suddenly his own legs gave way and he slid down into a sitting posture with his back to the wall. His mouth was as dry as a cinder and his face was wet with perspiration – and tears. What was it all about? He thought it must be a horrible illusion; he thought he was dreaming;

he thought – he was going mad! . . . After a while he collected his senses. What did they quarrel about? That sugar. How absurd! He would give it to him. – Didn't want it himself . . . And he began scrambling to his feet with a sudden feeling of security. But before he had fairly stood upright a common sense reflection occurred to him and drove him back into despair. He thought: If I give way now to that brute of a soldier, he will begin this horror again to-morrow – and the day after – every day – raise other pretensions; trample on me; torture me; make me his slave – and I will be lost! Lost! the steamer may not come for days – may never come . . . He shook so that he had to sit down on the floor again. He shivered forlornly. He felt he could not, would not move any more. He was completely distracted by the sudden perception that the position was without issue – that death and life had in a moment become equally difficult and terrible.

All at once he heard the other push his chair back; and he leaped to his feet with extreme facility. He listened and got confused . . . must run again . . . right or left? He heard footsteps . . . He darted to the left grasping his revolver and at the very same instant, as it seemed to him, they came into violent collision. Both shouted with surprise. A loud explosion took place between them; a roar of red fire, thick smoke – and Kayerts deafened and blinded rushed back thinking: I am hit – it's all over. He expected the other to come round – to gloat over his agony. He caught hold of an upright of the roof . . . All over! . . . Then he heard a crashing fall on the other side of the house, as if somebody had tumbled headlong over a chair . . . Then silence. Nothing more happened. He did not die. Only his shoulder felt as if it had been badly wrenched – and he had lost his revolver. He was disarmed and helpless! He waited for his fate. The other man made no sound. It was a stratagem. He was stalking him this very minute . . . Along what side? . . . Perhaps he was taking aim now! . . .

After a few moments of an agony frightful and absurd he decided to go and meet his doom. He was prepared for every surrender. He turned the corner steadying himself with one hand on the wall, made a few paces – and nearly swooned. He had seen on the floor, protruding past the other corner, a pair of turned up feet. A pair of white naked feet in red slippers. He felt deadly sick and stood for a time in profound darkness. Then Makola appeared before him saying quietly: 'Come along, Mr Kayerts. He is dead.' He burst into tears of gratitude; a loud, sobbing fit of crying. After a time he found himself sitting in a chair and looking at Carlier, who lay stretched on his back. Makola was kneeling over the body.

'Is this your revolver?' asked Makola, getting up.

'Yes!' said Kayerts, then he added very quickly: 'He ran after me to shoot me – You saw!'

'Yes, I saw,' said Makola. 'There is only one revolver. Where's his?'

'Don't know,' whispered Kayerts in a voice that had become suddenly very faint.

'I will go and look for it,' said the other gently. He made the round along the verandah while Kayerts sat still and looked at the corpse. Makola came back empty handed; stood in deep thought, then stepped quietly into the dead man's room and came out directly with a revolver, which he held up before Kayerts. Kayerts shut his eyes. Everything was going round. He found life more terrible and difficult than death. He had shot an unarmed man.

After meditating for a while Makola said softly, pointing at the dead man who lay there with his right eye blown out –

'He died of fever.'

Kayerts looked at him with a stony stare. 'Yes,' repeated Makola thoughtfully, stepping over the corpse. 'I think he died of fever. Bury him to-morrow.'

And he went away slowly to his expectant wife, leaving the two white men alone on the verandah.

Night came and Kayerts sat unmoving on his chair. He sat quiet as if he had taken a dose of opium. The violence of the emotions he had passed through produced a feeling of exhausted serenity. He had plumbed in one short afternoon the depths of horror and despair and now found repose in the conviction that life had no more secrets for him – neither had death! He sat by the corpse thinking – thinking very actively, thinking very new thoughts. He seemed to have broken loose from himself altogether. His old thoughts, convictions, likes and dislikes, things he respected and things he abhorred appeared in their true light at last! – appeared contemptible and childish, false and ridiculous. He revelled in his new wisdom while he sat by the man he had killed. He argued with himself about all things under heaven with that kind of wrong-headed lucidity which may be observed in some lunatics. Incidentally he reflected that the fellow dead there had been a noxious beast anyway; that men died every day in thousands; perhaps in hundreds of thousands – who could tell? – and that, in the number, that one death could not possibly make any difference, couldn't have any importance – at least to a thinking creature. He, Kayerts, was a thinking creature. He had been all his life – till that moment – a believer in a lot of nonsense like the rest of mankind – who are fools – but now he thought – he knew – he was at peace – he was familiar with the highest wisdom! Then he tried to imagine himself dead and Carlier sitting in his chair watching him; and his attempt met with such unexpected success, that in a very few moments he became not at all sure who was dead and who was alive. This extraordinary achievement of his fancy startled him however, and by a clever and timely effort of mind he saved himself just in time from becoming Carlier. His heart thumped and he felt hot all over at the thought of that danger . . . Carlier! What a beastly thing! . . . To compose his now disturbed nerves – and no wonder! – he tried to whistle a little . . . Then, suddenly, he fell asleep – or thought he had slept . . . but at any rate there was a fog – and somebody had whistled in the fog.

He stood up. The day had come and a heavy mist had descended upon the land; the mist penetrating, enveloping and silent; the morning mist of tropical lands, the mist that clings and kills, the mist white and deadly, immaculate and poisonous. He stood up; saw the body; and threw his arms above his head with a cry like that of a man who waking from a trance finds himself immured for ever in a tomb.

'*Help! My God!*'

A shriek inhuman, vibrating and sudden, pierced like a sharp dart the white shroud of that of sorrow. Three short, impatient screeches followed – and then, for a time, the fog-wreaths rolled on undisturbed, through a formidable silence. Then many more shrieks, rapid and piercing, like the yells of some exasperated and ruthless creature, rent the air. Progress was calling to Kayerts from the river. Progress, and civilization and all the virtues. Society was calling to its accomplished child, to come, to be taken care of, to be instructed, to be judged, to be condemned; it called him to return to that rubbish-heap from which he had wandered away – so that justice could be done.

Kayerts heard and understood. He stumbled out of the verandah leaving the other man quite alone for the first time since they had been thrown there together. He groped his way through the fog calling in his ignorance upon the invisible heaven to undo its work. Makola flitted by in the mist, shouting as he ran.

'Steamer! Steamer! They can't see. They whistle for the station. I go ring the bell. Go down to the landing, sir. I ring.' . . .

He disappeared. Kayerts stood still. He looked upwards; the fog rolled low over his head. He looked round like a man who has lost his way; and he saw a dark smudge, a cross-shaped stain upon the shifting purity of the mist. As he began to stumble towards it, the station bell rang in a tumultuous peal its answer to the impatient clamour of the steamer.

The Managing Director of the Great Civilizing Company (since we know that civilization follows trade) landed first – and incontinently lost sight of the steamer. The fog down by the river was exceedingly dense; above at the station the bell rang, unceasing and brazen.

The Director shouted loudly to the steamer:

'There is nobody down to meet us. There may be something wrong, though they are ringing. You had better come, too.'

And he began to toil up the steep bank. The captain and the engine-driver of the boat followed behind. As they scrambled up, the fog thinned and they could see their Director a good way ahead. Suddenly they saw him start forward, calling to them over his shoulder: 'Run! Run to the house. I've found one of them. Run, look for the other.'

He had found one of them! And even he, the man of varied and startling experience, was somewhat discomposed by the manner of this finding. He stood and fumbled in his pockets (for a knife) – while he faced Kayerts, who was hanging by a leather strap from the cross. He had evidently climbed the grave – which was high and narrow – and after tying the end of the strap to the arm had swung himself off. His toes were only a couple of inches above the ground. His arms hung stiffly down. He seemed to be standing rigidly at attention but with one purple cheek playfully posed on the shoulder. And, irreverently, he was putting out a swollen tongue at his Managing Director.

Members of the Bangala tribe in a canoe, *c.*1890. Bangala, located about halfway up the Congo, is where Conrad's 'Up-river Book' ends

The mutilation of children under Leopold's regime in the Congo by Government soldiers formed a crucial part of Casement's 1904 Congo Report

Two men, members of a chain gang, stand in their manacles in the Congo, *c.*1904. Conrad wrote to Casement in December 1903: 'It is an extraordinary thing that the conscience of Europe which seventy years ago has put down the slave trade on humanitarian grounds tolerates the Congo State to day. It is as if the moral clock had been put back many hours'

Joseph Conrad in a sketch by Sir William Rothenstein in 1916: 'The other day Will Rothenstein did another pencil drawing of me. Full face. A most successful piece of work and what's more an excellent likeness'

I N SENDING CONRAD GREETINGS for the new year about to begin, the Edinburgh publisher William Blackwood (1836–1912) in a letter of 30 December also requested a contribution from him to celebrate the thousandth issue of *Blackwood's Edinburgh Magazine* scheduled for February 1899. Conrad's stories 'Youth' and 'Karain' had first appeared in the monthly popularly known as *Maga*. Conrad's initial idea for the story that evolved into *Heart of Darkness* seems typically to have been for a shorter tale, but his contribution to *Blackwood's*, in the event, spread over three monthly issues and stretched to novella length. As usual, Conrad was also looking ahead to book publication, and the novella appeared in due course with 'Youth' and 'The End of the Tether' in 1902 in a volume given the title *Youth, A Narrative; and Two Other Stories*. Blackwood's nephew, George William Blackwood, was involved in running the firm with his uncle.

TO WILLIAM BLACKWOOD

[letterhead: Pent Farm]
31/12/98

Dear Mr Blackwood.

Come this moment to hand is your good le[t]ter whose kind wishes, believe me, I reciprocate with all my heart.

Your proposal delights me. As it happens I am (and have been for the last 10 days) working for *Maga*. The thing is far advanced and would have been finished by this only our little boy fell ill, I was disturbed and upset and the work suffered. I expect to be ready in a very few days. It is a narrative after the manner of *youth* told by the same man dealing with his experiences on a river in Central Africa. The *idea* in it is not as obvious as in *youth* – or at least not so obviously presented. I tell you all this, for tho' I have no doubts as to the *workmanship* I do not know whether the *subject* will commend itself to you for that particular number. Of course I should be very glad to appear in it and shall try to hurry up the copy for that express purpose, but I wish you to understand that I am prepared to leave the ultimate decision as to the date of appearance to your decision after perusal.

The title I am thinking of is '*The Heart of Darkness*' but the narrative is not gloomy The criminality of inefficiency and pure selfishness when tackling the civilizing work in Africa is a justifiable idea. The subject is of our time distinc[t]ly – though not topically treated. It is a story as much as my *Outpost of Progress* was but, so to speak 'takes in' more – is a little wider – is less concentrated upon individuals. I destine it for the vol: which is to bear Your imprint. Its lenght [*sic*] will be under 20.000 words as I see it now. If suitable and you wish to curtail it a couple of pars: could be taken out – from the proof, perhaps.

There is also the question of McClure securing copyright in the States. They bungled the *Youth* affair and I am not in a position to despise the almighty dollar – as yet.

All I can do is to hurry up. Meantime many thanks for thinking of me.

Friendly greetings to Your Nephew. I am delighted to be remembered by him.

I am dear Mr Blackwood, most sincerely yours
Jph. Conrad

HAVING MET CONRAD in the Congo in 1890 (see the 'Congo Diary'), Casement renewed his contact with the writer shortly before he co-founded with E. D. (Edmund Dene) Morel (né Georges-Edouard-Pierre-Achille Morel de Ville, 1873–1924) the Congo Reform Association, formed to bring attention to atrocities perpetrated under Belgian rule. The practice of cutting off natives' hands for infractions existed. The pamphlet that Casement sent to Conrad was either Morel's first, *The Congo Horrors*, or *The Congo Slave State*, both published in 1903 and both vivid and stern indictments of Belgian colonial rule.

TO ROGER CASEMENT

[letterhead: Pent Farm]
1903
17th Dec^{er}

My dear Casement

During my sojourn in the interior, keeping my eyes and ears well open too, I've never heard of the alleged custom of cutting off hands amongst the natives; and I am convinced that no such custom ever existed along the whole course of the main river to which my experience is limited. Neither in the casual talk of white men nor in the course of definite inquiries as to the tribal customs was ever such a practice hinted at; certainly not amongst the Bangalas who at that time formed the bulk of the State troops. My informants were numerous, of all sorts – and many of them possessed of abundant knowledge.

I have to thank you for Morel's pamphlet which reached me from L'pool a few days ago. There can be no doubt that his presentation of the commercial policy and the administrative methods of the Congo State is absolutely true. It is a most brazen breach of faith as to Europe. It is in every aspect an enormous and atrocious lie in action. If it were not rather appalling the cool completeness of it would be amusing.

My best wishes and cordial regards

Yours

Jph. Conrad

Casement's and Morel's work directly implicated Leopold II in the systematic brutalities of his Congo enterprises, with a counter-campaign launched to save the king's reputation. Parts of Conrad's next letter have the character of something written for public consumption, and Casement might have specifically requested him to write in such terms. Then British consul at Boma, Casement was on home leave, having completed a fact-finding mission that eventuated in the Casement Report. Conrad's wish to see Casement before he left England was granted: Casement called on him on 3 January 1904, an occasion he used to discuss his activities and the situation in the Congo.

TO ROGER CASEMENT

[letterhead: Pent Farm]
21st Dec 1903

My dear Casement

You cannot doubt that I form the warmest wishes for your success. A King, wealthy and unscrupulous, is certainly no mean adversary; for if the personality in this case be a rather discredited one, the wealth, alas, has never a bad odour – or this wealth in particular would tell its own suffocating tale.

It is an extraordinary thing that the conscience of Europe which seventy years ago has put down the slave trade on humanitarian grounds tolerates the Congo State to day. It is as if the moral clock had been put back many hours. And yet nowadays if I were to overwork my horse so as to destroy its happiness of physical wellbeing I should be hauled before a magistrate. It seems to me that the black man – say, of Upoto – is deserving of as much humanitarian regard as any animal since he has nerves, feels pain, can be made physically

miserable. But as a matter of fact his happiness and misery are much
more complex than the misery or happiness of animals and deserving of greater regard. He shares with us the consciousness of the universe in which we live – no small burden. Barbarism per se is no
crime deserving of a heavy visitation; and the Belgians are worse
than the seven plagues of Egypt insomuch that in that case it was a
punishment sent for a definite transgression; but in this the Upoto
man is not aware of any transgression, and therefore can see no end
to the infliction. It must appear to him very awful and mysterious;
and I confess that it appears so to me too. The amenities of the 'middle passage' in the old days were as nothing to it. The slave trade has
been abolished – and the Congo State exists to-day. This is very
remarkable. What makes it more remarkable is this: the slave trade
was an old established form of commercial activity; it was not the
monopoly of one small country established to the disadvantage of
the rest of the civilized world in defiance of international treaties and
in brazen disregard of humanitarian declarations. But the Congo
State created yesterday is all that and yet it exists. This is very mysterious. One is tempted to exclaim (as poor Thiers did in 1871) 'Il n'y
a plus d'Europe.' But as a matter of fact in the old days England had
in her keeping the conscience of Europe. The initiative came from
here. But now I suppose we are busy with other things; too much
involved in great affairs to take up cudgels for humanity, decency
and justice. But what about our commercial interests? These suffer
greatly as Morel has very clearly demonstrated in his book. There
can be no serious attempt to controvert his facts. Or [it] is impossible to controvert them for the hardest of lying won't do it. That
precious pair of African witch-men seem to have cast a spell upon
the world of whites – I mean Leopold and Thys of course. This is
very funny.

And the fact remains that in 1903, seventy five years or so after
the abolition of the slave trade (because it was cruel) there exists in
Africa a Congo State, created by the act of European Powers where
ruthless, systematic cruelty towards the blacks is the basis of
administration, and bad faith towards all the other states the basis
of commercial policy.

I do hope we shall meet before you leave. Once more my best wishes go with you on your crusade. Of course You may make any use you like of what I write to you. Cordially Yours

Jph Conrad

Conrad's friend R. B. (Robert Bontine) Cunninghame Graham (1852–1936), a socialist, wrote on the issues of the day and had been a Member of Parliament. He was an ardent Hispanophile, who travelled widely in Spain and South America, and his biography *Hernando de Soto*, which had just appeared, focused on an earlier story of colonisation and ruthless exploitation, a topic in mind after Casement's recent visit to Conrad's home. Conrad, who effected an introduction between Casement and Graham, recognised a confluence of interest and experience – Casement had held diplomatic posts in South America – if a wide difference in their personalities. Graham's social circle included the Colombian envoy extraordinary in London, Santiago Pérez Triana (1860–1916) with whom Conrad's former publisher but still friend at Heinemann's, S. S. (Sydney Southgate) Pawling (1862–1922), had been in touch. Graham's wife, Gabriela (née de la Balmondière, 1860?–1906), was also a writer, of poems, stories and a biography of the Spanish mystic St Teresa of Avila. The United States was then actively advocating that Panama, a province of Colombia, secede and become independent, an event Conrad played upon in *Nostromo*, on which he was then at work.

TO R. B. CUNNINGHAME GRAHAM

Pent Farm.
26th Dec 1903.

Cher Ami.

I snatch this piece of MS paper first of all to thank you for remembering the boy at this festive (?) season. Next to tell you that H. de Soto is most exquisitely excellent: your very mark and spirit upon a subject that only *you* can do justice to – with your wonderful English and your sympathetic insight into the souls of the Conquistadores. The glamour, the pathos and the romance of that time and of those men are only adequately, truthfully, conveyed to us by

your pen; the sadness, the glory and the romance of the endeavour
together with the vanity of vanities of the monstrous achievement
are reflected in your unique style as though you had been writing of
men with whom you had slept by the camp fire after tethering your
horses on the t[h]reshold of the unknown.

You have an eye for buried jewels! The Pizarro going about mourn-
fully with his hat pulled down on his ears after the death of Atahualpa
is new to me. He is made unforgettable at last. 'C'est *énorme* d'hu-
manité' as the great Flaubert would have yelled to the four winds of
heaven. What a touch. Behold in this Conquistador my long lost
brother together with those others: the Indio gentile hombre shouting insults underneath his tree and the thirty lances riding on to
the sea, some of them already with death sitting on the pillion
behind; to be received with the question: 'Have you seen any signs
of gold in the country?' One seems to hear the very voice. C'est la
vérité même! It's the most amazingly natural thing I've ever read; it
gives me a furious desire to learn Spanish and bury myself in the
pages of the incomparable Garcilasso – if only to forget all about our
modern Conquistadores.

Their achievement is monstrous enough in all conscience – but
not as a great human force let loose, but rather like that of a gigantic
and obscene beast. Leopold is their Pizarro, Thys their Cortez and
their 'lances' are recruited amongst the souteneurs, sous-offs,
maquereaux, fruit-secs of all sorts on the pavements of Brussels and
Antwerp. I send you two letters I had from a man called Casement,
premising that I knew him first in the Congo just 12 years ago. Perhaps you've heard or seen in print his name. He's a protestant Irishman, pious too. But so was Pizarro. For the rest I can assure you that
he is a limpid personality. There is a touch of the Conquistador in
him too; for I've seen him start off into an unspeakable wilderness
swinging a crookhandled stick for all weapons, with two bull-dogs:
Paddy (white) and Biddy (brindle) at his heels and a Loanda boy
carrying a bundle for all company. A few months afterwards it so
happened that I saw him come out again, a little leaner a little
browner, with his stick, dogs, and Loanda boy, and quietly serene as
though he had been for a stroll in a park. Then we lost sight of each

other. He was I believe Bsh Consul in Beira, and lately seems to have been sent to the Congo again, on some sort of mission, by the Br Gov[t]. I have always thought that some particle of Las Casas' soul had found refuge in his indefatigable body. The letters will tell you the rest. I would help him but it is not in me. I am only a wretched novelist inventing wretched stories and not even up to that miserable game; but your good pen, keen, flexible and straight, and sure, like a good Toledo blade would tell in the fray if you felt disposed to give a slash or two. He could tell you things! Things I've tried to forget; things I never did know. He has had as many years of Africa as I had months – almost. –

Another small matter. S. Perez Triana heard from Pawling of my longing to get away south (when possible) and has written me the kindest letter imaginable, offering information and even introductions. I am quite touched. But pray tell me whether he is Colombian Minister in Spain and if it behoves me to *lui donner de l'Excellence on the envelope*. I don't want faire une *bévue* and after all I know him very little. And à propos what do you think of the Yankee Conquistadores in Panama? Pretty, isn't it? Enfin. Veuillez presenter mes dévoirs les plus respectueux à Madame Votre Femme. Borys instructed me to send his love to you. Jessie's kind regards. Tout à vous

Jph Conrad

Graham, from a distinguished family – according to some sources, he had claims to the Scottish crown – was himself well connected in political and society circles. Belgravia's Chester Square would have proved a convenient meeting place for the two men: Graham's widowed mother lived at no. 39, and Casement's friend Herbert Ward (1863–1919) lived at no. 53. An aide to H. M. Stanley in Africa, Ward, the author of *Five Years with the Congo Cannibals* (1891), was a friend, like Casement, of E. D. Morel. Graham's club, the Devonshire, in St James's Street, brought Liberals together; Casement belonged to the Wellington in Grosvenor Place. Between 1900 and 1904 Graham, when not in Glasgow or abroad, lived in Sloane Street.

TO ROGER CASEMENT
                                    [letterhead: Pent Farm]
                                           29 Dec 1903

Private and Conf[identi]al

My dear Casement.

   I am overwhelming you with my scrawls!

   The cause of this one is that my friend R. B. Cunninghame Graham writing in answer to a letter of mine in which I'd mentioned Your presence in London wishes to communicate with you in person.

   The man is able and more than willing to help in your noble crusade; and you may safely give him your confidence. No doubt You have heard of him – in one way or another. Do not let his reputation for socialism influence your judgment upon the man. It has never been anything but a form of his hate for all oppression and injustice. His character is upright and unselfish; his talents (with the pen too) are great; he knows everybody worth knowing, and his social relations extend from Dukes to Labour-members. He may be of use to you, if only with his pen; and perhaps in other ways as well. Whatever may be the difference of Your political opinions I am sure that you will understand each other perfectly on humanitarian grounds.

   He has heard of you from me years ago and he is anxious to know you. His actual words which I transcribe are:

   'I think I could help. I would call in Chester Square or meet him at his club or mine (Devonshire).'

   There is more but the above is sufficient for practical purposes. His address is *7. Sloane Street*. He has not been very well of late but is better now and thinks of going to Spain soon for a month or so. If you want to enlist him there is no time to lose. Drop him a line. He is by some years your senior, so that there is no impropriety in you taking the first step – for which he is quite prepared. I honestly think that it would be worth your while, from the point of view of the *great Cause*. Besides he is a charming and in many ways an unique personality. Well; no more. God bless you and your work in the new year and in long years to come.

Yours cordially

J. Conrad

THIS SHORT STATEMENT served as the preface to the reprinting of 'An Outpost of Progress' in London's *Grand Magazine* in March 1906, Conrad having been asked by its editor to provide a comment and to make the selection. The magazine, in addition to its 'My Best Story' series, featured other series ('My Favourite Song', 'My First Appearance' and 'My First Play') with creators or performers likewise justifying their choices. Conrad's immediate colleagues in the story series for 1906 were all popular writers, who, apart from Jerome K. Jerome, have been forgotten. The story appeared in the magazine in a slightly truncated version.

MY BEST STORY AND WHY I THINK SO ['AN OUTPOST OF PROGRESS']

This story, for which I confess a preference, was difficult to write, not because of what I had to write, but of what I had firmly made up my mind not to write into it. What I have done is done with. No words, no regrets can atone now for the imperfections that stand there glaring, patent, numerous, and amusing. The story was written some ten years ago. And yet I remember perfectly well the inflexible and solemn resolve not to be led astray by my subject. I aimed at a scrupulous unity of tone, and it seems to me that I have almost attained it there. It is possible that I am deceiving myself, and that I have missed even that qualified success. But the story is endeared to me by the well-remembered severity of discipline and by one or two moments of flattering illusion.

And all this cannot possibly matter anything to the most benevolent soul amongst the readers of stories.

CONRAD BECAME FRIENDLY with Captain (later Major in the India Army Reserve) Ernest Dawson (1864–1949) through H. G. Wells and the poet and editor W. H. Henley, with Dawson being a connection as well through *Blackwood's Edinburgh Magazine*, to which he contributed reminiscences and stories about Australia and Burma, where he had served as a magistrate and been an officer in Rangoon's Volunteer Rifles. After his return from the Congo, Conrad convalesced in the German Hospital in Dalston, suffering both a physical and nervous collapse; he followed up treatment there with hydrotherapy in Geneva. Jessie Conrad suffered a fall in 1904, seriously injuring her knees, which gave her problems for the remainder of her life. Miss Ethel Gambrill (*c.* 1876–1964) was Dawson's half-sister; 'Jack', his brother (Alec John, 1872–1931), also a writer and traveller. Edward Noble's sea novel *The Grain Carriers* had recently been published; like Conrad, he was a sailor turned writer.

TO ERNEST DAWSON

Someries. Luton
25 June '08

My dear Ernest.

I am touched and a little appalled at the effort your letter must have cost you in your state of mysterious weakness. Pray don't do it again but just two words and your initials on a post-card shall be looked for from time to time to report progress. We are much concerned at your news.

I have been in a state resembling yours, some time after my Congo experience. It was not the convalescence from the fever. The convalescence was over for a year, and I was apparently as well as ever when that sort of weakness stole over me. I couldn't move *my fingers* (not hand, *fingers*) without sending the pulse up an incredible number of beats. I lay on my back in dismal lodgings and expected to go out like a burnt out candle any moment. That was nerves, and it was a six months job. But you being looked after ought to do this variety turn in 3 months at the outside.

Jessie is delighted with your charming offering – and still more with your thought of her. You don't know what a great store that girl sets on your and Your brother's friendship. She's awfully crippled. It's heart breaking for me simply.

The 'western-style' painting looks most fascinating in its proper place – that is on the wall above Jessie's writing table.

Her kindest regards to Miss Gambrill in which I join. She will be writing to you in a day or two. Dear old Jack! We are so sorry he is being constantly kept on the rack. I haven't read Noble's book. I know the man tho'. No more at present.

Yours ever,
J Conrad

This is a bracing place, 500 ft up. I don't think of the sea now. No one cares about it really, or I would have had as much success here as Loti in France. Borys after trying twice to leave this world (last year) is fairly well now, and at a little prep school in Luton. He will be pleased to hear when he comes home on Saturday that you remember him as a friend.

SERIALISED IN 1908–9 IN THE *English Review*, then edited by Conrad's friend and sometime collaborator Ford Madox Hueffer (1873–1939; later Ford Madox Ford), 'Some Reminiscences', later retitled *A Personal Record* for publication in 1912, is an impressionistic account of several moments of Conrad's life. Some doubts can be cast on the exactness of the 'recollection' dramatised here, similar moments being recounted in several books of memoirs, such as *In Savage Africa, Or Six Years of Adventure in Congo-Land* (1892) by the English explorer Edward James Glave (1862–95): 'But I remember that, even at school, Africa had a peculiar fascination for me. A great map of the "Dark Continent" hung on the walls of my classroom; the tentative way in which the geographers of that day had marked down localities in almost unknown equatorial regions seemed to me delightful and mysterious. There were rivers with great estuaries . . . and territories of whose extent and characteristics ignorance was openly confessed by vast unnamed blank spaces.' Conrad had taken with him to Africa the manuscript of his first novel, *Almayer's Folly* (1895), nearly losing it in the Congo River at Pointe de Kalina (now Pointe de la Gombe and in central Kinshasa). The Pointe was named after a young Austrian officer in the Belgian service, Ernest Kalina, who drowned there in December 1882, his boat having overturned. The loss of Conrad's belongings apparently occurred towards the close of October 1890. Kinshasa and Léopoldville, distinct at Conrad's time, have been amalgamated into present-day Kinshasa.

From *A Personal Record*

It was in 1868, when nine years old or thereabouts, that while looking at a map of Africa of the time and putting my finger on the
blank space then representing the unsolved mystery of that continent, I said to myself with absolute assurance and an amazing
audacity which are no longer in my character now:

'When I grow up I shall go *there*.'

And of course I thought no more about it till after a quarter of a
century or so an opportunity offered to go there – as if the sin of
childish audacity was to be visited on my mature head. Yes. I did go
there: *there* being the region of Stanley Falls which in '68 was the
blankest of blank spaces on the earth's figured surface. And the MS.
of 'Almayer's Folly,' carried about me as if it were a talisman or a
treasure, went *there* too. That it ever came out of *there* seems a special dispensation of Providence; because a good many of my other
properties, infinitely more valuable and useful to me, remained
behind through unfortunate accidents of transportation. I call to
mind, for instance, a specially awkward turn of the Congo between
Kinchassa and Leopoldsville – more particularly when one had to
take it at night in a big canoe with only half the proper number of
paddlers. I failed in being the second white man on record drowned
at that interesting spot through the upsetting of a canoe. The first
was a young Belgian officer, but the accident happened some
months before my time, and he, too, I believe, was going home; not
perhaps quite so ill as myself – but still he was going home. I got
round the turn more or less alive, though I was too sick to care
whether I did or not, and, always with 'Almayer's Folly' amongst my
diminishing baggage, I arrived at that delectable capital Boma,
where before the departure of the steamer which was to take me
home I had the time to wish myself dead over and over again with
perfect sincerity . . .

CONRAD'S CORRESPONDENT John Quinn (1870–1924) was a wealthy Ohio-born tax lawyer, of Irish descent, in practice in New York City, who had amassed a large collection of modernist pictures and manuscripts, including Conrad's. (Other enthusiasms were James Joyce and Picasso.) The *North American Review* had reprinted Conrad's 1904 essay 'Henry James: An Appreciation' in its April issue to mark the occasion of the novelist's death in February. James's 'The Younger Generation' in the *Times Literary Supplement* of 2 April 1914 discussed, among other works, Conrad's *Chance* (1914). The topics of moment raised include the Easter Rising of 1916, the execution of many of its leaders and Casement's arrest on 20 April, upon his landing in Ireland, for collaboration with Germany, an enemy power. An ardent supporter of Ireland, Quinn, like Conrad, knew Casement personally and, well connected in Washington as well as New York, made moves to appeal for leniency. Associated with Belgian enterprises in the Congo in 1884 and 1886, Casement, engaged for a year by the Société Anonyme Belge du Haut-Congo on 11 May 1890, arrived in Matadi on 11 June. The Johnson Club (not Society), founded in 1884, was a dining club convened to listen to papers on the eighteenth-century writer Samuel Johnson, Conrad's first publisher, T. Fisher Unwin, figuring among its founders. At the time it had no permanent premises, unlike the Sports Club, which was located in St James's Square. Conrad also recalls Casement's 1896 visit to his home in Kent and a chance meeting in London that had occurred between January and August 1911, when Casement, during the first months of his home leave, was writing a report (published in July 1912) on the exploitative and cruel methods of the rubber barons of Colombia's Putumayo basin. Salisbury, thrice prime minister, and his Conservatives opposed Home Rule for Ireland, but Casement's attitudes towards the issue date to later than the time suggested; Salisbury's patronage saw him posted to Lourenço Marques (now Maputo), Mozambique. In 1906, he was posted to Brazil as consul in Pará and later promoted to consul general in Rio de Janeiro. Will Rothenstein (1872–1945), a friend of Whistler and Degas (and, coincidentally, acquainted with Casement), did his first portrait of Conrad in 1903; the pencil drawing mentioned figured in the 1916 exhibition at the Leicester Galleries, then located off Leicester Square. (Both works are now in the National Portrait Gallery.) The drawing was not used as a frontispiece in Conrad's collected edition, a project, in any case, delayed until after the war, and published in England and America, by Heinemann and Doubleday, Page, & Co. respectively, only in 1920–1. James Gibbons Huneker (1857–1921), an American novelist, had interviewed Conrad for the *New York Times* in 1912.

TO JOHN QUINN

[letterhead: Capel House]
24 May '16

My dear Quinn

Many thanks for your letter. It was very good of you to send me the N.A.R with the 'James' Article. I had forgotten it completely. I don't agree with you that if I were to write about him now I would have to say more and pitch the note higher. That last would be impossible. Henry James at that time had given his measure and I believe I did give him then the fullest measure of appreciation. I said he was great and incomparable – and what more could one say? His autobiographical 2 books are admirable; but what makes them so wonderful are the very same qualities which make his novels admirable. And after all the article was professedly 'An Appreciation' nothing more – nothing less. I didn't write like a professional critic would write. I spoke of his art in a large relation, as a fellow writer, in the spirit in which you, for instance, might have spoken of a distinguished colleague's at the bar forensic eloquence – as distinct from his learning and from his method of conducting a case. The sheer great art of it, where not so much the mind as the soul finds its expression. At any rate that's what I meant to do.

The only time he did me the honour of speaking of me in print (about 2 years ago) he confined himself to the analysis of method which he rather airily condemned in relation to the methods of two young writers. I may say, with scrupulous truth, that this was the *only time* a criticism affected me painfully. But in our private relations he has been always warmly appreciative and full of invariable kindness. I had a profound affection for him. He knew of it and he accepted it as if it were something worth having. At any rate that is the impression I have. And he wasn't a man who would pretend. What need had he? . . . even if he had been capable of it.

The S[inn] F[ein] outburst has thrown Irish affairs into lurid relief. But that's only momentary. It has saddened me but has not shaken my confidence in the future of Anglo-Irish relations. One only wonders, in one's grief, what it was all for? With Britain smashed and the German fleet riding the seas the very shadow of Irish Independence would have passed away. The Island Republic (if that is what they wanted) would have become merely a strongly held German outpost – a despised stepping stone towards the final aim of the Welt-Politik. I needn't labour the theme. You can see it better perhaps than I do.

I met Casement for the first time in the Congo in 1890. For some three weeks he lived in the same room in the Matadi Station of the Belgian Société du Haut Congo. He was rather reticent as to the exact character of his connection with it; but the work he was busy about then was recruiting labour. He knew the coast languages well. I went with him several times on short expeditions to hold 'palavers' with neighbouring village-chiefs. The object of them was procuring porters for the Company's caravans from Matadi to Leopoldville – or rather to Kinchassa (on Stanley Pool). Then I went up into the interior to take up my command of the stern-wheeler 'Roi des Belges' and he, apparently, remained on the coast.

Next time we met was in 1896 in London, by chance, at a dinner of the Johnson Society. We went away from there together to the Sports Club and talked there till 3 in the morning. I asked him down to Pent Farm (where we lived then). He came for the night. Lord Salisbury had taken him up or was going to take him up. Certain Liberal circles were making rather a pet of him; well-connected Irishman, Protestant Homeruler, of romantic aspect – and so on.

In 1911 (I think – but anyhow before the Putumayo atrocities Report) we came upon each other in Surrey St Strand. He was more gaunt than ever and his eyes still more sunk in his head. There was a strange austerity in his aspect. He told me he was Bsh Consul in Rio de Janeiro on leave home for 3 months. We parted after 5 minutes conversation an[d] I never even heard of him (except the Putumayo Report) till I read the news of him being in Germany.

We never talked politics. I didn't think he had really any. A Homeruler accepting Lord Salisbury's Patronage couldn't be taken very seriously. He was a good companion; but already in Africa I judged that he was a man, properly speaking, of no mind at all. I don't mean stupid. I mean that he was all emotion. By emotional force (Congo report Putumayo – etc) he made his way, and sheer emotionalism has undone him. A creature of sheer temperament – a truly tragic personality: all but the greatness of which he had not a trace. Only vanity. But in the Congo it was not visible yet.

I hope I have not bored you with those old reminiscences.

The other day Will Rothenstein did another pencil drawing of me. Full face. A most successful piece of work and what's more an excellent likeness. I would be happy if Doubleday Page would use it for the portrait for the Coll^d Edition de Luxe. Will is having an exhibition of heads at Leicester Galleries – opened today.

I am grateful to you for the interest you take in the aforesaid Edition. This is the moment for my friends to rally round me; and in a matter like this a friend like you is invaluable. I have written to D. P. telling them I would be glad if they would consult you on all the material points of this affair. I am anxious for its success so as to add a little actual cash to the little fund I want to leave to my wife – for goodness only knows whether my copyrights will be worth anything. The boys will have to scout around for themselves.

Borys writes often and, without grumbling, complains a little. Here he is a Second Lieut in sole command of a section of 120 men and 15 cars, in charge of all the ammunition of a heavy battery which is almost constantly engaged. He feels the responsability in addition to the actual hard work. As he has no other officer with him he is kept on the stretch continuously. After all he is only just 18. He can't have the mental and physical stamina of a mature man. I daresay writing all this to father in a six page letter has done him good. I wrote at once a sympathetic reply, patting him on the back as it were. He had had no sleep for 30 hours when he sat down to write (a horrible scrawl) because he says, he didn't feel a bit sleepy. Under those circumstances I think he's excusable even if he throws a few cuss-words at the Head-Quarters of his corps. On the other hand he talks affectionately of his Non-Com. officers who are very good to him, he says, and the men who are 'dear fellows'. He hadn't had to punish one of them ever since he is in command. In reality this means that they like the boy. And that's all right. Well, enough. My wife sends her most friendly regards. Believe me

always yours
Joseph Conrad

PS Remember me affec^{ly} to Huneker. We are glad to hear he's out of the wood.

CONRAD WROTE THIS ESSAY, which he first thought to call 'Geography and Exploration', to serve as the introduction to *Countries of the World*, a photo-illustrated gazetteer of the world's countries and regions. He composed it in October and November 1923. It was first printed privately, as a pamphlet, and then in *Countries of the World*, under the title 'The Romance of Travel', in February 1924. It also appeared in *National Geographic Magazine*'s March 1924 issue.

The essay passes in review various figures important in the European exploration of Africa, including the Scottish explorer and missionary David Livingstone (1813–73), who wanted to introduce Christianity to the continent in part to combat the slave trade. Reshid bin Mohammed (1855?–?) was the nephew of the notorious Tippu Tibb (or Hamid Ibn Muhammad, 1837?–1905) and, like his uncle and many other Arabs in the Congo, was involved in both the slave and the ivory trade, based at the Arabs' seat of power near Stanley Falls.

FROM 'GEOGRAPHY AND SOME EXPLORERS'

Education is a great thing, but Doctor Barth gets in the way. Neither will the monuments left by all sorts of empire builders suppress for me the memory of David Livingstone. The words 'Central Africa' bring before my eyes an old man with a rugged, kind face and a clipped, gray moustache, pacing wearily at the head of a few black followers along the reed-fringed lakes towards the dark native hut on the Congo headwaters in which he died, clinging in his very last hour to his heart's unappeased desire for the sources of the Nile.

That passion had changed him in his last days from a great explorer into a restless wanderer refusing to go home any more. From his exalted place among the blessed of militant geography and with his memory enshrined in Westminster Abbey, he can well afford to smile without bitterness at the fatal delusion of his exploring days, a notable European figure and the most venerated perhaps of all the objects of my early geographical enthusiasm.

Once only did that enthusiasm expose me to the derision of my schoolboy chums. One day, putting my finger on a spot in the very middle of the then white heart of Africa, I declared that some day I would go there. My chums' chaffing was perfectly justifiable. I myself was ashamed of having been betrayed into mere vapouring. Nothing was further from my wildest hopes. Yet it is a fact that, about eighteen years afterwards, a wretched little stern-wheel steamboat I commanded lay moored to the bank of an African river.

Everything was dark under the stars. Every other white man on board was asleep. I was glad to be alone on deck, smoking the pipe of peace after an anxious day. The subdued thundering mutter of the Stanley Falls hung in the heavy night air of the last navigable reach of the Upper Congo, while no more than ten miles away, in Reshid's camp just above the Falls, the yet unbroken power of the Congo Arabs slumbered uneasily. Their day was over. Away in the middle of the stream, on a little island nestling all black in the foam of the broken water, a solitary little light glimmered feebly, and I said to myself with awe, 'This is the very spot of my boyish boast.'

A great melancholy descended on me. Yes, this was the very spot. But there was no shadowy friend to stand by my side in the night of the enormous wilderness, no great haunting memory, but only the unholy recollection of a prosaic newspaper 'stunt' and the distasteful knowledge of the vilest scramble for loot that ever disfigured the history of human conscience and geographical exploration. What an end to the idealized realities of a boy's daydreams! I wondered what I was doing there, for indeed it was only an unforeseen episode, hard to believe in now, in my seaman's life. Still, the fact remains that I have smoked a pipe of peace at midnight in the very heart of the African continent, and felt very lonely there.

Appendix 1

THE FIRST MEETING BETWEEN CONRAD and the society hostess Lady Ottoline Morrell (née Ottoline Violet Anne Cavendish-Bentinck, 1873–1938) took place in early August 1913 at Conrad's home, Capel House, near Ashford, Kent, with the novelist Henry James providing the introduction. The later meeting she recalls, with her husband Philip (1870–1943), a politician and sometime Liberal Member of Parliament, was at Conrad's new home, Oswalds, near Canterbury, not far from their mutual friend Bernard Henry Holland (1856–1926), who lived at Harbledown Lodge in Canterbury. A barrister, Holland was active in local government and had worked in the Charity Commission Office; he and Philip Morrell had been at Eton together.

FROM LADY OTTOLINE MORRELL, *MEMOIRS* (1913 AND 1923)

The next really interesting event was my visit to Joseph Conrad at Ashford in Kent . . .

He talked English with a strong accent, as if he tasted his words in his mouth before pronouncing them; but he talked extremely well, though he had always the talk and manner of a foreigner. It seemed difficult to believe that this charming gentleman with high square shoulders, which he shrugged now and again so lightly, and the unmistakably foreign look, had been a captain in the English Merchant Service, and was, too, such a master of English prose. He was dressed very carefully in a blue double-breasted jacket. He talked on apparently with great freedom about his life – more ease and freedom indeed than an Englishman would have allowed himself. He spoke of the horrors of the Congo, from the moral and physical shock of which he said he had never recovered, the impression had been so deep that he felt he would never lose it – but that out of this experience had come *The Heart of Darkness* and *The Outpost of Duty*, which he wrote on his honeymoon in Brittany, as he also did *The Idiots*; but of this story he obviously didn't think very highly – it was too much derived from Guy de Maupassant. I wondered what his wife thought of these strange and haunting companions of their honeymoon! . . .

I visited him again once or twice, but as he was very patriotic I did not dare go during the war, as I felt sure he would disapprove of my views, but in 1923 while Philip and I were staying with Bernard Holland not far from Conrad's new home in Kent we all went over to see him (he had not met Philip before) . . .

He also spoke again of the Congo. Knowing that he had met Casement there I asked about him. All that I now remember of what he said was that he met him emerging from one of the densest and most perilous jungles in a white linen jacket and white tennis shoes, and for arms and protection a walking-stick and a native boy. As he described it I felt that in spite of disapproving of what Casement did in the war he bowed before such quixotic and aristocratic behaviour and nonchalant courage . . .

Conrad's friend John Galsworthy (1867–1933), who had sailed to the South Pacific to mend a broken heart and possibly to meet Robert Louis Stevenson in Samoa, was later to win fame with his series of novels *The Forsyte Saga*, and international recognition with the Nobel Prize. Their meeting aboard the *Torrens* proved the beginning of a lifelong friendship, made towards the end of Conrad's career at sea. The ship departed Adelaide on 23 March 1893, arriving in London on 26 July. Conrad remembered 'Old Andy', a Norwegian named Claes Anderson, in his short essay 'A Friendly Place' (1912), written to help a funding campaign for the London Sailors' Home. His captain was Walter Henry Cope (1849–1918), master of the *Torrens* during six voyages undertaken from 1890 to 1895. Conrad's 'youthful Carlist gun-running adventure' is almost certainly a tall tale, Conrad having arrived in Marseilles in 1874, when the Carlist cause – the attempt to put Don Carlos de Bourbon, Duke of Madrid, on the Spanish throne – was already almost spent. Conrad's London diggings were at 17 Gillingham Street (now marked with a Greater London Council blue plaque) near Victoria Station in what was then a louche area.

FROM JOHN GALSWORTHY, 'REMINISCENCES OF CONRAD' (1924)

Many writers knew my dead friend, and will write of him better than I; but no other writer knew him quite so long, or knew him both as sailor and novelist.

It was in March 1893 that I first met Conrad on board the English sailing ship 'Torrens' in Adelaide Harbour. He was superintending the stowage of cargo. Very dark he looked in the burning sunlight – tanned, with a peaked brown beard, almost black hair, and dark brown eyes, over which the lids were deeply folded. He was thin, not tall, his arms very long, his shoulders broad, his head set rather forward. He spoke to me with a strong foreign accent. He seemed to me strange on an English ship. For fifty-six days I sailed in his company.

The chief mate bears the main burden of a sailing ship. All the first night he was fighting a fire in the hold. None of us seventeen passengers knew of it till long after. It was he who had most truck with the tail of that hurricane off the Leeuwin, and later with another storm. He was a good seaman, watchful of the weather, quick in handling the ship; considerate with the apprentices – we had a long, unhappy Belgian youth among them, who took unhandily to the sea and dreaded going aloft; Conrad compassionately spared him all he could. With the crew he was popular; they were individuals to him, not a mere gang; and long after he would talk of this or that among them, especially of old Andy the sailmaker: 'I likéd that old fellow, you know.' He was friendly with the young second mate, a cheerful, capable young seaman, very English; and respectful, if faintly ironic, with his whiskered, stout old English captain. I, supposed to be studying navigation for the Admiralty Bar, would every day work out the position of the ship with the captain. On one side of the saloon table we would sit and check our observations with those of Conrad, who from the other side of the table would look at us a little quizzically. For Conrad had commanded ships, and his subordinate position on the 'Torrens' was only due to the fact that he was then still convalescent from the Congo experience which had nearly killed him. Many evening watches in fine weather we spent on the poop. Ever the great teller of a tale, he had already nearly twenty years of tales to tell. Tales of ships and storms, of Polish revolution, of his youthful Carlist gun-running adventure, of the Malay seas, and the Congo; and of men and men: all to a listener who had the insatiability of a twenty-five-year-old . . .

Between his voyages in those last days of his sailor's life Conrad used to stay at rooms in Gillingham Street, near Victoria Station. It was there that he read so prodigiously, and there that he suffered from bouts of that lingering Congo fever which dogged his health and fastened a deep, fitful gloom over his spirit. In a letter to me he once said: 'I don't say anything of actual bodily pain, for, God is my witness, I care for that less than nothing.' He was, indeed, truly stoical, and his naturally buoyant spirit reacted with extreme suddenness. But all the years I knew him – thirty-one – he had to fight for decent health. Such words as 'I have been abominably ill – abominably is the right word,' occur again and again in his letters, and his creative achievement in a language not native to him, in face of these constant bouts of illness, approaches the marvellous . . .

Writing to the *Times Literary Supplement*, Jessie Conrad characterised the published recollections by her husband's sometime collaborator and friend Ford Madox Ford as a 'detestable book' (4 December 1924), objecting to Ford's claims with regard to the sources of Conrad's art and his closeness to the writer. Its impressionistic method famously mingles fact and part-fact with outright invention. Conrad's political letters 'written from aboard ship to a compatriot' are possibly the handful addressed to Józef Spiridion Kliszczewski (1849–1932), the son of a Polish watchmaker and goldsmith born in Cardiff, written in 1885 from Singapore and Calcutta. No letters to the Brussels liberal daily *L'Indépendance Belge*, founded in 1831, are known, and mention of them has a characteristically Fordian note of invention.

FROM FORD MADOX FORD,
JOSEPH CONRAD: A PERSONAL REMEMBRANCE
(1924)

Part I: VI

... Of Conrad's deep-sea life the writer proposes to say next to nothing. Intimately mixed up as he was with the writing of so many of Conrad's sea-stories he could not disentangle to his own satisfaction which version of a semi-autobiographic story, like *Heart of Darkness*, was the printed story, which the preparation for the printed story, as Conrad told it to the writer, which the version that Conrad told for the pleasure of chance hearers and which was, as it were, the official autobiographic account. Occasionally, as in his account of his meeting with Roger Casement on the fringe of the bush outside Boma, Conrad would turn to the writer and say: 'You'll keep that, *mon vieux*, for my biography . . .' speaking semi-jocularly.

However, by a curious fatality, during the late war the writer happened to come across a largish body of writing in the form of letters written by Conrad from aboard ship to a compatriot. By Conrad as politician, not as seaman! It was precisely a body of writing since each of the letters was a sort of essay on international politics and it was curious in that it was to all intents and purposes completely uninteresting. It was in a sense passionate in that it was filled with aspirations that Great Britain should join in one combination or another against Russia. She was to join Germany, Austria, France – any one, so long only as she fought the Bear. But all these letters were written with a fluency, such that, had they come before the writer editorially he would at once have thrown them into the waste-paper basket. It was as if Lord Macaulay had been writing leaders for a popular paper . . . Before that one of Conrad's relatives had showed the writer a number of letters that Conrad had written to the *Indépendance Belge*. These were quite another matter – admirably written, intensely emotional. As if Pierre Loti had had some heart!

They had in fact, as is to be expected, a great deal of the body and substance of *Heart of Darkness*.

At both of these documents, however, the writer did no more than glance. The lady had treasured up as cuttings her nephew's correspondence and, when Conrad was out of the room, presented the bundle to Conrad's *ami le poête*. He read them for perhaps half an hour before Conrad came in again: then their author exhibited so much perturbation that the writer desisted. The probability is that Conrad burned the bundle . . . It was very similar with the other letters. They were lent to the writer by their addressee at a time when the writer was extremely occupied; he glanced at them for long enough to form the opinion expressed above and then put them away. Before he had had time to look at them again it occurred to him that Conrad might prefer him not to read them. He accordingly wrote to Conrad and received the answer that Conrad would extremely prefer that the letters should not be re-read and the author returned them to their owner. It is to be hoped that they will not be disinterred.

It should not be inferred that Conrad had anything to hide. He disliked the writer's reading his early works out of the shyness that attends the maturity of every author. This writer would give a good deal if the shelf in the British Museum that contains his early writings could be burned, and Conrad would occasionally say that the idea of the writer or anyone else reading certain of the stories of the *Outpost of Progress* or even certain paragraphs of his later work caused him to have *chair de poule* all down his spine. It is like a feeling of physical modesty . . .

We had left Lowestoft and passed for master . . . We made the voyage in the *Judea, Do or Die* – actually the *Palestine* – that you find narrated in *Youth*. In the East we passed so and so many years. You find the trace of them in the *End of the Tether*, to go no further outside the *Youth* volume. We commanded the Congo Free State navy – for the sake of *Heart of Darkness*. So we have the whole gamut of youth, of fidelity and of human imbecility . . . And if the writer write 'we' – that is how it feels. For it was not possible to be taken imperiously through Conrad's life, in those unchronological and burning passages of phraseology, and not to feel – even to believe – that one had had, oneself, that experience. And the feeling was heightened by Conrad's affecting to believe that one had, at least to the extent of knowing at all times where he had been, what seen, and what performed.

The scenes of Conrad's life as afterwards rendered, say in *Heart of Darkness*, are really as vivid in the writer's mind from what Conrad said as from what Conrad there wrote. It is a curious affair. Actually under the writer's eyes are the bright, lit up keys of a typewriter. Yet perfectly definitely he sees *both* the interior and the outside of a palm-leaf hut, daylight shining through the interstices. A man lies on the floor of the hut, reaching towards a pile of condensed milk tins. The man is half in shadow – half Conrad, half the writer: too tall for Conrad; stretched out a full eight feet, trunk and arms. Outside an immense grey tide, the other shore hardly visible: a few darkish trees of irregular outline. And a man – Coming. In a planter's dress: breeches, leggings, a flannel shirt, a sombrero . . . Some time before he had lifted up the branches of the forest on the opposite shore and looked across at our hut . . . He makes a fire and gives us some soup . . . He comes once a fortnight . . .

We had been at the sources of the Congo: nearly to Fashoda, says the ungeographical part of our minds that once pored over a map of Africa to see everywhere *Terra Incognita* – in the eighties – and that has never again looked at a map of Africa. We had belonged to the Humanitarian Party. The Humanitarian Party did not approve of feeding our black troops on black prisoners: the Conservatives did. So the Conservatives had poisoned us or something the equivalent. And had put our quasi corpse in charge of native bearers to take us, dead or alive, down to Boma on the coast. It was all one to the natives whether at Boma they delivered us quick or dead: they were paid the same.

Half down the Congo they had dumped us in a hut that was a cache for condensed milk. They had gone away for a fortnight to their own village . . . We extracted the condensed milk from the tins by suction, having first pierced them with a pocket knife . . . The condensed milk was the very antidote for the poison! . . . The bearers, black, their white teeth protruding, come back, not displeased to find us alive. Not pleased . . . Astonished! . . . They carried Conrad down to Boma, a sweltering collection of tin huts. The Bomese took great pains to keep you alive: you must die at sea, otherwise the death rate of the Congo Free State rises by one . . .

At Boma then, listless from the abominable huts, we strolled out one day along the coast, between the satin sea and the steaming trees. A man, with the sunlight on his face, in white tennis shoes with two bulldogs at his heels stepped out of the dark forest. He said Hullo! He had strolled across Africa from the Zanzibar side in his tennis shoes, with no bearers, no escort but his bulldogs, no arms. He had such a fascination for the black fellows. That was Roger Casement . . . There was a great deal of light, the sky blue, the sea dove-coloured and oily, the forest black-green, a wall; the beach pink, the bulldogs crashed over it to sniff at our heels . . .

Part II: I

. . . We met at first as two English gentlemen do in a Club : upon that footing we continued. We took it for granted that each *was* a gentleman, with the feelings, views of the world and composure of a member of the ruling classes of the days of Lord Palmerston – tempered of course with such eccentricities as go with the spleen of the *milor anglais*. Such eccentricities we allowed each to the other, but without question. Thus during the South African War, as has been said, the writer was an active and sometimes uproarious Pacifist. Not a pro-Boer: he would have hanged President Kruger on the same gallows as Mr Chamberlain. Or, later with an equal enthusiasm he supported Miss Christabel Pankhurst and the Suffragettes. Now and then on idle occasions after lunch he would declaim about either of these causes. Conrad would listen.

From time to time, particularly whilst writing *Heart of Darkness* Conrad would declaim passionately about the gloomy imbecility and cruelty of the Belgians in the Congo Free State. Still more would he so declaim now and then, after he had been up to London and had met Casement who had been British Commissioner on the Congo and was passionately the champion of the natives. Then the writer would listen . . .

. . . for Conrad the universe was the ship-shape. Any soul wandering outside that corral in the abyss was for him a matter purely of gloomy indifference . . . 'The fellow simply does not exist!' That was the formula . . . That anyone with whom he was on terms of intimacy should, all unsuspected, hold such a philosophy was to him unspeakably painful: as if it were a treachery to the British flag. It was as unspeakably painful to him as when later Casement, loathing the Belgians so much for their treatment of the natives on the Congo, took up arms against his own country and was, to our eternal discredit, hanged, rather than shot in the attempt to escape . . . We might have achieved *that* effort of our wooden imaginations . . .

And as soon as the writer had let Conrad know that this [*The Inheritors: An Extravagant Story*, 1901] was a novel, not a short story, he knew that he was in for another collaboration. Every word spoken added to that conviction . . . The novel was to be a political work, rather allegorically backing Mr Balfour in the then Government; the villain was to be Joseph Chamberlain who had made the war. The sub-villain was to be Leopold II, King of the Belgians, the foul – and incidentally lecherous – beast who had created the Congo Free State in order to grease the wheels of his harems with the blood of murdered negroes and to decorate them with fretted ivory cut from stolen tusks in the deep forests . . . For the writer, until that moment, it had appeared to be an allegorico-realist romance: it showed the superseding of previous generations and codes by the merciless young who are always alien and without remorse . . . But the moment Conrad spoke, he spoke with the voice of the Conrad who was avid of political subjects to treat, and the writer knew that this indeed was the Conrad subject . . .

Part III: I

. . . From time to time gentlemen of the Press anxious to depreciate the writer have said that he imitated the work of Conrad. This was not the case. It is a curious characteristic of the work of Conrad that, not only can you not recognisably imitate it, you hardly ever feel even the impulse to do so, and the one writer who really sedu- lously be-aped the more exotic romances of the author of *An Outpost of Progress* achieved performances so lugubrious that he seems to have warned off any other imitators of his example. The fact is that Conrad, like Turgenev, is very little mannered; his tem- perament had no eccentricities that could be easily imitated; his vocabulary was as much the result of difficulties as of arbitrary selection; his cadences were so intimately his own that they were practically unimitable. The writer probably more than any other man must have had opportunities of studying the way prose came to Conrad but the writer does not remember more than three sen- tences that he ever wrote – apart from sentences that he actually composed for Conrad himself – in which he either consciously tried for some purpose or other to get the cadence of a sentence of Conrad's, or as to which he felt, after having written them, the satis- faction which he might imagine himself feeling if he *had* written a Conrad sentence. If the accusation had been of imitation of Mr Henry James it might have been just enough, though a pastiche is not exactly the same thing as an imitation – being an exercise in the manner of a writer rather than an attempt to make a living by con- cealed plagiarism . . .

Part IV

. . . Indeed, in that frame of mind, Conrad was very impartial. He used to shock the writer who, as a Briton, knows nothing about his Imperial possessions, by declaring that the French were the only European nation who knew how to colonise: they had none of the spirit of Mr Kipling's 'You-bloody-niggerisms' about them, but regarded black or tan or black and tan as all one humanity with themselves, intermarrying, working peacefully side by side, and side by side in Algerian cafés of an evening sitting and drinking their aperitifs. And they provided the nigger with exactly the same mairies, frescoes, statuary in the midst of jungles, representation in

Paris and maddening regulations for obtaining *permis de chasse* or money from the Post Office as are provided in any French town from Pont l'Evèque to Aigues Mortes. That seemed to Conrad the way to colonise: and indeed one never heard of any Secessionist movements in the French colonies, from Algeria to Annam. But be that as it may, with all his gloomily fatalistic views of the incapacity of Anglo-Saxons as colonists other than by butchery and the sjam-bok, in *Heart of Darkness* it is a French, not a British, ship-of-war that bombards the unanswering bush from the tepid seas of the African coasts . . .

Conrad's friend and mentor at the beginning of his career, Edward William Garnett (1868–1937), befriended the writer when Garnett was a reader for T. Fisher Unwin, encouraging him in the writing of his second novel, *An Outcast of the Islands* (1896), set like his first in the Malay world and deal-ing with the disintegration of a Dutch adventurer, Peter Willems. Jean Fréderic-Emile Aubry (1882–1949), a French journalist and music critic who wrote under the pen name 'Jean-Aubry', was Conrad's first biographer and the author of *Joseph Conrad au Congo* (1925). Garnett's memory of being regaled with the telling of Conrad's African experience at his home, The Cearne in Crockham Hill, Kent, rings true only in part. Conrad's story of being succoured by a native woman whilst ill is possibly true; but Con-rad is known to have embroidered his biographical recollections, and it is strongly reminiscent of a situation dealt with under the subheading 'Com-passionate Treatment of a Negro Woman' in the Scottish explorer Mungo Park's *Travels in the Interior of Africa* (1799), which he recalls in the essay 'Geography and Some Explorers'.

FROM EDWARD GARNETT, *LETTERS FROM CONRAD 1895 TO 1924* (1928)

Introduction

Conrad, exhilarated by my praise, then described his ideas of the downhill path of Willems and foreshadowed Aissa's part in the drama. The plot had already taken shape in his mind, but most of the action was still in a state of flux. Conrad's attitude to *The Outcast* was from the first a strange blend of creative ardour and scepticism. He spoke deprecatingly of his knowledge of Malay life, but all the same the figures of Willems, Joanna and Aissa captivated his imagination. His sardonic interest in Willems' disintegration reflected, I believe, his own disillusionment over the Congo. I agree with M. Jean-Aubry that Conrad's Congo experiences were the turning-point in his mental life and that its effects on him determined his transformation from a sailor to a writer. According to his emphatic declaration to me, in his early years at sea he had 'not a thought in his head'. 'I was a perfect animal,' he reiterated, meaning, of course, that he had reasoned and reflected hardly at all over all the varieties of life he had encountered. The sinister voice of the Congo with its murmuring undertone of human fatuity, baseness and greed had swept away the generous illusions of his youth, and had left him gazing into the heart of an immense darkness . . . That Conrad's memory had extraordinary wealth of observation to draw on I had an illuminating proof in *Heart of Darkness*. Some time before he wrote this story of his Congo experience he narrated it at length one morning while we were walking up and down under a row of Scotch firs that leads down to the Cearne. I listened enthralled while he gave me in detail a very full synopsis of what he intended to write. To my surprise when I saw the printed version I found that about a third of the most striking incidents had been replaced by others of which he had said nothing at all. The effect of the written narrative was no less sombre than the spoken, and the end was more consummate; but I regretted the omission of various scenes, one of which described the hero lying sick to death in a native hut, tended by an old negress who brought him water from day to day, when he had been abandoned by all the Belgians. 'She saved my life,' Conrad said; 'the white men never came near me.'

The Cambridge philosopher and social critic the Hon. Bertrand Arthur William Russell (1872–1970; 3rd Earl Russell, 1931) quickly followed

upon the heels of his then mistress Ottoline Morrell to see Conrad at his
Kentish home, the meeting occurring on 10 September 1913. (Conrad paid
a return visit to Russell in Cambridge about a week later.) Conrad's wish to
go to sea was expressed not, so far as is known, to his parents but to his
maternal uncle and guardian Tadeusz Bobrowski; however, for a Russian
subject the dream of enrolling in the Hapsburg Empire's naval academy on
the Adriatic at Pola (now Pula, Croatia) was simply that.

FROM BERTRAND RUSSELL, 'PORTRAITS FROM MEMORY, V: JOSEPH CONRAD' (1956)

I made the acquaintance of Joseph Conrad in September, 1913,
through our common friend Lady Ottoline Morrell. I had been for
many years an admirer of his books, but should not have ventured to
seek acquaintance without an introduction. I travelled down to his
house near Ashford in Kent in a state of somewhat anxious expectation. My first impression was one of surprise. He spoke English with
a very strong foreign accent, and nothing in his demeanour in any
way suggested the sea. He was an aristocratic Polish gentleman to
his finger-tips. His feeling for the sea, and for England, was one of
romantic love – love from a certain distance, sufficient to leave the
romance untarnished. His love for the sea began at a very early age.
When he told his parents that he wished for a career as a sailor, they
urged him to go into the Austrian navy, but he wanted adventure
and tropical seas and strange rivers surrounded by dark forests; and
the Austrian navy offered him no scope for these desires. His family
were horrified at his seeking a career in the English merchant
marine, but his determination was inflexible.

He was, as anyone may see from his books, a very rigid moralist
and politically far from sympathetic with revolutionaries. He and I
were in most of our opinions by no means in agreement, but in
something very fundamental we were extraordinarily at one.

My relation to Joseph Conrad was unlike any other that I have
ever had. I saw him seldom, and not over a long period of years. In
the out-works of our lives, we were almost strangers, but we shared

a certain outlook on human life and human destiny, which, from the very first, made a bond of extreme strength. I may perhaps be pardoned for quoting a sentence from a letter that he wrote to me very soon after we had become acquainted. I should feel that modesty forbids the quotation except for the fact that it expresses so exactly what I felt about him. What he expressed and I equally felt was, in his words, 'A deep admiring affection which, if you were never to see me again and forgot my existence tomorrow, would be unalterably yours *usque ad finem*.'

Of all that he had written I admired most the terrible story called *The Heart of Darkness*, in which a rather weak idealist is driven mad by horror of the tropical forest and loneliness among savages. This story expresses, I think, most completely his philosophy of life. I felt, though I do not know whether he would have accepted such an image, that he thought of civilized and morally tolerable human life as a dangerous walk on a thin crust of barely cooled lava which at any moment might break and let the unwary sink into fiery depths. He was very conscious of the various forms of passionate madness to which men are prone, and it was this that gave him such a profound belief in the importance of discipline. His point of view, one might perhaps say, was the antithesis of Rousseau's: 'Man is born in chains, but he can become free.' He becomes free, so I believe Conrad would have said, not by letting loose his impulses, not by being casual and uncontrolled, but by subduing wayward impulse to a dominant purpose . . .

Appendix 2

HAVING, AS BRITISH CONSUL at Matadi, apprised the Foreign Office of the deleterious effects on the native population of the coerced labour system in effect and the systematic brutalisation of native peoples, Casement actively agitated for reform upon returning to London, being joined by the Aborigines' Protection Society and the Congo Reform Society. Pressed, the House of Commons passed a resolution that enjoined Casement to make a formal and extensive inquiry into conditions in the Belgian territory. Addressed to Lord Lansdowne (né Henry Charles Keith Petty-Fitzmaurice, 1845–1927; 5th Marquess of Lansdowne, 1866) as Secretary of State for Foreign Affairs, and formally part of the British Parliamentary Papers, Casement's report, which was greeted with a public outcry, was communicated to the governments of the nations that had signed the Berlin Treaty (1885), the legal instrument regulating European colonisation and trade. The report, which details Casement's travels through the Congo, is most notable for its description, in its inclosures, of atrocities committed by Belgian nationals. These were investigated – and corroborated by an independent commission established by the Belgian Parliament – leading, in the end, to the prosecution and punishment of those responsible for them. The report constituted a severe indictment of Leopoldine policies, brought to widespread public attention for the first time; in 1908 the Congo, annexed by the Belgian state, which took over its administration, ceased to be the private property of the King of the Belgians.

THE MAIN REPORT

Mr Casement to the Marquess of Lansdowne
London, December 11, 1903

My Lord,
I have the honour to submit my Report on my recent journey on the Upper Congo.

    I left Matadi on the 5th June, and arriving at Léopoldville on the

6th, remained in the neighbourhood of Stanley Pool until the 2nd July, when I set out for the Upper Congo. My return to Léopoldville was on the 15th of September, so that the period spent in the Upper River was one of only two and a half months, during which time I visited several points on the Congo River itself, up to the junction of the Lulongo River, ascended that river and its principal feeder, the Lopori, as far as Bongandanga, and went round Lake Mantumba.

Although my visit was of such brief duration, and the points touched at nowhere lay far off the beaten tracks of communication, the region visited was one of the most central in the Congo State, and the district in which most of my time was spent, that of the Equator, is probably one of the most productive. Moreover, I was enabled, by visiting this district, to contrast its present day state with the condition in which I had known it some sixteen years ago. Then (in 1887) I had visited most of the places I now revisited, and I was thus able to institute a comparison between a state of affairs I had myself seen when the natives lived their own savage lives in anarchic and disorderly communities, uncontrolled by Europeans, and that created by more than a decade of very energetic European intervention. That very much of this intervention has been called for no one who formerly knew the Upper Congo could doubt, and there are to-day widespread proofs of the great energy displayed by Belgian officials in introducing their methods of rule over one of the most savage regions of Africa.

Admirably built and admirably kept stations greet the traveller at many points; a fleet of river steamers, numbering, I believe, forty-eight, the property of the Congo Government, navigate the main river and its principal affluents at fixed intervals. Regular means of communication are thus afforded to some of the most inaccessible parts of Central Africa.

A railway, excellently constructed in view of the difficulties to be encountered, now connects the ocean ports with Stanley Pool, over a tract of difficult country, which formerly offered to the weary traveller on foot many obstacles to be overcome and many days of great bodily fatigue. To-day the railway works most efficiently, and I noticed many improvements, both in the permanent way and in the general management, since the date of my last visit to Stanley Pool in January 1901. The cataract region, through which the railway passes, is a generally unproductive and even sterile tract of some 220 miles in breadth. This region is, I believe, the home, or birthplace of the sleeping sickness – a terrible disease, which is, all too rapidly, eating its way into the heart of Africa, and has even traversed the entire continent to well-nigh the shores of the Indian Ocean. The population of the Lower Congo has been gradually reduced by the unchecked ravages of this, as yet, undiagnosed and incurable disease, and as one cause of the seemingly wholesale diminution of human life which I everywhere observed in the regions revisited, a prominent place must be assigned to this malady. The natives certainly attribute their alarming death-rate to this as one of the inducing causes, although they attribute, and I think principally, their rapid decrease in numbers to other causes as well. Perhaps the most striking change observed during my journey into the interior was the great reduction observable everywhere in native life. Communities I had formerly known as large and flourishing centres of population are to-day entirely gone, or now exist in such diminished numbers as to be no longer recognizable. The southern shores of Stanley Pool had formerly a population of fully 5,000 Batekes, distributed through the three towns of Ngaliema's (Léopoldville), Kinchasa and Ndolo, lying within a few miles of each other. These people, some twelve years ago, decided to abandon their homes, and in one night the great majority of them crossed over into the French territory on the north shores of Stanley Pool. Where formerly had stretched these populous native African villages, I saw to-day only a few scattered European houses, belonging either to Government officials or local traders. In Léopoldville to-day there are not, I should estimate, 100 of the original natives or their descendants now residing. At Kinchasa a few more may be found dwelling around one of the European trading depôts, while at Ndolo none remain, and there is nothing there but a station of the Congo Railway Company and a Government post. These Bateke people were not, perhaps, particularly desirable subjects for an energetic Administration, which desired, above all things, progress and speedy results. They were themselves interlopers from the northern shores of the Congo River, and derived a very profitable existence as trading middlemen, exploiting the less sophisticated population among whom they had established themselves. Their loss to the southern shores of Stanley Pool is none the less to be deplored, I think, for they formed, at any rate, a connecting link between an incoming European commercial element and the background of would-be native suppliers.

Léopoldville

Léopoldville is sometimes spoken of as a Congo town, but it cannot rightly be so termed. Apart from the Government station, which, in most respects, is very well planned, there is nothing at all resembling a town – barrack would be the correct term. The Government station of Léopoldville numbers, I was informed by its Chief, some 148 Europeans, and probably 3,000 native Government workmen, who all dwell in well-ordered lines of either very well-built European houses, or, for the native staff, mud-built huts. Broad paths, which may be termed streets, connect the various parts of this Government Settlement, and an elementary effort at lighting by electricity has already evolved three lights in front of the house of the Commissaire-Général. Outside the Government staff, the general community, or public of Léopoldville, numbers less than one dozen Europeans, and possibly not more than 200 native dependents of their households or trading stores. This general public consists of two missionary establishments, numbering in all 4 Europeans; a railway station with, I think, 1 European; 4 trading establishments – 1 Portuguese, 1 Belgian, 1 English, and 1 German – numbering 7 Europeans, with, perhaps, 80 or 100 native dependents; 2 British West African petty traders, and a couple of Loango tailor boys, who make clothes for the general community. This, I think, comprises almost all those not immediately dependent upon the Government.

These shops and traders do scarcely any business in native produce, of which there may be said to be none in the district, but rely upon a cash trade in Congolese currency, carried on with the large staff of Government employés, both European and native. Were this cash dealing to cease, the four European shops would be forced to put up their shutters. During the period of my stay at Léopoldville it did actually cease, and, for reasons which were not known publicly, the large native staff of Congo Government workmen, instead of receiving a part of their monthly wages in cash to spend locally – as also those being paid off on the expiry of their contracts – were remunerated by the Government in barter goods, which they were issued from a Government store. This method of payment did not satisfy either the native Government employés or the local traders, and I heard many complaints on this score. The traders complained, some of them to myself, that as they had no other form of trading open to them, save this with the Government staff against cash, for the Government to itself now pay these men in goods was to end, at a blow, all trade dealings in the district. The native workmen complained, too, that they were paid in cloth which often they did not want in their own homes, and in order to have the wherewithal to purchase what they wanted, a practice at once arose amongst these men to sell for cash, at a loss to themselves, the cloth they had been forced to receive in payment from the Government store. The workmen lost on this transaction, and so did the traders. Pieces of cloth which were charged by the Government at 10 fr. each in paying off the workmen, these men would readily part with for 7 fr., and even for 6 fr. I myself, one day in June, bought for 7 fr. a-piece, from two just-discharged Government workmen, two pieces of cloth which had been charged against them at 10 fr. each. These men wished to buy salt at one of the local stores, and to obtain the means of doing so, they readily sacrificed 3 fr. in each 10 fr. of their pay. The traders, too, complained that by this extensive sale, at reduced rates by the Government employés, of cotton goods, their own sales of cloth at current prices were rendered well-nigh impossible throughout the district.

The 3,000 Government workpeople at Léopoldville are drawn from nearly every part of the Congo State. Some, those from the cataract district especially, go voluntarily seeking employment, but many – and I believe a vast majority – are men, or lads, brought from districts of the Upper Congo, and who serve the authorities not primarily at their own seeking. On the 16th June last, five

Government workpeople brought me their contracts of engagement with a request that I might tell them how long a period they still had to serve. They were all Upper Congo men, and had already nearly completed the full term of their engagement. The contracts, in each case, appeared as having been signed and drawn up at Boma on behalf of the Governor-General of the Congo State, and were, in each case, for a term of seven years. The men informed me that they had never been to Boma, and that the whole of their period of service had been spent either at Léopoldville or on the Upper Congo. In three of these cases I observed that an alteration had been made in the period of service, in the following terms:

> I reduce from seven to five years, the term of service of . . .

This entry was signed by the acting State Inspector of the district. It seemingly had not been observed, for it was struck out by his successor, and, as a matter of fact, the full period of seven years was, in each case, within a few months of completion.

On the whole the Government workmen at Léopoldville struck me as being well cared for, and they were certainly none of them idle. The chief difficulty in dealing with so large a staff arises from the want of a sufficiency of food supply in the surrounding country. The staple food of the entire Upper Congo is a preparation of the root of the cassava plant, steeped and boiled, and made up into loaves or puddings of varying weight [kwanga]. The natives of the districts around Léopoldville are forced to provide a fixed quantity each week of this form of food, which is levied by requisitions on all the surrounding villages. The European Government staff is also mainly dependent upon food supplies obtained from the natives of the neighbourhood in a similar manner. This, however necessary, is not a welcome task to the native suppliers who complain that their numbers are yearly decreasing, while the demands made upon them remain fixed, or tend even to increase.

The Government station at Léopoldville and its extensive staff exist almost solely in connection with the running of Government steamers upon the Upper Congo.

A hospital for Europeans and an establishment designed as a native hospital are in charge of a European doctor. Another doctor also resides in the Government station whose bacteriological studies are unremitting and worthy of much praise. The native hospital – not, I am given to understand, through the fault of the local medical staff – is, however, an unseemly place. When I visited the three mud huts which serve the purpose of the native hospital, all of them dilapidated, and two with the thatched roofs almost gone, I found seventeen sleeping sickness patients, male and female, lying about in the utmost dirt. Most of them were lying on the bare ground – several out on the pathway in front of the houses, and one, a woman, had fallen into the fire just prior to my arrival (while in the final, insensible stage of the disease) and had burned herself very badly. She had since been well bandaged, but was still lying out on the ground with her head almost in the fire, and while I sought to speak to her, in turning she upset a pot of scalding water over her shoulder. All the seventeen people I saw were near their end, and on my second visit two days later, the 19th June, I found one of them lying dead out in the open.

In somewhat striking contrast to the neglected state of these people, I found, within a couple of hundred yards of them, the Government workshop for repairing and fitting the steamers. Here all was brightness, care, order, and activity, and it was impossible not to admire and commend the industry which had created and maintained in constant working order this useful establishment. In conjunction with a local missionary, some effort was made during my stay at Léopoldville to obtain an amelioration of the condition of the sleeping sickness people in the native hospital, but it was stated, in answer to my friend's representations, that nothing could be done in the way of building a proper hospital until plans now under consideration had been matured elsewhere. The structures I had visited, which the local medical staff, I believe, greatly deplored – had endured as the only form of hospital accommodation for several years – provided for the numerous native staff of the district.

The Government stores at Léopoldville are large and well built, and contain not only the goods the Government itself sends up river in its fleet of steamers, but also the goods of the various Concession Companies. As a rule, the various produce brought down river by the Government steamers is transhipped direct into the railway trucks which run alongside the wharf, and is carried thence by train to Matadi for shipment to Europe. The various Companies carrying on operations on the Upper Congo, and who hold concessions from the Congo Government, are bound, I was told, by Conventions to abstain from carrying, save within the limits of their Concessions, either goods or passengers. This interdiction extends to their own merchandise and to their own agents. Should they carry, by reason of imperative need outside these limits any of their own goods or their own people, they are bound to pay to the Congo Government either the freight or passage money according to the Government tariff, just as though the goods or passengers had been conveyed on one of the Government vessels. The tariff upon goods and passengers carried along the interior waterways is a fairly high one, not perhaps excessive under the circumstances, but still one that by reason of this virtual monopoly, can produce a yearly revenue which must go far towards maintaining the Government flotilla. By the estimates for 1902, published in the 'Bulletin Officiel' of January this year, the transport service is credited with a production of 3,100,000 fr. of public revenue for 1902, while the expenditure for the same year is put at 2,023,376 fr. That this restriction of public conveyance by Government vessel alone is not altogether a public gain my own experience demonstrated. I had wished to leave Stanley Pool for the Upper Congo at an early date after my arrival in Léopoldville, but as the Government vessels were mostly crowded, I could not proceed with any comfort by one of these. The steamship 'Flandre', one of the largest of these vessels, which left Léopoldville for Stanley Falls on the 22nd June, and by which I had, at first, intended to proceed, quitted port with more than twenty European passengers over her complement, all of whom, I was informed, would have to sleep on deck. I accordingly was forced to seek other means of travelling, and through the kindness of the Director of one of the large commercial Companies (the 'Société Anonyme Belge du Haut-Congo'), I found excellent accommodation, as a guest, on one of his steamers. Although thus an invited guest and not paying any passage money, special permission had to be sought from the Congo Government before this act of courtesy could be shown me, and I saw the telegram from the local authority, authorizing my conveyance to Chumbiri.

This commercial Company has three other steamers, but the interdiction referred to applies to the entire flotilla of trading vessels of Congolese nationality on the Upper River. Despite the fact that these vessels are not allowed to earn freight or passage, they are all, for their tonnage, heavily taxed, while the Government vessels, which earn considerable sums on transport of general goods and passengers, pay no taxes. The four vessels of the Société Anonyme Belge du Haut-Congo referred to, of which the largest is only, I believe, one of 30 tons, pay annually, I was informed, the following taxes:

	Fr.
For permission to cut firewood	17,870
Licence for each steamer, according to her tonnage	400 to 600

The master of each vessel must be licensed, for which a tax of 20 fr. per annum is levied.

Himself and each European member of the crew must then pay 30 fr. per annum as 'imposition personnelle' [personal tax] whilst each native member of the crew costs his employers 3 fr. per head for engagement licence annually, and 10 fr. per head per annum as 'imposition personnelle'.

The 'President Urban', the largest steamer of the Company referred to, under these various heads pays, I was informed, a sum of not less that 11,000 fr. in taxes per annum. Should she carry any of the agents of the Company owning her, or any of its goods, her owners must pay to the Congo Government both passage money and freight on these, just as though they had been sent by one of the Government vessels.

No firewood may be cut by the public within half-an-hour's steaming distance of any of the Government wooding posts, which are naturally chosen at the best wooding sites available along the various waterways, so that the 10,000 fr. wood-cutting licence which the 'President Urban' pays, entitles her only to cut up for fuel such suitable timber as her crew may be able to find in the less accessible spots . . .

Bolobo

At Bolobo, where I spent ten days waiting for a steamer to continue my journey, a somewhat similar state of affairs prevails to that existing at Chumbiri. Bolobo used to be one of the most important native Settlements along the south bank of the Upper Congo, and the population in the early days of civilized rule numbered fully 40,000 people, chiefly of the Bobangi tribe. To-day the population is believed to be not more than 7,000 or 8,000 souls. The Bolobo men were famous in their former days for their voyages to Stanley Pool and their keen trading ability. All of their large canoes have to-day disappeared, and while some of them still hunt hippopotami – which are still numerous in the adjacent waters – I did not observe anything like industry among them.

Indeed, it would be hard to say how the people now live or how they occupy their own time. They did not complain so much of the weekly enforced food supplies required of them, which would, indeed, seem to be an unavoidable necessity of the situation, as to the unexpected calls frequently made upon them. Neither rubber nor ivory is obtained in this neighbourhood. The food supply and a certain amount of local labour is all that is enforced. As woodcutters, station hands in the Government post, canoe paddlers, workers on the telegraph route or in some other public capacity, they are liable to frequent requisition.

The labour required did not seem to be excessive, but it would seem to be irregularly called for, unequally distributed, and only poorly remunerated, or sometimes not remunerated at all.

Complaints as to the manner of exacting service are much more frequent than complaints as to the fact of service being required. If the local official has to go on a sudden journey men are summoned on the instant to paddle his canoe, and a refusal entails imprisonment or a beating. If the Government plantation or the kitchen garden require weeding, a soldier will be sent to call in the women from some of the neighbouring towns. To the official this is a necessary public duty which he cannot but impose, but to the women suddenly forced to leave their household tasks and to tramp off, hoe in hand, baby on back, with possibly a hungry and angry husband at home, the task is not a welcome one.

One of the weightier tasks imposed upon the neighbourhood during my stay at Bolobo was the construction of a wooden pier at the Government beach whereat Government vessels might come alongside.

I visited this incompleted structure several times, and estimated that from 1,500 to 2,000 trees and saplings had already been used in its partial construction. All of these were cut down and carried in by the men of some of the neighbouring towns, and for this compulsory service no remuneration had, up to that date, I was on all sides informed, been made to any one of them. They were ordered, they said, to do it as a public duty. The timber needed had to be sought at a considerable distance, most of the trees had been carried some miles, and the task was not altogether an agreeable one. The chief complaint I heard directed against this work, however, was that the pier was being so badly put up that when finished it would be quite useless, and all their work would thus be thrown away. My own opinion of the structure was that this criticism was well-founded, and that the first annual rise of the river would sweep most of the ill-laid timbers away.

The Bolobo people do not object, they said, so much to the regular food tax, just because this is regular, and they can prepare and regularly meet it, as to the sudden and unexpected labour tasks, such as canoe journeys, or this more onerous pier building. They could, I perceived, trace no connection between this hastily conceived exaction on their time and labour and a system of general contribution in the public interest, which, to be readily admitted, should be clearly defined. Were a regular annual tax levied in money, or some medium of barter exchange serving as a legal currency, the people would in time be brought to see that a payment of this kind evenly distributed and enforced was, indeed, a public duty they were

bound to acquit themselves of, and one their Government was justi-
fied in strictly enforcing; but they do not assign any such value to the
unsystematic calls upon them which prevail to-day. To be hastily
summoned from their usual home avocations, or even from their
possibly habitual idleness, to perform one or other of the tasks indicated above, and to get neither food nor pay for their exertions, as is
often the case, seems to these unprogressive people not a public
service they are called upon to perform in the public interest, but a
purely personal burden laid upon their bodies and their time by the
local agent of an organization which, to them, would seem to exist
chiefly for its own profit.

The weight of the kwanga required at Bolobo seemed to be less
than that enforced at Chumbiri, and I found that this variance
existed throughout the Upper Congo. At Bolobo the kwanga loaves
supplied to the Government post weighed each a little over 3 lb. That
made for ordinary sale in the public market just over 1 lb.: one of
each that I weighed myself gave 3 lb. 2 oz. to the Government loaf,
and 13 oz. to that made for general consumption. The price paid in
each case was the same – viz., one brass rod.

At the village of Litimba, some 4 or 5 miles from the Government post, which I visited, I found the village to number some forty
adult males with their families. This village has to supply weekly to
the Government post 400 of these loaves (say 1,250 lb. weight of
food) for which a payment of 20 fr. (400 rods) is made. The people
of Litimba told me that when short of cassava from their own fields
for the preparation of this supply, they bought the root in the local
market and had to pay for it in the raw state just twice what they
received for the prepared and cooked product they delivered at the
post. I had no means of verifying this statement, but I was assured
by many persons that it was strictly true. In addition to supplying
this food weekly, Litimba is liable to the usual calls for canoe paddlers, day labourers at the Government station (male and female),
timber gatherers for the pier, and woodcutters at the local wood-
post of the Government steamers.

There was a good deal of sickness in this town, and in that beyond
it at the date of my visit. Sleeping sickness and, still more, small-pox.

Both diseases have done much to reduce the population. Emigration to the French shore, once active, would seem now to have ceased. Efforts are made locally, both by Government officials and by the Baptist Missionary Society, who have a very flourishing station at Bolobo, to improve the physical and sanitary condition of the people, and improvements due to these efforts are becoming apparent, but I was given to understand that progress is very slow.

The insufficiency of the food generally observable in this part of the Congo would seem to account for much sickness, and probably for the mental depression of the natives I so often observed, itself a frequent cause of disease. The Chief of the Government post at Bolobo during a part of my stay there told me that he thought the district was quite exhausted, and that it must be ever increasingly difficult to obtain food from it for the public requirements of the local administration.

Some 40 miles above Bolobo a large 'camp d'instruction', with from 600 to 800 native recruits and a staff of several European officers, is established at a place called Yumbi. I had, to my regret, no opportunity of visiting this camp, although I met one of its officers who very kindly invited me there, promising a hearty welcome. He informed me that native food supplies were fairly plentiful in the neighbourhood of this camp, and that the principal rations of the soldiers consisted of hippopotamus meat, the Congo in that neighbourhood affording a seemingly inexhaustible supply of these creatures.

In front of the house of one of the natives in a Bolobo village, close to the English Mission, I saw some seventy hippopotamus skulls. The animals, I was told, had all been killed by one man. Many are speared, and some are shot by the native hunters with cap-guns. A somewhat considerable trade in these weapons appears to have been done until recently by the Government Agents in the district, and I found several of the Bolobo young men with guns of this description which they had bought at different times from the local official, generally paying for them with ivory tusks. The sale of these arms by Representatives of the Congo Government would seem to have ceased somewhat more than a year ago, since which date the holders of the guns have been exposed to some trouble in order to obtain licences. Dealing in or holding guns of this description would seem to be regulated by clearly drawn up Regulations, which, however, do not seem to have been observed until last year. A tax of 20 fr. is now levied on the issue of a licence to bear arms, which the law renders obligatory on every gun holder.

I learned while at Bolobo that a large influx from the Lake Léopold II district (which comprises the 'Domaine de la Couronne') had lately taken place into the country behind Bolobo. The nearest Settlement of these emigrants was said to be about 20 to 25 miles from Bolobo and I determined to visit this place. I spent the 20th, 21st, and 22nd July on this journey, visited two large villages in the interior belonging to the Batende tribe, wherein I found that fully half the population now consisted of refugees belonging to the Basengili tribe who had formerly dwelt near Lake Léopold II. I saw and questioned several groups of these people, whom I found to be industrious blacksmiths and brass-workers. These people consisted of old and young men, women and children. They had fled from their country and sought an asylum with their friends the Batende during the last four years. The distance they had travelled in their flight they put at about six or seven days' march – which I should estimate at from 120 to 150 miles of walking. They went on to declare, when asked why they had fled, that they had endured such ill-treatment at the hands of the Government officials and the Government soldiers in their own country that life had become intolerable, that nothing had remained for them at home but to be killed for failure to bring in a certain amount of rubber or to die from starvation or exposure in their attempts to satisfy the demands made upon them. The statements made to me by these people were of such a nature that I could not believe them to be true. The fact remained, however, that they had certainly abandoned their homes and all that they possessed, had travelled a long distance and now preferred a species of mild servitude among the Batende to remaining in their own country. I took careful note of the statements made to me by these people, which will be found in the transcript attached (Inclosure 1). I subsequently found when at Lukolela some days later, other Basengili, who confirmed the truth of the statements made to me at Mpoko.

On my return to Bolobo in September I found that the Rev. A. E. Scrivener, of the Baptist Missionary Society, who had accompanied me in July on my journey to Mpoko, had in the interval made a six weeks' journey on foot from Bolobo to the shores of Lake Léopold II. This journey had carried him through the homelands of some of the very refugees I had seen and spoken to at Mpoko. He found the truth of their statements made to me amply confirmed, both by his own observation on the spot and statements made to him by the present Government officer in charge of the district. My own further inquiries at Lukolela and Mr Scrivener's statements to me are also embodied in the accompanying document (Inclosure 1).

Lake Mantumba

From Irebu I proceeded some 25 miles to Ikoko, once a large village on the north shore of Lake Mantumba, where there is a Mission station belonging to the American Baptist Missionary Union. I remained in Lake Mantumba seventeen days, visiting, during that time, the Government post at Bikoro on the east shore of the lake and many native towns scattered round the lake side. I also ascended by boat one of the rivers falling into the lake, and visited three native villages in the forest situated along this waterway. Lake Mantumba is a fine sheet of water about 25 or 30 miles long and some 12 or 15 miles broad at the broadest part, surrounded by a dense forest. The inhabitants of the district are of the Ntomba tribe and are still rude savages, using very fine bows and arrows and ill-made spears as their weapons. There are also in the forest country many families or clans of a dwarf race called Batwas, who are of much more savage and untameable disposition than the Ntombas, who form the bulk of the population. Both Batwas and Ntombas are still cannibals and cannibalism, although repressed and not so openly indulged in as formerly, is still prevalent in the district. The Mantumba people were, in the days before the establishment of Congo State rule, among the most active fishermen and traders of the Upper Congo.

In fleets of canoes they used to issue out upon the main waters of the Congo and travel very great distances, fighting their way if necessary, in search of purchasers of their fish or slaves, or to procure these latter. All this has ceased and, save for small canoes used in catching fish, I saw neither on the lake itself nor at the many villages I touched along its shores, any canoes comparable to those so frequently seen in the past. One State-invested Chief of a village I visited told me that he had recently bought a fine canoe for 2,000 brass rods (100 fr.), in which he had sent his weekly imposition of fish to the local State post. The canoe had been kept by the official there, had been used to transport Government soldiers in, and was now attached to a Government wood-cutting post, which he named, out on the main river. He had received nothing for the loss of this canoe, and when I urged him to lay the matter before the local official responsible, who had doubtless retained the canoe in ignorance, he pulled up his loin cloth and, pointing to where he had been flogged with a chicotte, said: 'If I complained I should only get more of these.' Although afraid to complain locally, this Chief declared he would be perfectly willing to accompany me if I would take him before one of the Congo Judges or, above all, down to Boma. I assured him that a statement such as that he had made to me would meet with attention at Boma, and that if he could prove its truth he would get satisfaction for the loss of his canoe.

Statements of a similar character, often supported by many witnesses, were made to me more than once during my journey around the lake, some of them pointing to far greater derelictions of duty. The same Chief told me, on the same occasion, that one of the Government officials of the district (the same man, indeed, who had retained his canoe) had recently given him three wives. The official, he declared, had been 'making war' on a town in the forest I was then in, for failing to bring in its fixed food supply, and as a result of the punitive measures undertaken the town had been destroyed and many prisoners taken. As a result, several women so taken were homeless and were distributed among some of the State-invested Chiefs of the district. 'Wives were being given away that day,' said my informant, 'he gave me three, but the Chief of Bokoti got four.'

The Chief went on to say that one of these 'wives' had since escaped, aided, as he complained, by one of his own townsmen, who was a slave from her own native town.

The population of the lake-side towns would seem to have diminished within the last ten years by 60 or 70 per cent. It was in 1893 that the effort to levy an india-rubber imposition in this district was begun, and for some four or five years this imposition could only be collected at the cost of continual fighting. Finding the task of collecting india-rubber a well nigh impossible one, the authorities abandoned it in this district, and the remaining inhabitants now deliver a weekly supply of food-stuffs for the upkeep of the military camp at Irebu, or the big coffee plantation at Bikoro. Several villages I visited supply also to the latter station a fortnightly tax of gum-copal, which the surrounding forests yield abundantly. Gum-copal is also exposed and washed up on the shores of the lake. The quantity of this commodity supplied by each village on which it is assessed is put at 10 bags per fortnight. Each bag is officially said to contain 25 kilog., so that the imposition would amount to a quarter of a ton weight per fortnight. I found, when trying to lift some of these bags I saw being packed at a native village I was in, that they must weigh considerably more than 25 kilog., so that I concluded that each sack represents that quantity net of gum-copal. There is a considerable loss in cleaning, chipping, and washing crude gum as collected. The quantity brought by each village would thus work out at 6½ tons per annum. When I visited the Government station at Bikoro on the 31st July, the chief of that post, M. Wauters, showed me ten sacks of gum which he said had been just brought in by a very small village in the neighbourhood. For this quarter of a ton of gum-copal he said he had paid the village one piece of blue drill – a rough cotton cloth which is valued locally, after adding the cost of transport, at 11½ fr. a-piece. By the Congo Government 'Bulletin Officiel' of this year (No. 4, April 1903) I found that 339½ tons of gum-copal were exported in 1902, all from the Upper Congo, and that this was valued at 475,490 fr. The value per ton would, therefore, work out at about £56. The fortnightly yield of each village would therefore seem to be worth a maximum of £14 (probably

less), for which a maximum payment of 11½ fr. is made. At one village I visited I found the majority of the inhabitants getting ready
the gum-copal and the supply of fish which they had to take to
Bikoro on the morrow. They were putting it into canoes to paddle
across the lake – some 20 miles – and they left with their loads in
the night from alongside my steamer. These people told me that
they frequently received, instead of cloth, 150 brass rods (7½ fr.) for
the quarter of a ton of gum-copal they took fortnightly.

The value of the annual payment in gum-copal by each town
would seem to be about £360, while at an average of 9 fr. as the remuneration each receives fortnightly, they would appear to receive
some £10 in annual return.

{In the village of Montaka, at the south end of the lake, where I spent
two days, the people seemed, during my stay, to be chiefly engrossed
in the task of chipping and preparing the gum-copal for shipment to
Bikoro, and in getting ready their weekly yield of fish for the same
post. I saw the filling with gum of the ten basket-sacks taking place
under the eyes of the Chief – himself contributed – and a State sentry
who was posted there. Each household in the town was represented
at this final task, and every adult householder of Montaka shared
in the general contribution. Assuming the population of Montaka
at from 600 to 800 – and it cannot now be more although a town of
4,000 souls ten years ago – fully 150 householders are thus directly
affected by the collection and delivery, each fortnight, of this 'impôt
en nature' [tax in kind], and are affected for the great majority of
the days throughout the year. Since [for] the 6½ tons of gum-copal
which the 150 householders of Montaka contribute annually, they are
seen to receive not more than a total payment of £10 in the year – viz.,
26 fortnightly payments of, on an average, say 9 fr. 50c., giving 247 fr.
annually – it follows that the remuneration each adult householder
of Montaka receives for his entire year's work is the one hundred
and fiftieth part of that total – or just 1s. 4d. This is just the value of
an adult fowl in Montaka. I bought ten fowls, or chickens rather,
the morning of my going away, and for the only reasonably sized
one among them I gave 30 rods (1 fr. 50c.), the others, small fledg-

lings, ranging from 15 to 20 rods each (75 cents. to 1 fr.).

The 6½ tons of gum-copal supplied annually by these 150 house-holders being valued at about £364, it follows that each householder had contributed something like £2. 8s. per annum in kind.

The labour involved may or may not be unduly excessive – but it is continuous throughout the year – each man must stay in his town and be prepared each week and fortnight to have his contribution ready under fear of summary punishment.

The natives engaged as workmen on my steamer were paid each a sum of 20 rods (1 fr.) per week for food rations only, and 100 rods (5 fr.) per month wages. One of these native workmen thus earned more in one week of my service – which was that of any other private estab-lishment employing ordinary labour – than the Montaka house-holder got in an entire year for his compulsory public service rendered to the Government.}

At other villages which I visited, I found the tax to consist of bas-kets, which the inhabitants had to make and deliver weekly as well as, always, a certain amount of food-stuffs – either kwanga or fish. These baskets are used at Bikoro in packing up the gum-copal for conveyance down the river and to Europe – the river transport being effected by Government steamers. The basket-makers and other workers complained that they were sometimes remunerated for their labour with reels of sewing cotton and shirt buttons (of which they had no use) when supplies of cloth or brass wire ran short at Bikoro. As these natives go almost entirely naked, I could believe that neither thread or shirt buttons were of much service to them. They also averred that they were frequently flogged for delay or inability to complete the tale of these baskets, or the weekly sup-ply of food. Several men, including a Chief of one town, showed broad weals across their buttocks, which were evidently recent. One, a lad of 15 or so, removing his cloth, showed several scars across his thighs, which he and others around him said had formed part of a weekly payment for a recent shortage in their supply of food. That these statements were not all untrue was confirmed by my visit to Bikoro on the 31st July, when the 'domaine privé' store was shown to me by the Chief of the post. It had very little in it, and M. Wauters confessed that his barter stock of goods had not been replenished for some time. There appeared to be from 200 to 300 pieces of coarse cotton cloth, and nothing else, and as the cloth was visibly old, I estimated the value of the entire stock at possibly £15. It certainly would not have fetched more if put up to auction in any part of the Upper Congo.

{The instructions regulating the remuneration of the native contributors and the mode of exploitation of the 'forêts domaniales' [state-owned forests] were issued in the 'Bulletin Officiel' of 1896, under authority of Decrees dated the 30th October and the 5th December, 1892. These general instructions require that:

> All operations are to be carried out by the agents of the Administration, under the direction of the District Commissaire. Everything connected to operations in the Private Domain should be distinctly separated from any Government services.
>
> The agents responsible for the Private Domain operations shall devote all their energies towards the collection of rubber and other forest products.
>
> Whatever mode of operation used to this effect, they must remunerate the natives in a manner consistent with the cost of the necessary labour needed to collect the raw-material; this rate of pay shall be fixed by the District Commissioner, who will submit such a tariff for the Governor-General's approval.
>
> The State Inspector of the area shall verify if this tariff is linked to the price of the labour; he shall oversee its strict application, and he shall ascertain whether the general operational conditions give cause for any justified complaint.
>
> The agents entrusted with this task must understand that, by justly rewarding the natives, they are using the only efficient method to assure good administration in the domain and to implant in the native the taste and habit of work.

Both from the condition of the Domaine Privé Store I inspected at Bikoro and the obvious poverty and universal discontent of the native contributors, whose towns I visited during the seventeen days spent in Lake Mantumba, it was clear that these instructions had long since ceased to be operative. The responsibility for the non-application of such necessary regulations could not be attributed to the local officials, who, obviously, if left without the means of adequate remuneration could not themselves make good the oversights or omissions of their superiors. That these omissions form part of a systematic breach of instructions conceived in the interest of the native I do not assert, but it was most apparent that neither in Lake Mantumba nor the other portions of the Domaine Privé which I visited was any adequate provision made for inculcating the natives with any just appreciation of the value of work.

The station at Bikoro has been established as a Government plantation for about ten years. It stands on the actual site of the former native town of Bikoro, an important Settlement in 1893, now reduced to a handful of ill-kept, untidy huts, inhabited by only a remnant of its former expropriated population.

Another small village, Bomenga, stands on the other side of the Government houses, the plantation enveloping both villages, and occupying their old cassava fields and gardens, which are now planted with coffee trees. Further inland these give place to cocoa and india-rubber trees (fantumia elastica), and also to the indigenous Landolphia creeper, which is being extensively cultivated. The entire plantation covers 800 hectares. There are 70 kilom. of well-cleared pathway through it, one of these roads measuring 11 kilom. in almost a straight line; 400 workmen are employed, consisting in small part of local natives, but chiefly of men brought from a distance. One numerous group I saw I was informed were 'prisoners' from the Ruki district. There are 140,000 coffee trees and 170,000 cocoa trees actually in the ground, the latter a later planting than the coffee. Last year the yield was: coffee 112 tons, and cocoa 7 tons, all of which, after cleaning and preparing at the Government depôt at Kinchasa, was shipped to Europe on the Government account. India-rubber planting was not begun until November 1901. There are now 248 hectares already under cultivation, having 700,000 young Landolphia creepers, and elsewhere on the plantation, on portions mainly given up to coffee growing, there are 50,000 fantumia elastica and 50,000 manihot glaziovii trees. The station buildings are composed entirely of native materials, and are erected entirely by local native labour. The Chief of the Post has very ably directed the work of this plantation, which engrosses all his time, and until quite recently he had no assistant. A subordinate official is now placed under his orders. When he took over the district he told me there were sixty-eight native soldiers attached to the post, which number he has now been able to reduce to nineteen. In the days when the india-rubber tax prevailed in Lake Mantumba there were several hundreds of soldiers required in that region. No rubber is now worked in the neighbourhood I am informed.

Despite the 70 kilom. of roadway through the plantation, much of which has to be frequently – indeed daily – traversed, the two Europeans have no means of locomotion provided them, and must make their daily inspection to various points of this large plantation on foot.

In addition to the control of this flourishing establishment, the Chief of the Post is the Executive Chief of the entire district, but it is evident that but little time or energy could be left to the most energetic official for duties outside the immediate scope of his work as a coffee and india-rubber grower, in addition to those 'engrossing cares' the general instructions cited above impose upon the agents who exploit the State domain.}

. . . A careful investigation of the conditions of native life around the lake confirmed the truth of the statements made to me both by M. Wauters, the local American missionary, and many natives, that the great decrease in population, the dirty and ill-kept towns, and the complete absence of goats, sheep, or fowls – once very plentiful in this country – were to be attributed above all else to the continued effort made during many years to compel the natives to work india-rubber. Large bodies of native troops had formerly been quartered in the district, and the punitive measures undertaken to this end had endured for a considerable period. During the course of these operations there had been much loss of life, accompanied, I fear, by a somewhat general mutilation of the dead, as proof that the soldiers had done their duty. Each village I visited around the lake, save that of Ikoko, where a Mission station had existed throughout these troublous times, and one other, had been abandoned by its inhabitants. To some of these villages the people have only just returned; to others they are only now returning. In one I found the bare and burnt poles of what had been dwellings left standing, and at another – that of Mwebi – the people had fled at the approach of my steamer, and despite the loud cries of many native guides on board that our steamer belonged to a Mission, nothing could induce them to return, and it was impossible to hold any intercourse with them. At the three succeeding villages I visited beyond Mwebi, in traversing the lake towards the south, the inhabitants all fled at the approach of the steamer, and it was only when they found that the vessel belonged to a missionary society and had Mission men on board that they could be induced to return.

At one of these villages, Montaka, at the extreme south end of the lake, after confidence had been restored and the fugitives had been induced to come in from the surrounding forest, where they had hidden themselves, I saw women coming back carrying their babies, their household utensils, and even the food they had hastily snatched up, up to a late hour of the evening. Meeting some of these returning women in one of the fields I asked them why they had run away at my approach, and they said, smiling: 'We thought you were Bula Matadi' (*i.e.*, 'Men of the Government'). Fear of this kind was formerly unknown on the Upper Congo; and in much more out-of-the-way places visited many years ago the people flocked from all sides to greet a white stranger. But to-day the apparition of a white man's steamer evidently gave the signal for instant flight.

M. Wauters, the chief of the Bikoro post, told me that a similar alarm reigned almost everywhere in the country behind his station, and that when he went on the most peaceful missions only a few miles from his house the villages were generally emptied of all human beings when he entered them, and it was impossible in the majority of cases to get into touch with the people in their own homes. It was not so in all cases, he said, and he instanced certain villages where he could go certain of a friendly reception, but with the majority, he said, he had found it quite impossible to ever find them 'at home'. He gave, as an explanation, when I asked for the reason of this fear of the white man, that as these people were great savages, and knew themselves how many crimes they had committed, they doubtless feared that the white man of the Government was coming to punish their misconduct. He added that they had undoubtedly had 'an awful past' at the hands of some of the officials who had preceded him in the local administration and that it would take time for confidence to be restored. Men, he said, still came to him whose hands had been cut off by the Government soldiers during those evil days, and he said there were still many victims of this species of mutilation in the surrounding country. Two cases of the kind came to my actual notice while I was in the lake. One, a young man, both of whose hands had been beaten off with the butt ends of rifles against a tree, the other a young lad of 11 or 12 years of age, whose right hand was cut off at the wrist. This boy described the circumstances of his mutilation and, in answer to my enquiry, said that although wounded at the time he was perfectly sensible of the severing of his wrist, but lay still fearing that if he moved he would be killed. In both these cases the Government soldiers had been accompanied by white officers whose names were given to me. Six natives (one a girl, three little boys, one youth and one old woman) who had been mutilated in this way during the rubber regime, had been cared for and kept by the local American Mission, but all except one were dead on the date of my visit. The old woman had died at the beginning of this year and her niece described to me how the act of mutilation in her case had been accomplished. The day I left Lake Mantumba five men whose hands had been cut off came to the village of Nyange across the lake to see me, but hearing I had already gone away they returned to their homes. A messenger came in to tell me, and I sent to Nyange to find them, but they had then dispersed. Three of them subsequently returned, but too late for me to see them. These were some of those, I presume, to whom M. Wauters had referred, for they came from the country in the vicinity of Bikoro station. Statements of this character, made both by the two mutilated persons I saw and by others who had witnessed this form of mutilation in the past, are appended (Inclosure 4).

The taxes levied on the people of the district being returnable each week or fortnight, it follows that they cannot leave their homes. At some of the villages I visited near the end of Lake Mantumba the fish supplies have to be delivered weekly to the military camp at Irebu, or when the water is high in the lake and fish harder to catch, every ten days. The distance from Irebu of one of these towns could not have been less than 45 miles. To go and come between their homes and the camp involved to the people of this town 90 miles of canoe paddling, and with the lake stormy and its waters rough – as is often the case – the double journey would take at least four days. This consumption of time must be added to that spent in the catching of the fish, and as the punishment for any falling off in quantity or delay in delivery is not a light one, the Chief responsible for the tax stoutly opposes any one quitting the town. Some proof of this incidentally arose during my stay, and threatened to delay my journey. Being short-handed I sought, when at Ikoko, to engage six or seven young men of the town as woodcutters to travel on board the steamer. I proposed to engage them for two or three months, and offered good wages, much more than by any local service they could hope to earn. More men offered than I needed, and I selected six. The State Chief of the village hearing of this at once came to me to protest against any of his people leaving the town, and said that he would have all the youths I had engaged tied up and sent over to the Government official at Bikoro. There were at the time three soldiers armed with Albini rifles quartered at Ikoko, and the Chief sent for them to arrest my would-be crew. The Chief's argument, too, was perfectly logical. He said, 'I am responsible each week for 600 rations of fish which must be delivered at Bikoro. If it fails I am held responsible and will be punished. I have been flogged more than once for a failure in the fish supply, and will not run any risks. If these men go I shall be short-handed, therefore they must stay to help in getting the weekly tax.' I was forced to admit the justice of this argument, and we finally arrived at a compromise. I promised the Chief that, in addition to paying wages to the men I took, a sum representing the value to him of their labour should be left at Ikoko, so that he might hire extra hands to get the full quantity of fish required of him. The Chief of the local State post admitted that he had been forced to flog men from villages which failed in their weekly supplies, but that he had for some months discontinued this course. He said that now he put defaulters into prison instead. If a village which was held to supply, say, 200 rations of fish each week brought only 180 rations, he accepted no excuse, but put two men in 'block'. If thirty rations were wanting he detained three of the men, and so on – a man for each ten rations. These people would remain prisoners, and would have to work at Bikoro, or possibly would be sent to Coquilhatville, the administrative head-quarters of the Equator district, until the full imposition came in.

I subsequently found when in the neighbourhood of Coquilhatville that summary arrest and imprisonment of this kind for failure to complete the tale of local imposition is of constant occurrence. The men thus arrested are kept often in the 'chain gang', along with other prisoners, and are put to the usual class of penitential work. They are not brought before or tried by any Court or sentenced to any fixed term of imprisonment, but are merely detained until some sort of satisfaction is obtained, and while under detention are kept at hard work.

Indeed, I could not find that a failure to meet the weekly tax is punishable by law and no law was cited to me as a warrant for this summary imprisonment, but if such a law exists it is to be presumed that it does not treat the weekly taxpayers' failure as a grave criminal offence. The men taken are frequently not those in fault, the requisitioning authority cannot discriminate. He is forced to insure compliance with the demands imposed on each village, and the first men to hand from the offending community of necessity have to pay in the chain-gang the general failure and possibly the individual fault of others. Men taken in this way are sometimes not seen again in their own homes. They are either taken to distant Government stations as workmen, or are drafted as soldiers into the Force Publique. The names of many men thus taken from the Mantumba district were given to me, and in some cases their relatives had heard of their death in distant parts of the country. This practice was, I believe, more general in the past, but that it still exists to-day, and on an extensive scale, I had several instances of observing in widely separated districts. The officials effecting these arrests do not seem to have any other course open to them, unless it be a resort to punitive measures or to individual corporal punishment; while the natives assert that, as the taxes are unequally distributed, and their own numbers constantly decreasing, the strain upon them each week often becomes unbearable, and some of their number will shirk the constantly recurring unwelcome task. Should this shirking become general instead of being confined to individuals, punitive measures are undertaken against the refractory community. Where these do not end in fighting, loss of life and destruction of native property, they entail very heavy fines which are levied on the defaulting village. An expedition of the minor kind occurred some five months before my presence in Lake Mantumba. The village in fault was that of Mwebi, the one where when I sought to visit it no people would remain to face me. This village was said to have been some three weeks in arrears with the fish it was required to supply to the camp at Irebu. An armed force occupied it, commanded by an officer, and captured ten men and eight canoes. These canoes and the prisoners were conveyed by water to Irebu, the main force marching back by land.

My informant, who dwelt in a village near Mwebi, which I was then visiting, said he saw the prisoners being taken back to Irebu under guard of six black soldiers, tied up with native rope so tightly that they were calling aloud with pain. The force halted the night in his town. These people were detained at Irebu for ten days until the people of Mwebi had brought in a supply of fish and had paid a fine. Upon their release two of these men died, one close to Irebu and the other within sight of the village I was in, and two more, my informant added, died soon after their return to Mwebi. The Chief, who saw them, said the prisoners were ill and bore the marks on wrists and legs of the thongs used in tying them. Of the canoes captured only the old ones were returned to Mwebi, the better ones being confiscated.

The native relating this incident added that he thought it stupid of the white men to take both men and canoes away from a small place like Mwebi as a punishment for a shortage in its fish supply.

'The men were wanted to catch fish and so were the canoes,' he said, 'and to take both away only made it harder for the people of Mwebi to perform their task.' I went to Mwebi in the hope of being able to verify the truth of this and other statements made to me as to the hardships recently inflicted on its people by reason of their dis-obedience, but owing to their timidity, to whatever cause this might have been due, it was impossible for me to get into touch with any of them. That a very close watch is kept on the people of the district and their movements is undoubted. In the past they escaped in large numbers to the French territory, but many were prevented by force from doing this.

To-day the Congolese authorities discourage intercourse of this kind, not by the same severe measures as formerly, but probably none the less effectively. By a letter dated the 2nd July, 1902, the present Commandant of the camp of Irebu wrote as follows to the Rev. E. V. Sjöblom, a Swedish Missionary (since dead), who was then in charge of the Mission at Ikoko:

> I should be very much obliged if you would stop your young people landing on the French side (of the river) and having commerce with the native French who have fled from our bank, selling them food-stuffs produced by the work of our natives who have not fled and who do not evade the work which we have imposed on them.

Return to Stanley Pool

I decided, owing to pressure of other duties, to return from Coquil-hatville to Stanley Pool. The last incident of my stay in the Upper Congo occurred the night prior to my departure. Late that night one of the native scholars of the Catholic Mission at Coquilhatville came with some natives of the Bangala district, represented as his friends, who were fleeing from their homes, and whom he begged me to carry with me to the French territory at Lukolela. These were the Chief Manjunda of Monsembi and seven of his people. The Chief stated that, owing to his inability to meet the impositions of the Commissaire of the Bangala district, he had, with his family, abandoned his home and was trying to reach Lukolela. He had already come 80 miles downstream by canoe, but was now hiding with friends in one of the towns near Coquilhatville. Part of the imposition laid upon his town consisted of two goats which had to be supplied each month for the white man's table at Bangala.

As all the goats in the neighbourhood had long since disappeared in meeting these demands, he could now only satisfy this imposition by buying in inland districts such goats as were for sale. For these he had to pay 3,000 rods each (150 fr.), and as the Government's remuneration amounted to only 100 rods (5 fr.) per goat, he had no further means of maintaining the supply. Having appealed in vain for the remission of this burden, no other course was left him but to fly. I told this man I regretted I could not help him, that his proper course was to appeal for relief to the authorities of the district; and this failing, to seek the higher authorities at Boma. This, he said, was clearly impossible for him to do. On the last occasion when he had sought the officials at Bangala he had been told that if his next tax were not forthcoming he should go into the 'chain gang'. He added that a neighbouring Chief who had failed in this respect had just died in the prison gang, and that such would be his fate if he were caught. He added that, if I disbelieved him, the Protestant missionary at Monsembi – of whose church he was a member – could vouch for his character and the truth of his statement; and I told him and his Catholic friend that I should inquire in that quarter, but that it was impossible for me to assist a fugitive. I added, however, that there was no law on the Congo Statute Book which forbade him or any other man from travelling freely to any part of the country, and his right to navigate in his own canoe the Upper Congo was as good as mine in my steamer or anyone else's. He and his people left me at midnight, saying that unless they could get away with me they did not think it possible they could succeed in gaining Lukolela.

The resident missionary at Monsembi, the Rev. John H. Weeks, to whom I referred this statement informed me by letter, dated the 7th October, that Manjunda's statement was true. He said: 'What Manjunda told you, *re*. price of goats, was perfectly true. At

Bolombo they are 3,000; and here they are 2,500 to 3,000 rods. We have not bought a goat here for more than eight years. Ducks are from 200 to 300 rods, and these we never buy. Fowls are from 60 to 100 rods, and these we should not be able to buy, only we can get them cheap for articles of barter goods, such as mugs, &c. *Re.* "dying in the chains", he had every reason to fear this for recently two Chiefs died in the chain; viz., the Chief of a little town above Bolombo; his crime: because he did not move his houses a few hundred yards to join them to Lobolu as quickly as the Commissaire thought he should do; secondly, the Chief of this town of Monsembi; his crime: because he did not go up every fortnight with the tax. These two men were chained together and made to carry heavy loads of bricks and water, and were frequently beaten by the soldiers in charge of them. There are witnesses to prove this.'

Leaving the township of Coquilhatville on the 11th September I reached Stanley Pool on the 15th September.

I have &c.

(Signed) R. Casement

INCLOSURES TO THE CONGO REPORT

1 Notes on Refugee Tribes from District of Lake Léopold II
   Mr Casement Encountered Near Bolobo in July 1903

Hearing of the Basengele refugees from Lake Léopold II, I decided to visit the nearest Settlement of these fugitives, some 20 miles away, to see them for myself.

July 20. – Left Bolobo on the 12th for Bodzandongo, where we picked up Mr Scrivener, and arrived Bongendi 4.35. Stopped night alongside bank.

July 21. – Left Bongendi 8 a.m. on foot, going about 3 miles an hour. Arrived Mpoko at 12.15. Crossed five streams and swamps, which delayed us; calculated distance about 10 miles from the

Congo. Passed several Batende villages removed from path we traversed. People going to market, near but very timid and kept always
at a distance.

At Mpoko found large town of Batende, and scattered through it
many small settlements of Basengele refugees. The town of Mpoko
consists approximately of seventy-one Batende houses and seventy-
three occupied by Basengele. These latter seemed industrious, simple folk, many weaving the Mpusu palm fibre into mats or native
cloth; others had smithies, working brass wire into bracelets, chains,
and anklets; some iron workers making knives. Sitting down in one
of these blacksmith's sheds, the five men at work ceased and came
over to talk to us. I counted ten women, six grown-up men, and
eight lads and women in this one shed of Basengeles. I then asked
them through Scrivener and Lusala – the native interpreter – to tell
me why they had left their homes. Three of the men sat down in
front of me, and told a tale which I cannot think can be true, but it
seemed to come straight from their hearts. It was translated to me
almost word for word by Scrivener and Lusala, and I repeatedly asked
certain parts to be gone over again while I wrote in my note book.
The fact of my writing down and asking for names, &c., seemed to
impress them, and they spoke with what certainly impressed me as
being great sincerity.

I asked, first, why they had left their homes around Lake Léopold II,
and to come to live in a strange far-off country among the Batende,
where they owned nothing, and were little better than servitors?
All, when this question was put, women as well, shouted out, 'On
account of the rubber tax levied by the Government posts around
the Lake and along the Mfini.'

I asked particularly the names of the places whence they had
come. They answered they were from Bangongo. Other Basengele
refugees here at Mpoko were Bakutu, others again were Bateto, but
all had fled from their homes for the same reason – it was the 'rubber
tax'.

I asked then how this tax was imposed. The chief of them, who
had been hammering out an iron neck collar on my arrival, spoke
first. He said:

'I am Moyo. These other two beside me are Wankaki and Nkwa-bali, all of us Bandongo [*sic*]. From our country each village had to take twenty loads of rubber. These loads were big: they were as big as this . . .' (Producing an empty basket which came nearly up to the handle of my walking-stick.) 'That was the first size. We had to fill that up, but as rubber got scarcer the white man reduced the amount. We had to take these loads in four times a-month.'

Q. 'How much pay did you get for this?'

A. (Entire audience). 'We got no pay! We got nothing!'

And then Moyo, whom I asked, again said:

'Our village got cloth and a little salt, but not the people who did the work. Our Chiefs eat up the cloth, the workers get nothing. The pay was a fathom of cloth and a little salt for every big basket full, but it was given to the Chief, never to the men. It used to take ten days to get the twenty baskets of rubber – we were always in the forest and then when we were late we were killed. We had to go further and further into the forest to find the rubber vines, to go without food, and our women had to give up cultivating the fields and gardens. Then we starved. Wild beasts – the leopards – killed some of us when we were working away in the forest, and others got lost or died from exposure and starvation, and we begged the white man to leave us alone, saying we could get no more rubber, but the white men and their soldiers said: "Go! You are only beasts yourselves, you are nyama (meat)." We tried, always going further into the forest, and when we failed and our rubber was short, the soldiers came to our towns and killed us. Many were shot, some had their ears cut off; others were tied up with ropes around their necks and bodies and taken away. The white men sometimes at the posts did not know of the bad things the soldiers did to us, but it was the white men who sent the soldiers to punish us for not bringing in enough rubber.'

Here Nkwabali took up the tale from Moyo:

'We said to the white men, "We are not enough people now to do what you want us. Our country has not many people in it and we are dying fast. We are killed by the work you make us do, by the stoppage of our plantations and the breaking up of our homes." The white man looked at us and said: "There are lots of people in Mputu" (Europe, the white man's country). "If there are lots of people in the white man's country there must be many people in the black man's country." The white man who said this was the chief white man at Ibale, his name was Kwango, he was a very bad man. Other white men of Bula Matadi who had been bad and wicked were Mfuami Bonginda, Malu Malu (Quick! Quick!), Mpampi. These had killed us often, and killed us by their own hands as well as by their soldiers. Some white men were good. These were Nkango, Bako Mobili, Nyambi, Nyeli, and Fuashi.'

These ones told them to stay in their homes and did not hunt and chase them as the others had done, but after what they had suffered they did not trust more any one's word, and they had fled from their country and were now going to stay here, far from their homes, in this country where there was no rubber.

Q. 'How long is it since you left your homes, since the big trouble you speak of?'

A. 'It lasted for three full seasons, and it is now four seasons since we fled and came into the Batende country.'

Q. 'How many days is it from Mpoko to your own country?'

A. 'Six days of quick marching. We fled because we could not endure the things done to us. Our Chiefs were hanged, and we were killed and starved and worked beyond endurance to get rubber.'

Q. 'How do you know it was the white men themselves who ordered these cruel things to be done to you? These things must have been done without the white man's knowledge by the black soldiers.'

A. (Nkwabali): 'The white men told their soldiers: "You kill only women; you cannot kill men. You must prove that you kill men." So then the soldiers when they killed us' (here he stopped and hesitated, and then pointing to the private parts of my bulldog – it was lying asleep at my feet), he said: 'then they cut off those things and took them to the white men, who said: "It is true, you have killed men." '

Consul: 'You mean to tell me that any white man ordered your bodies to be mutilated like that, and those parts of you carried to him?'

Nkwabali, Wankaki, and all (shouting): 'Yes! many white men. Malu Malu did it.'

Consul: 'You say this is true? Were many of you so treated after being shot?'

All (shouting out): 'Nkoto! Nkoto!' (Very many! Very many!)

There was no doubt that these people were not inventing. Their vehemence, their flashing eyes, their excitement, was not simulated. Doubtless they exaggerated the numbers, but they were clearly telling what they knew and loathed. Scrivener, beside me, said that these stories had been told to him before when he had first found these Basengele refugees ten months previously in the back country behind Bolobo. They often became so furious at the recollection of what had been done to them that they lost control over themselves, and he had ceased to question them. One of the men before me (Wankaki) was getting into this state now.

I asked whether Basengele tribes were still running from their country, or whether they now stayed at home and worked voluntarily.

Moyo answered: 'They cannot run away now – not easily; there are sentries in the country there between the Lake and this; besides, there are few people left.'

Nkwabali said: 'We heard that letters came to the white men on the Lake to say that the people were to be well treated. We heard that these letters had been sent by the big white men in "Mputu" (Europe); but our white men tore up these letters, laughing, saying: "We are the 'basango' and 'banyanga' (fathers and mothers, *i.e.* elders). Those who write to us are only 'bana' (children)." Since we left our homes the white men now around the Lake have asked us to go home again. We have heard that they want us to go back, but we will not go. We are not warriors, and do not want to fight. We only want to live in peace with our wives and children, and so we stay here among the Batende, who are kind to us, and will not return to our homes.'

Q. 'Would you not like to go back to your homes? Would you not, in your hearts, all wish to return?'

A. (By many.) 'We loved our country, but we will not trust ourselves to go back.'

Nkwabali: 'Go, you white men, with the steamer to Lake Léopold and see what we have told you is true. Perhaps if other white men, who do not hate us, go there, Bula Matadi may stop from hating us, and we may be able to go home again.'

I asked to be pointed out any refugees from other tribes, if there were such, and they brought forward a lad who was a Bateto, and a man of the Baboma, on the Kasai, or Mfini. These two, answering me, said there were many with them from their tribes who had fled from their country.

Went on about fifteen minutes to another Basengele group of houses in the midst of the Batende town. Found here mostly Bakuti, the old Chief sitting in the open village Council-house with a Baboma man and two lads. An old woman soon came and joined, and another man. The woman began talking with much earnestness. She said the Government had worked them so hard they had had no time to attend their fields and gardens, and they had starved to death. Her children had died; her sons had been killed. The two men, as she spoke, muttered murmurs of assent.

The old Chief said: 'We used to hunt elephants long ago, there were plenty in our forests, and we got much meat; but Bula Matadi killed the elephant hunters because they could not get rubber, and so we starved. We were sent out to get rubber, and when we came back with little rubber we were shot.'

Q. 'Who shot you?'

A. 'The white men, Malu Malu, Mpampi, Fuami, sent their soldiers out to kill us.'

Q. 'How do you know it was the white man who sent the soldiers? It might be only these savage soldiers themselves.'

A. 'No, no. Sometimes we brought rubber into the white man's stations. We took rubber to Malu Malu's station, Mbongo, and to Ibali and to Fuami's station. When it was not enough rubber the white man would put some of us in lines, one behind another, and would shoot through all our bodies. Sometimes he would shoot us like that with his own hand; sometimes his soldiers would do it.'

Q. 'You mean to say you were killed in the Government posts

themselves by the Government white men themselves, or under their eyes?'

A. (Emphatically.) 'We were killed in the stations of the white men themselves. We were killed by the white man himself. We were shot before his eyes.'

The names Malu Malu, Fuami, and Mpampi were names I heard repeatedly uttered.

The Baboma man, Nciele, said he, too, had fled; now he lived at peace with the Batende.

The abnormal refugee population in this one Batende town must equal the actual Batende population itself. On every hand one finds these refugees. They seem, too, to pass busier lives than their Batende hosts, for during all the hot hours of the afternoon, wherever I walked through the town – and I went all through Mpoko until the sun set – I found Basengele weavers, or iron and brass workers, at work.

Slept at Lusala's house. Many people coming to talk to us after dark.

July 22. – Left Mpoko about 8 to return to the Congo bank. On the way back left the main path and struck into one of the side towns, a village called Makesi. This lies only some 4 or 5 miles from the river. Found here thirty-two Basengele houses with forty-three Batende, so that the influx of fugitives here is almost equal to the original population. Saw many Basengele. All were frightened, and they and the Batende were evidently so ill at ease that I did not care to pause. Spoke to one or two men only as we walked through the town. The Basengele drew away from us, but on looking back saw many heads popped out of doors of the houses we had passed.

Got back to steamer about noon.

At Lukolela, July 26. – Heard that Basengele came sometimes to Lukolela from Lake Léopold II District. I am now 100 miles (about) up-river from Mpoko. Went into one of the Lukolela country farm towns called Bwonzola. Found on entering plantation two huts with five men and one woman who I at once recognized by their head-dress as Basengele, like those at Mpoko. Spoke to them through

Whitehead and the interpreter. The chief speaker, a young man named Bakotembesi, who lives at Bwonzola. He seems about 22 or 23, and speaks with an air of frankness. He says: 'The Basengele here and others who come to Lukolela, come from a place near Lake Léopold II, called Mbelo. It is connected with the lake by a stream. His own town in the district of Mbelo is Mpenge. Mbele is a big district and had many people. They now bring the Government india-rubber, kwanga, and fowls, and work on broad paths connecting each village. His own village has to take 300 baskets of india-rubber. They get one piece of cotton cloth, called locally a sanza, and no more.' (Note. – This cannot be true. He is doubtless exaggerating.) Four other men with him were wearing the rough palm-fibre cloth of the country looms, and they pointed to this as proof that they got no cloth for their labours. Bakotambesi continuing said: 'We were then killed for not bringing in enough rubber.'

Q. 'You say you were killed for not bringing in rubber. Were you ever mutilated as proof that the soldiers had killed you?'

A. 'When we were killed the white man was there himself. No proof was needed. Men and women were put in a line with a palm tree and were shot.'

Here he took three of the four men sitting down and put them one in line behind the other, and said: 'The white men used to put us like that and shoot all with one cartridge. That was often done, and worse things.'

Q. 'But how, if you now have to work so hard, are you yourselves able to come here to Lukolela to see your friends?'

A. 'We came away without the sentries or soldiers knowing, but when we get home we may have trouble.'

Q. 'Do you know the Basengele who are now at Mpoko, near Bolobo?' (Here I gave the names of Moyo, Wankaki, and Nkwa-bali.)

A. 'Yes; many Basengele fled to that country. Moyo we know ran away on account of the things done to them by the Government white men. The Batende and Basengele have always been friends. That is why the Basengele fled to them for refuge.'

Q. 'Are there sentries or soldiers in your villages now?'

A. 'In the chief villages there are always four soldiers with rifles. When natives go out into the forest to collect rubber they would leave one of their number behind to stay and protect the women. Sometimes the soldiers finding him thus refused to believe what he said, and killed him for shirking his work. This often happens.'

Asked how far it was from Lukolela to their country they say three days' journey, and then about two days more on to Lake Léopold by water, or three if by land. They begged us to go to their country, they said: 'We will show you the road, we will take you there, and you will see how things are, and that our country has been spoiled, and we are speaking the truth.'

Left them here and returned to the river bank.

The foregoing entries made at this time in my note-book seemed to me, if not false, greatly exaggerated, although the statements were made with every air of conviction and sincerity. I did not again meet with any more Basengele refugees, for on my return to Bolobo, on the 12th September, I stayed only a few hours. I was there told, however, that since I had been to Mpoko in July, Mr Scrivener, who then accompanied me, had set out with the intention of reaching Lake Léopold II by land, a journey which would apparently carry him through the very country of the people I had seen and questioned at Mpoko. Mr Scrivener had then been nearly seven weeks absent from Bolobo, but was expected shortly to return. A few days afterwards, while I was at Stanley Pool, I received from him an account of this journey, written from Bolobo on his return on the 22nd September. His letter to me contains the following:

Bolobo, September 22, 1903.

I was sorry not to see you as you passed down, and so missed the opportunity of conveying to you personally a lot of evidence as to the terrible maladministration practised in the past in the lake district. I was for three weeks in the district, and was for three days the guest of an official at the post of Mbongo, or, as he put it 'Bongo'. He is the successor of the infamous wretch Malu Malu, of whom you heard so much yourself from the refugees at Mpoko. This Malu

Malu (his name is Massard) was in this district in 1898, 1899, and 1900, and he it was that depopulated the country.*

His successor, Auguste Dooms, is very vehement in his denunciations of him, and declares that he will leave nothing undone that he can do to bring him to justice.

He is now stationed at Umanghi, near our station at Bopoto.[†]

Of Dooms I have nothing to say but praise. In a very difficult position he has done wonderfully. The people are beginning to show themselves and gathering about the many posts under his charge. Dooms told me that when he took over the station at Bongo from Massard he visited the prison, and almost fainted, so horrible was the condition of the place and the poor wretches in it. He told me of many things he had heard of from the soldiers, of Massard shooting with his own hand man after man who had come with an insufficient quantity of rubber. Of his putting several one behind the other and shooting them all with one cartridge. My teachers, who accompanied me, also heard from the soldiers many frightful stories and abundant confirmation of what was told us at Mpoko about the taking to Massard of the organs of the men slain by the sentries of the various posts. I saw a letter from the present Commandant of Ibali to Dooms, in which he upbraids him for not using more vigorous means, telling him to talk less and shoot more, and reprimanding him for not killing more than one in a district under his care where there was a little trouble. Dooms is due in Belgium in about three months, and says he will land one day and begin denouncing his predecessor the next. I received many favours from him, and should be sorry to injure him in any way . . . He has already accepted a position in one of the Kasai Companies, being unable to continue longer in the service of the State. I have never seen in all the different parts of the State which I have visited a neater station, or a district more under control than that over which this Dooms presides. He is the Bafe the people of Mpoko told us of, whom they said was kind.

If I can give you any more information, or if there are any

* He would seem to have been only one. – R.C.
[†] I was informed at Matadi that this man had just returned to Europe. – R.C.

questions you would like to put to me, I shall be glad to serve you, and through you these persecuted people.

From a separate communication, dealing with his journey to the lake, which Mr Scrivener transmitted at the same time, I extract the following paragraphs:

. . . About seven weeks ago, when a fortnight out on an itineration, I heard of some half-dozen Basengele who were anxious to visit their old home, and would be willing to go with me; so, after procuring some necessary articles in the shape of provisions and barter, I started from our post at Mpoko. It was the end of the dry season, and many of the watercourses were quite dry, and during some days we even found the lack of water somewhat trying. The first two days' travelling was through alternating forest and grass plain, our guides, as far as possible, avoiding the villages . . . Getting fresh guides from a little village, we got into a region almost entirely forested, and later descended into a gloomy valley still dripping from the rain. According to our guides we should soon be through this, but it was not until the afternoon of the second day after entering that we once more emerged from the gloom. Several times we lost the track, and I had little inclination to blame the guides, for several times the under-growth and a species of thorn palm were trodden down in all directions by the elephants. It would seem to be a favourite hunting ground of theirs, and once we got very close to a large herd who went off at a furious pace, smashing down the small trees, trumpeting, and making altogether a most terrifying noise. The second night in this forest we came across, when looking for the track, a little village of runaways from the rubber district. When assured of our friendliness they took us in and gave us what shelter they could. During the night another tornado swept the country and blew down a rotten tree, some branches of which fell in amongst my tent and the little huts in which some of the boys were sleeping. It was another most narrow escape.

Early the next day we were conducted by one of the men of this village to the right road, and very soon found ourselves travelling along a track which had evidently been, at only a recent date, opened up by a number of natives. 'What was it?' 'Oh! It is the road along which we used to carry rubber to the white men.' 'But why used to?' 'Oh, all the people have either run away, or have been killed or died of starvation, and so there is no one to get rubber any longer.'

That day we made a very long march, being nearly nine and a half hours walking, and passing through several other large depopulated districts. On all sides were signs of a very recent large population, but all was as quiet as death, and buffaloes roamed at will amongst the still growing manioc and bananas. It was a sad day, and when, as the sun was setting, we came upon a large State post we were plunged into still greater grief. True, there was a comfortable house at our service, and houses for all the party; but we had not been long there before we found that we reached the centre of what was once a very thickly populated region, known as Mbelo, from which many refugees in the neighbourhood of Bolobo had come. It was here a white man, known by the name of Malu Malu, lived . . . He came to the district, and, after seven months of diabolical work, left it a waste. Some of the stories current about him are not fit to record here, but the native evidence is so consistent and so universal that it is difficult to disbelieve that murder and rapine on a large scale were carried on here. His successor, a man of a different nature, and much liked by the people, after more than two and a half years has suc- ceeded in winning back to the side of the State post a few natives, and there I saw them in their wretched little huts, hardly able to call their lives their own in the presence of the new white man (myself), whose coming among them had set them all a-wondering. We spent the Sunday there, and once more clean and dry, made an early start on Monday morning. From this on to the Lake there was no fear of losing the track. For many miles it was a broad road, from 6 to 10 feet in width, and wherever there was a possibility of water settling logs were laid down. Some of these viaducts were miles in length, and must have entailed immense labour; whilst rejoicing in the great facility with which we could continue our journey, we could not help picturing the many cruel scenes which, in all probability, were a constant accompaniment to the laying of these huge logs. I wish to emphasize as much as possible the desolation and emptiness of the country we passed through. That it was only very recently a well-populated country, and, as things go out here, rather more densely than usual, was very evident. After a few hours we came to a State rubber post. In nearly every instance these posts are most imposing, some of them giving rise to the supposition that several white men were residing in them. But in only one did we find a white man – the successor of the famous (or infamous) Malu Malu. At one place I saw lying about in the grass surrounding the post, which is built on the site of several very large towns, human bones, skulls, and, in some places, complete skeletons. On inquiring the reason for this unusual sight: 'Oh!' said my informant, 'When the bambote (soldiers) were sent to make us cut rubber there were so many killed we got tired of burying, and sometimes when we wanted to bury we were not allowed to.'

'But why did they kill you so?'

'Oh! Sometimes we were ordered to go, and the sentry would find us preparing food to eat while in the forest, and he would shoot two or three to hurry us along. Sometimes we would try and do a little work on our plantations, so that when the harvest time came we should have something to eat, and the sentry would shoot some of us to teach us that our business was not to plant but to get rubber. Sometimes we were driven off to live for a fortnight in the forest without any food and without anything to make a fire with, and many died of cold and hunger. Sometimes the quantity brought was not sufficient, and then several would be killed to frighten us to bring more. Some tried to run away, and died of hunger and privation in the forest in trying to avoid the State posts.'

'But,' said I, 'if the sentries killed you like that, what was the use? You could not bring more rubber when there were fewer people.'

'Oh! As to that, we do not understand it. These are the facts.'

And looking around on the scene of desolation, on the untended farms and neglected palms, one could not but believe that in the main the story was true. From State sentries came confirmation and particulars even more horrifying, and the evidence of a white man as to the state of the country – the unspeakable condition of the prisons at State posts – all combined to convince me over and over again that, during the last seven years, this 'domaine privé' [private domain] of King Léopold has been a veritable 'hell on earth'.

The present régime seems to be more tolerable. A small payment is made for the rubber now brought in. A little salt – say a penny-worth – for 2 kilogrammes of rubber, worth in Europe from 6 to 8 fr. The collection is still compulsory, but, compared with what has gone before, the natives consider themselves fairly treated. There is a com-ing together of families and communities and the re-establishment of villages; but oh! in what sadly diminished numbers, and with what terrible gaps in the families . . . Near a large State post on the Lake we saw the only large and apparently normal village we came across in all the three weeks we spent in the district. One was able to form here some estimate of what the population was before the advent of the white man and the search for rubber . . .

It will be observed that the devastated region Mr Scrivener passed through, and whence had come the refugees I saw at Mpoko, com-prises a part of the 'Domaine de la Couronne' [Crown Domain].

4 Notes in the Case of Mola Ekulite, a Native of Mokili in the Mantumba District, both of whose hands have been hacked or beaten off, and with reference to other similar cases of Mutilation in that District

I found this man in the Mission station at Ikoko on the 29th July, and learned that he had been kept by the missionaries for some years, since the day when a party of native teachers had found him in his own town, situated in the forest some miles away from Ikoko. In answer to my inquiry as to how he came to lose his hands, Mola's statement was as follows:

State soldiers came from Bikoro, and attacked the Bwanga towns, which they burned, killing people. They then attacked a town called Mauto and burned it, killing people there also. From that they went

on to Mokili. The Mokili people fled into the forest, leaving some few
of their number behind with food to offer to the soldiers – among
whom was Mola. The soldiers came to Mokili, under the command
of a European officer, whose native name was 'Ikatankoi' ('the Leop-
ard's Paw').* The soldiers took prisoner all the men left in the town,
and tied them up. Their hands were tied very tight with native rope,
and they were tied up outside in the open; and as it was raining very
hard, and they were in the rain all the time and all the night, their
hands swelled, because the thongs contracted. His (Mola's) hands
had swollen terribly in the morning, and the thongs had cut into the
bone. The soldiers, when they came to Mokili, had only one native a
prisoner with them; he was killed during the night. At Mokili itself
eight people, including himself (Mola) were taken prisoners; all were
men; two were killed during the night. Six only were taken down in
the morning to the lake side at Ianga. On reaching the lake side the
white man ordered four of the prisoners to be released; the fifth was a
Chief, named Iyeli Etumba. This Chief had come back to Mokili in
the night to try secretly to get some fire to take back into the forest,
where the fugitives were hiding. His wife had become sick during the
heavy rain in the forest, and the Chief wanted the fire for her; but the
soldiers caught him, and he was taken along with the rest. This Chief
was taken to Bikoro, but he believes that on the way, at Nyange, he
tried to escape, and was killed. Mola's hands were so swollen that they
were quite useless. The soldiers seeing this, and that the thongs had
cut into the bone, beat his hands against a tree with their rifles, and
he was released. He does not know why they beat his hands. The
white man 'Ikatankoi' was not far off, and could see what they were
doing. Ikatankoi was drinking palm-wine while the soldiers beat his
hands off with their rifle-butts against the tree. His hands subsequently fell off (or sloughed away). When the soldiers left him by the
waterside, he got back to Mokili, and when his own people returned
from the forest they found him there. Afterwards some boys from the
Mission – one of whom was a relation – came to preach at Mokili,
and they found him without his hands; and later on he came to the

* I subsequently found that this officer is reported to have died when on his
way home in March 1900. His name is known to me.

Mission, where he has since been helped and maintained by Mr Clark.

There was some doubt in the translation of Mola's statement whether his hands had been cut with a knife; but later inquiry established that they fell off through the tightness of the native rope and the beating of them by the soldiers with their rifle-butts.

With regard to the foregoing statement, Mr Clark, upon my further inquiry, gave me the following additional particulars relative to Mola:

The boy was found, Mr Clark said, as he had related to me, by some of the evangelists, and brought to the Mission. His mother sometimes came to visit him from Mokili. Although both his hands are gone, he tries to make himself useful herding the Mission sheep.

In April 1901, when Mr Clark was on his way home to America, on completing eight years' continued residence at Lake Mantumba, he wrote to Governor-General Wahis, pointing out the unhappy state of this man, and requesting that some provision should be made for him out of the public funds. This letter Mr Clark had hoped to present personally at Boma, but the steamer remaining there only a short time, he had been forced to send it instead. Strange to say, I found that I myself had taken charge of this very letter, and had sent it to Government House, then in entire ignorance of its contents, explaining that Mr Clark had himself been unable to call upon the Governor. I had never heard of Mola Ekulite in my life until I saw him on the beach at Ikoko on the 29th July last; but it was a somewhat remarkable coincidence that I should, in April 1901, have been the means of conveying to the local authorities at Boma an appeal on his behalf. Mr Clark went on to say that he had received, neither at the time nor since, any acknowledgment of the letter he had written to the Governor-General. On arriving in Europe he had addressed a second and similar appeal on Mola's behalf to the Central Administration at Brussels, inclosing a photograph of the maimed or mutilated boy. To this second appeal no reply had been received. The only acknowledgment it would seem to have drawn from those in authority at Brussels was that, within a week of its despatch, a paragraph appeared in one of the Brussels newspapers (Mr Clark thinks it was the 'Petit Bleu') to the effect that an American missionary was going about with a faked-up photograph purporting to be that of a native of the Congo who had been mutilated by Government soldiers.

Since that date, seeing the reception his two appeals had met with, Mr Clark had made no further attempt to draw attention to Mola's case. To convince me, however, of his *bona fides*, he handed me a copy he found in his note-book of the first letter addressed to Governor-General Wahis, which I myself had been the means of delivering. That letter was as follows:

Steam-ship 'Sobo', Boma
April 4, 1901.

Sir,

At our station, Ikoko, Lac Ntomba, there is a youth who was mutilated by State soldiers some years ago. His right hand was cut off, and his left so beaten on the side of a canoe that all the fingers were destroyed. I write to beg that you will in some way arrange for his support at the Mission station. When you visited us at Ikoko you gave orders that one young man who had been mutilated should be supported by the post at Bikoro, but he refused to go there. Permit me to suggest that the 'Chef de Poste' at Bikoro be authorized to pay 1 fr. per week to the Mission for the lad.

I am now returning to Europe and America, and I am anxious to say that the Government has undertaken the support of the young man, as an officer who recently returned to Europe obtained, without my consent or knowledge, a copy of the photo I made of the young man.

There are two other cases, one a man and one a boy, who each had one hand cut off by soldiers in our district, but they are both able to do some work and provide for themselves. Let me assure you that these cases are not recent cases of mutilation. I am not aware of any cases of mutilation during the term of service of those now in authority in our district.

If you cannot decide this matter before the departure of the steam-ship 'Sobo', might I ask that you give instructions that your reply be forwarded to me at my address in Scotland.

'Congolia,'
Arduthie Road,
Stonehaven.
          I beg, &c.

(Signed) Joseph Clark

The statement made in this letter, that one of the hands was cut off against the side of a canoe, was evidently inaccurate. That would, however, appear to have been a not uncommon way of mutilating those who underwent this process in the Lake region, for it was one of the methods M. Wauters himself informed me the mutilated men around Bikoro said had been employed in their cases. I mentioned Mola's case to M. Wauters when visiting Bikoro on the 31st July, and it was in reference to it that I was informed that there were several similar cases in the neighbourhood. Apart from Mr Clark's two letters to the higher authorities, Mola's presence as a dependent upon the Mission charity was well known, I found, in the neighbourhood.

On leaving Lake Mantumba on the 14th August, I again visited the State camp at Irebu, where, in the course of conversation with the officer in command, I made passing but intentional reference to the fact that I had seen Mola, and had heard his story from himself. I added that from the boy's statement it would seem that the loss of his hands was directly attributable to an officer who was apparently close at hand and in command of the soldiers at the time. I added that I had heard of other cases in the neighbourhood. The Commandant at once informed me that such things were impossible, but that in this specific case of Mola he should cause inquiry to be instantly made.

On my return from the Lulongo River I found that this remark in passing conversation had borne instant fruit. The Commissaire-Général of the Equator District had, learning of it, at once proceeded to Lake Mantumba, and a judicial investigation as to how Mola lost his hands had been immediately instituted. The boy was taken to Bikoro, and I have since been informed that he is now provided for life with a good brick house, a wife, and a weekly allowance. This commendable provision for the maimed man might have been made, it would have been thought, rather when Mr Clark, two years and a half previously, appealed for help.

It is to be regretted that the double appeal he then addressed to the highest quarters in the Congolese Administration should have met with no response save an insulting newspaper paragraph, while the casual remark of His Majesty's Consul, made to a quite subordinate officer, should have at once evoked judicial inquiry and immediate relief.

When at the village of Bokoti on the 7th August, I had found there a boy of not more than 12 years of age with the right hand gone. This child, in answer to my inquiries, said that the hand had been cut off by the Government soldiers some years before. He could not say how long before, but judging from the height he indicated he could not then have been more than 7 years if now 12. His statement was fully confirmed by the Chief and his relatives, who stood around him while I questioned him. The soldiers had come to Bokoti from Coquilhatville by land through the forest. They were led by an officer whose name was given as 'Etunbanbilo'. His father and mother were killed beside him. He saw them killed, and a bullet hit him and he fell. He here showed me a deep cicatrized scar at the back of the head, just at the nape of the neck, and said it was there the bullet had struck him. He fell down, presumably insensible, but came to his senses while his hand was being hacked off at the wrist. I asked him how it was he could possibly lie silent and give no sign. He answered that he felt the cutting, but was afraid to move, knowing that he would be killed if he showed any sign of life.

I made some provision for this boy, and begged the Mission at Ikoko, who had never heard of him until my visit, to send and bring him from Bokoti, and provide for him.

The names of six other persons mutilated in a similar way, who had, from time to time, been kept at the Mission, were given to me by Mrs Clark. The last of these, an old woman, had died only a few months previously to my visit, and her niece who is the wife of one of the principal natives attached to the Mission, stated that her aunt had often told her how she came to lose her hand. The town had been attacked by Government troops and all had fled, pursued into the forest. This old woman (whose name was Eyeka) had fled with her son, when he fell shot dead, and she herself fell down beside him – she supposed she fainted. She then felt her hand being cut off, but had made no sign. When all was quiet and the soldiers had gone, she found her son's dead body beside her with one hand cut off and her own also taken away.

Of acts of persistent mutilation by Government soldiers of this nature I had many statements made to me while at Lake Mantumba, some of them specifically, others in a general way. Of the fact of this mutilation and the causes inducing it there can be no shadow of doubt. It was not a native custom prior to the coming of the white man; it was not the outcome of the primitive instincts of savages in their fights between village and village; it was the deliberate act of the soldiers of a European Administration, and these men themselves never made any concealment that in committing these acts they were but obeying the positive orders of their superiors. Mrs Clark, who had resided at Ikoko with her husband through all the period from 1893 to 1901, when the rubber régime originated and culminated, gave me several specific instances of this practice of mutilation having been carried out in the town of Ikoko itself, when the Government soldiers had come across from Bikoro to raid it or compel its inhabitants to work.

On one of these days the killing had gone on close to the Mission-house, some of the native fugitives flying for refuge into the church where Mrs Clark and her school-girls were. At mid-day, when about to sit down to dinner, her husband had told her that one of the soldiers was going back with a basket of severed hands which he had laid down outside their verandah whilst getting the canoe ready at the lake side, in which to return to Bikoro. She had then, along with her husband, gone out and seen with her own eyes, the hands, four of which were those of infants, and Mr Clark (who confirmed his wife's statement) told me it had contained seventeen human hands. The excuse made to me by State officers when I sometimes touched upon this revolting practice was that, although wholesale mutilation might have occurred in the past, it had always been due to the primitive instincts of savages, either savage soldiers employed by the Government or the savage natives themselves, but that in no case had a European officer had cognizance of these occurrences or been responsible for them.

The statements made to me, on the other hand, by the natives or the witnesses of these acts, being not vague generalizations but positive declarations, left in my mind the conviction that this and other forms of mutilation had been carried out by the soldiers of the Government as a part of the general policy of the time – which would seem to have been chiefly designed to crush all organized resistance by the natives to the imposition of a general scheme of taxation.

Sources and Acknowledgements

Every effort has been made to contact copyright holders; in the event of an inadvertent omission or error, the editorial department should be notified at The Folio Society Ltd, 44 Eagle Street, London WC1R 4FS.

Joseph Conrad:

Letters: Frederick R. Karl, Laurence Davies et al. (eds), *The Collected Letters of Joseph Conrad* (9 vols, Cambridge: Cambridge University Press, 1983–2008), vols 1–5. © the Estate of Joseph Conrad, 1983, published by Cambridge University Press and reproduced with permission

'The Congo Diary' and 'Up-river Book': Harold Ray Stevens and J. H. Stape (eds), *Last Essays* (Cambridge: Cambridge University Press, 2010). © the Estate of Joseph Conrad, 2010, published by Cambridge University Press and reproduced with permission

'My Best Story and Why I Think So': Zdzisław Najder (ed.), *Congo Diary and Other Uncollected Pieces* (Garden City, NY: Doubleday & Company, 1978).

'An Outpost of Progress': Allan H. Simmons and J. H. Stape (eds), *Tales of Unrest* (Cambridge: Cambridge University Press, 2009). © the Estate of Joseph Conrad, 2012, published by Cambridge University Press and reproduced with permission

A Personal Record (London: J. M. Dent & Sons, 1919).

'Geography and Some Explorers': *Last Essays* (London: J. M. Dent, 1928).

Roger Casement, extracts from the Congo Report: Séamas Ó Síocháin and Michael O'Sullivan (eds), *The Eyes of Another Race: Roger Casement's Congo Report and 1903 Diary* (Dublin: University College Dublin Press, 2003).

Ford Madox Ford, extracts from *Joseph Conrad: A Personal Remembrance*: Ford Madox Ford (Ford Madox Hueffer), *Joseph Conrad:*

A Personal Remembrance (London: Duckworth & Co., 1924).

John Galsworthy, extracts from 'Reminiscences of Conrad': John Galsworthy, *Castles in Spain and Other Screeds* (London: William Heinemann, 1927).

Edward Garnett, extracts from introduction to *Letters from Conrad 1895 to 1924*: Edward Garnett (ed.), *Letters from Conrad 1895 to 1924* (London: Nonesuch Press, 1928).

Lady Ottoline Morrell, extracts from *Memoirs*: Robert Gathorne-Hardy (ed.), *Ottoline: The Early Memoirs of Lady Ottoline Morrell* (London: Faber and Faber, 1963).

Bertrand Russell, extract from 'Portraits from Memory': Bertrand Russell, *Portraits from Memory, and Other Essays* (London: Allen & Unwin, 1956). © 1956, The Bertrand Russell Peace Foundation Ltd. Reproduced by permission of The Bertrand Russell Peace Foundation.

Bibliography

Biographical Studies

Batchelor, John, *The Life of Joseph Conrad: A Critical Biography* (Oxford: Blackwell, 1994).

Knowles, Owen, *A Conrad Chronology* (Basingstoke: Macmillan, 1990).

Najder, Zdzisław, *Joseph Conrad: A Chronicle*, translated by Halina Carroll-Najder (Cambridge University Press, 1983); rpt. and revised as *Joseph Conrad: A Life* (Rutgers University Press, 2007).

Najder, Zdzisław (ed.), *Conrad under Familial Eyes*, translated by Halina Carroll-Najder (Cambridge University Press, 1983).

Ray, Martin (comp.), *Joseph Conrad: Interviews and Recollections* (Basingstoke: Macmillan, 1990).

Stape, John, *The Several Lives of Joseph Conrad* (London: Heinemann, 2007).

Letters

The Collected Letters of Joseph Conrad, Frederick R. Karl and Laurence Davies (eds) 9 vols (Vol. 6 with Owen Knowles, Vol. 7 with J. H. Stape and Vol. 8 with Gene M. Moore) (Cambridge University Press, 1983–2009).

Conrad's Polish Background: Letters to and from Polish Friends, Zdzisław Najder (ed.) (Oxford University Press, 1964).

A Portrait in Letters: Correspondence to and about Conrad, J. H. Stape and Owen Knowles (eds) (Amsterdam: Editions Rodopi, 1996).

Reference

Knowles, Owen, *An Annotated Critical Bibliography of Joseph Conrad* (Hemel Hempstead: Harvester/Wheatsheaf, 1992).

Knowles, Owen, and Gene M. Moore, *Oxford Reader's Companion to Conrad* (Oxford University Press, 2000).

Simmons, Allan H., John G. Peters, and J. H. Stape (gen. eds),

Conrad: The Contemporary Reviews (Cambridge University Press, 2012).

Critical Studies

Berthoud, Jacques, *Conrad: The Major Phase* (Cambridge University Press, 1978).

Gordan, John D., *Joseph Conrad: The Making of a Novelist* (Cambridge, Mass.: Harvard University Press, 1941).

Guerard, Albert J., *Conrad the Novelist* (Cambridge, Mass.: Harvard University Press, 1958).

Lothe, Jakob, *Conrad's Narrative Method* (Oxford University Press, 1989).

Moser, Thomas, *Achievement and Decline* (Cambridge, Mass.: Harvard University Press, 1957).

Najder, Zdzisław, *Conrad in Perspective: Essays on Art and Fidelity* (Cambridge University Press, 1997).

Stape, J. H. (ed.), *The Cambridge Companion to Joseph Conrad* (Cambridge University Press, 1996).

Watt, Ian, *Conrad in the Nineteenth Century* (London: Chatto & Windus, 1980).

Watts, Cedric, *Preface to Conrad* (London: Longman, 1990; 2nd edn 1993).

Journals

The Conradian: Journal of the Joseph Conrad Society (UK), published twice yearly by Rodopi of Amsterdam.

Conradiana: A Journal of Joseph Conrad Studies, published thrice yearly by Texas Tech University Press, Lubbock, Texas.

L'Epoque Conradienne, published once yearly by the Société Conradienne Française at Les Presses Universitaires Limoges, Limoges, France.

Index

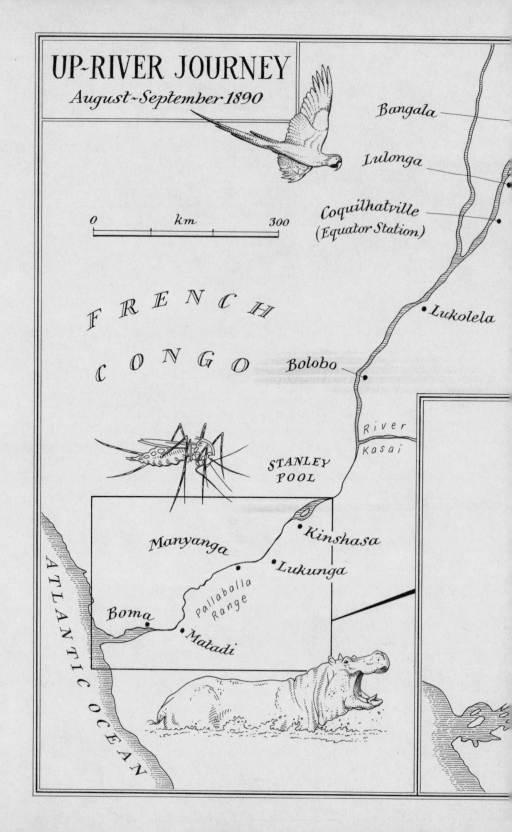

UP-RIVER JOURNEY
August~September 1890

Bangala

Lulonga

Coquilhatville
(Equator Station)

0   km   300

• Lukolela

F R E N C H

C O N G O

Bolobo

River
Kasai

STANLEY
POOL

Manyanga   • Kinshasa

                • Lukunga

Pallaballa
Range

Boma •

• Matadi

A T L A N T I C   O C E A N